How to Write a Cookbook and Get It Published

How to Write a
COOKBOOK
and Get It Published

By Sara Pitzer

Writer's
Digest
Books

Cincinnati, Ohio

HOW TO WRITE A COOKBOOK AND GET IT PUBLISHED

LIBRARY OF CONGRESS CATALOGING IN PUBLICATION DATA

Pitzer, Sara.
    How to write a cookbook and get it published.

    Bibliography: p.
    Includes index.
    1. Cookery—Authorship. I. Title.

TX644.P58   1984   808'.0666415021   84-5058
ISBN 0-89879-132-4

Design by Janet Czarnetzki

PERMISSIONS ACKNOWLEDGMENTS

Illustrations by Kate Barnes from *Cross Creek Kitchens—Seasonal Recipes and Reflections* by Sally Morrison, copyright 1983, reprinted by permission of Triad Publishing Company, Gainesville, Florida.

Pages from *Moosewood Cookbook* by Mollie Katzen, copyright 1977, reprinted by permission of Ten Speed Press.

Illustrations by Karl W. Stuecklen from *Beard on Pasta* by James Beard, copyright 1983, reprinted by permission of Alfred A. Knopf, Inc. Illustrations copyright 1983 by Karl W. Stuecklen.

Photos by Glen Millward from *Whole Grains: Grow, Harvest and Cook Your Own* by Sara Pitzer, copyright 1981 by Garden Way, Inc., reprinted by permission of Storey Communications.

Illustrations by Mike Nelson from *Wok: A Chinese Cookbook* by Gary Lee, copyright 1970, reprinted by permission of Nitty Gritty Productions.

Illustration by Craig Torlucci from *Casseroles and Salads* by Lou Siebert Pappas, copyright 1977, reprinted by permission of Nitty Gritty Productions.

Pages from *Secrets from Pocono Kitchens* by the Women's Auxiliary of the First Presbyterian Church of Stroudsburg, Pennsylvania, copyright 1942, reprinted by permission.

Pages from *Christmas at Our House*, copyright 1979, reproduced by permission of Drake-Chenault Enterprises, Inc.

Illustrations by Elizabeth P. Miller from *Best of Cook's Corner* are reproduced by permission of The South Carolina Women Involved in Rural Electrification.

Illustration by Sheila Lukins from *The Silver Palate* by Julee Rosso and Sheila Lukins, copyright 1979, 1980, 1981, 1982, reprinted by permission of Workman Publishing.

Illustrations by Anne S. Samson from *Forum Feasts*, copyright 1973, reprinted by permission of the Forum School, Waldwick, New Jersey.

Illustration by Janet Rabideau from *Cooking with Dried Beans* by Sara Pitzer, copyright 1982 by Garden Way, Inc., reprinted by permission of Storey Communications.

Illustration by Dennis Abbe from *The Picnic Gourmet* by Joan Hemingway and Connie Maricich, copyright 1975 and 1977, reprinted by permission of Random House.

Illustrations by Jeni Bassett from *Sunsational*, copyright 1982, reprinted by permission of the Junior League of Orlando-Winter Park, Florida, Inc., 125 North Lucerne Circle, East, Orlando, FL 32801.

Illustration by Linda Newberry from a *Private Collection*, copyright 1980, reprinted by permission of the Junior League of Palo Alto, Inc.

Illustration by Joan Blume from The *Early American Cookbook* by Hyla O'Connor, copyright 1974, reprinted by permission of Rutledge Books.

DEDICATION

This book is for
Al Munson,
my high school English teacher
to whom I promised it about twenty years ago,
and for
Charlie Brown,
my college journalism professor
who pointed out that unless I learned to spell
I would never be able to deliver.

ACKNOWLEDGMENTS

*I can hardly be too effusive in my thanks
to the authors, editors, publishers, photographers,
artists, food stylists, distributors, booksellers, cooks,
and readers who contributed to this book.
My wisdom, if I have any at all,
is essentially a compilation of theirs.*

Table of Contents

6 Looking at Trade Publishing 137

If you decide to serve your book up to a commercial publisher, you'll need to learn who's publishing what, whom to approach and how to approach them, what happens to your proposal once it gets there, and what to do if you're offered a contract. You'll see a sample query and proposal, and get lots of advice on making a professional presentation.

7 Illustrating Your Cookbook 173

How a cookbook is illustrated has a lot to do with its character—and cost. Possibilities range from simple line art and black-and-white photography to full-color illustrations. This chapter offers suggestions on where to find free or inexpensive art for your cookbook and some tips on how to photograph food, as well as what to look for in food illustration.

8 Beyond Cookbooks 197

Now that you're into it, you may want to find more outlets for your food writing. Almost everything that's printed seems to have recipes in it somewhere. Magazines, newspapers, premium cookbooks—maybe you can even teach a class!

*How to Write a Cookbook
and Get It Published*

Introduction

You love to eat.
You're a good cook.
And you're genuinely interested in food.

You can write a cookbook! If you're always fooling around with new recipes or collecting old ones, if your family and friends talk about your cooking and suggest wistfully that your best dishes could be duplicated if you would only write things down, and if you've always had an urge to write a cookbook, you're a natural. The main difference between you and the people who have already written cookbooks is merely a stack of typewritten pages.

Sometimes I think the urge to write a cookbook is as universal as the popular fantasy about opening our own restaurant. I think this passion has its roots in the generations of American women who essentially did write their own cookbooks. They collected and exchanged recipes, copying them carefully to pass from generation to generation, even including them in letters and diaries. As they encountered new foods and unfamiliar conditions, they told other women what they had learned about turning these strange things into meals that would sustain and please their families. Could an old English way with mutton tame the gaminess in squirrel? Was it possible to make bread from cornmeal? Did maple syrup substitute for sugar? Pass it on. It all deserved to be shared, sometimes as a matter of survival, sometimes as a courtesy.

Even today this desire seems to motivate cookbook authors. In the introduction to *From Julia Child's Kitchen* Julia Child explains that the book is a "very personal" summation of her twenty-five years in the kitchen. And in her foreword to the classic *Thousand Recipe Chinese Cookbook*, Gloria Bley Miller writes about the joy of learning from Chinese friends that Chinese cooking could be simple and logical. "I felt these discoveries should be shared," she writes. The discoveries, which started out as a magazine article, ended up as a book of more than 900 pages. Claudia Rosen presents her *Book of Middle Eastern Food* as a collection of recipes from many other Middle Easterners who now live in the Western world. She says they share so as not to forget. Margaret and Ancel Keys wrote one of the earliest "health food" cookbooks, *The Benevolent Bean*, to tell all who would read about the value of an underappreciated food. Similarly, Ellen Buchman Ewald offers *Recipes for a Small Planet* as an extension of the work in cooking balanced proteins without meat begun by Frances Moore Lappé. Even Jacques Pépin, the prolific writer of French cookbooks, who wrote *Everyday Cooking* mainly to amplify his cooking show on public television, says he is not creating something new, but is offering recipes from his head, heart, and memory, as he learned them at home.

Share and Share Alike

Your own impulse may stem from a conviction that everyone could eat more healthfully if they just had the right recipes, or perhaps from a wish to preserve historic recipes that have been in your family for generations. No matter what the motivation, few things are more personal than the foods we love and the ways we have learned to prepare them. When we let others see our recipes, we're often sharing a part of our lives about which we feel passionately.

The most dramatic illustration I can think of is the work of Nikki and David Goldbeck, authors of *The Supermarket Handbook*, *The Dieter's Companion*, and *The Good Breakfast Book*. They call themselves "food ecologists." Sally Lodge, who interviewed the Goldbecks for *Publishers Weekly*, observed that they are "consumed by their interest in nutrition—and are eager to spread their word." Nikki worked on food accounts for a public relations firm for a while, and discovered that people get most of their knowledge about food from the food industry itself. She wanted to spread the word about whole foods, those not treated with additives or preservatives or refined unnecessarily, which she and David consider significantly superior to processed foods. This "consuming" passion led the Goldbecks to spend several years testing and developing recipes for their 580-page tome, *Nikki and David Goldbeck's American Wholefoods Cuisine*.

My own passion for cooking and writing about food must stem from the day I was born. My earliest memories revolve around holidays when grandparents, cousins, uncles, and aunts gathered for wonderful dinners of roast chicken, served with mountains of mashed potatoes and three or four different vegetables. For dessert, chocolate

You don't necessarily have to use pictures of food in illustrating a cookbook. Pictures that call up the pleasant associations we have with food or remind us of the special places where it has been cooked and served can be equally effective. This watercolor by Kate Barnes, "Majorie's Kitchen," is from Cross Creek Kitchens—Seasonal Recipes and Reflections, *by Sally Morrison. The accompanying text describes the smell of frying sausage and gingerbread baking on a cool day in the country. The kitchen originally belonged to Marjorie Rawlings, author of the* Yearling. *Morrison writes about food and the places where it is grown and prepared in a way that makes them seem inseparable. Barnes' illustrations of the kitchens and countryside capture the mood of the text more effectively than could pictures of individual dishes.*

cake, coconut cake, and apple pie, and, in winter, homemade ice cream. Everybody brought something good to eat. When you opened the door you were immediately welcomed by the steamy, warm aroma of roasting meats and simmering sauces.

I especially remember the mashed potatoes, heaped into a warmed china serving bowl and topped with a huge chunk of cold butter. Gradually the butter would melt, and during grace, while the grownups sat with their heads bowed and their eyes closed, I would watch it run in little streams down the mound of potatoes. Then, while Grandpa or Dad or Uncle Lloyd was asking who wanted a leg and who wanted a wing, the mashed potatoes would make the rounds. A grownup whose hands were big enough to hold the bowl would always see to it that I had a large helping with a nice little well pressed into the top for gravy.

Right behind the potatoes came the peas and carrots, with green and orange contrasting so brightly that the bowl hardly seemed able to contain them. Cold pickled beets broke the richness of butter and gravy. I learned that if you arranged everything carefully on the plate you could eat the whole meal without turning the mashed potatoes pink from beet juice.

Sometimes we would have ham loaf. I knew from the grownups' talk that Grandma had the butcher grind a special mixture of pork and ham for the loaf. Something about the combination made it bake up so that it was deep brown and lightly crisp on the outside and firm, pink, and full of juice inside. To go with the ham loaf, raisin sauce was passed in a pitcher. If you poured carefully, you could cover the top of a thick slice of ham loaf with soft plumped raisins and have just a tiny bit of the clear brown syrup run over the edges.

After a meal, when the table was cleared and Grandpa had crumbed the tablecloth with the ivory crumber and the women had washed the dishes, everyone sat around in the living room, talking about absent relatives and *food*. They'd reminisce about Great-Grandma Eyer's pie crust and her pickled stuffed peppers. Or someone would tell how they used to bring in buckets of fresh "huckaberries" to be made into three or four pies that were eaten hot. To use a phrase I heard just the other day, my family treated food as a sacrament.

When I was grown, I learned recipes for more exotic dishes, but I never lost my love for the meals we ate when I was a child. To duplicate them, I set about collecting and, when necessary, recreating, the old recipes. After that, writing to share was inevitable. Some people's roots may be traced through family trees; mine can be found in the food we ate.

Preserve Culinary Heritage

In recent years, interest in old recipes has also grown in two less personal ways. Many people want to know how earlier cooking methods evolved into today's practices. These food historians trace the development of recipes through generations, noting when certain ingredients became available and began to appear in common use, and studying the relationship between cultural developments and what people ate. Such interest has resulted in a spate of books reproducing the favorites of Thomas Jefferson, Martha Washington, early Quakers, Southern plantation dwellers, and scores of other ancestral cooks.

This coin has another interesting side. Today, by studying old recipes, we can draw conclusions about how the people who used them thought and behaved. For instance, anyone studying the old cream-and-butter-laden recipes of the Pennsylvania Dutch would soon deduce that these ingredients were readily available to nearly all, and that people at that time apparently didn't worry about being too fat or consuming too much cholesterol.

Preserving ethnic family recipes is especially important, because "authentic" ethnic food changes as the people who cook it accommodate to their circumstances. For instance, the best Chinese restaurant in town makes a soup in which tomato catsup is a major ingredient. Julia Child uses lasagna noodles in concoctions that never graced an Italian table. Revised editions of Southern cookbooks contain recipes from the wrong side of the Mason-Dixon Line because boundaries have blurred, and Rebs and Yanks now have a few cooking habits in common. Jewish cooking is famous for picking up and adapting whatever ingredients can be found in the neighborhood where a Jewish cook finds herself.

This all makes wonderful eating, but quickly obscures the old culinary traditions. The family cookbook, created to preserve on paper a record of the way we used to eat, keeps us from losing these details of our heritage. Someday such records will be part of history for future generations.

But history is only one motivation for writing a cookbook. A passion for a particular food is another. (I could have written a book about my years-long search for the perfect sticky bun.) Or you may be answering your children's pleas to write down how you make your pancakes so they can do it too. Whether you are writing for the delight of family and friends, for posterity, or for a little fame and fortune, your effort to share what you know about cooking puts you into an exciting class of people—those who *do*. Cooking experts.

Can Do!

Too often, these urges to communicate what we know get bogged down in details and confusion about how to proceed. A friend of mine who used to be the food editor for the *St. Petersburg Times* once collected recipes from all the cooks she admired most, to put into a personally published cookbook called *With A Little Help from My Friends.* She was going to give it to all her friends for Christmas. She selected, tested, and organized the recipes with no trouble, but the idea of typing them so overwhelmed her that she abandoned the project. I still mourn losing what that book could have been; she knows some fabulous cooks. That's why I have included a chapter in this book about how to publish a "personal" book in small quantities for your friends, along with suggestions about how to do it without typing.

A group of big eaters and excellent cooks published a cookbook to raise money for their church. Their cookbook is outstanding, but they printed too many copies, got into too many fights about how to manage the project, and ended up losing not only money, but also esprit de corps. For people like them, I have written a long chapter on self-publishing, with advice on how to manage the committee aspects and plenty of information about the business decisions involved. You *can* self-publish without losing money or friends.

And because during my years of working in publishing houses I have seen many good ideas rejected because they were shown to the wrong publisher or presented the wrong way, I have written a chapter on how trade publishing works and what to do if you choose to try publishing your book commercially.

If you are like most of us, when someone talks about publishing, you probably think first of the large, well-known publishers in New York. Their books seem to be in the majority in bookstores and book-club catalogs. Random House, Barnes and Noble, Macmillan, Prentice-Hall, Doubleday, and Simon and Schuster come to mind. Or Harcourt Brace Jovanovich, or Harper and Row. In a book about publishing cookbooks, you may expect to read first about how to approach one of these giants in the commercial world (known as "trade publishers" within the book-publishing and selling industry). Or if you have worked long enough as a writer, you may believe that the best place to start is with a smaller trade publisher, still in the business of selling other authors' books for profit but on a smaller scale and usually operating outside the New York area, and you may expect me to begin with a pragmatic discussion of breaking into print with one of them.

In this book, however, I have written about almost everything else before I discuss trade publishing. That's because no matter how you publish, you have to go through the same steps in working up recipes and writing them coherently, and I thought it best to examine the stuff of which cookbooks are made *before* talking about the various publishing processes. Moreover, considering the numbers of cookbooks published privately by individuals and groups, I thought it was important to tell you first about those alternatives which—in cookbook publishing—are often more desirable than trade publishing.

But if all these preliminaries make you impatient, and if you believe that "real publishing" is trade publishing, you can begin with that chapter and read later about gathering, testing, and writing the recipes. The same is true if you are planning a self-publishing project and are more concerned with how to get your group started than with the nitty-gritty of the recipes. In that case, start with the self-publishing chapter. If a particular kind of publishing does not interest you at all, you can even skip it.

Eventually, though, you will have to get down to business and work through the early chapters on recipes and writing. In those chapters, I tell you how to find and create more recipes, how to attribute those you borrow, and how to avoid nasty problems like plagiarism. I go into detail on testing, writing up the ingredients and methods clearly, preparing your manuscript, and dealing with illustrations.

Publishing a book is a big project. If you would prefer to start on a smaller scale, Chapter Eight introduces you to other food-writing possibilities: newspaper columns, premium booklets, company publications, and magazine articles.

In every chapter I've told stories of people like you, who wanted to write a cookbook—and did it. I hope they will inspire you to go ahead and try the project you've been contemplating, to move from the category of dreamers into the world of doers. For no matter how your book finally finds its readers, through a trade publisher, by self-publishing, or with the special intimacy of personal publishing, you're in for a good time once you've accomplished it.

Increasing Culinary Awareness

While you are learning about cookbooks, another good thing will happen. Your perception will expand. By now, I suppose, everybody knows the famous example of the Eskimos; they have more than twenty different words for snow because they know so much about it that they actually perceive twenty different kinds. Closer to home, after I learned about sewing I began to notice little things like where the seams in turtleneck collars were located. Hanging around with upholsterers, I began to observe whether couch cushions were zipped or tucked into their covers, and whether the skirts on chairs were mitered or square-folded at the corners. From a birdwatcher I learned to see that different birds move their wings differently as they fly. Where once I saw only clothes, furniture, and birds, all in general, now I can see details about them that I didn't know existed before. That's what I mean by expanding perceptions.

The same thing happens when you begin to learn about cookbooks. You become aware of the kind and quality of illustrations, their effectiveness, and their reason for being there, beyond just being pretty. You learn about format and different ways of listing ingredients. You develop a concept of internal consistency and of clear directions. You see things you never noticed before. Years ago a creative writing teacher told me that I would probably never write any great fiction, but that the attempt would make me an outstandingly perceptive reader of fiction. He was right on both points. Similarly, you'll begin to evaluate cookbooks as you look at them. Some, which you used to think were spectacular, may disappoint you on reexamination; others, to which you gave scant attention, may please you with newly discovered subtleties.

Your familiarity with cookbooks will be obvious to other people. You'll become the expert to whom people come for help when they try recipes and end up with too much difference between the print on the page and the pastry in the pan. You'll get calls when souffles don't puff, fudge won't harden, and yogurt won't set. You'll get questions about how to hard-boil eggs so they don't turn green, how to roll pie crust that doesn't fall apart, and how to bake bread that doesn't have big holes the jelly runs through. But—I hate to tell you this—once you're known as the expert, you will intimidate people. The one thing you won't get is lots of invitations to dinner.

CHAPTER *1*

Where to Start

W hy do you want to write a cookbook?
Whom do you want to read it?

Before you read on, stop and think about these questions, because your answers will influence every decision you make about your cookbook: its contents, its style, even the illustrations. The answers to these questions will determine the focus and theme of your cookbook, whether you write alone or with collaborators, and whether you choose trade publishing, self-publishing, or personal publishing.

Let's suppose for a moment that you want to write a cookbook because you are famous in your community for your Italian cooking, which is based on old family recipes not found in print anywhere. You want to give these recipes in book form to all the younger members of your large family. To complicate matters, an entrepreneurial woman's club in town has hinted that they would pay you a little something to write an Italian cookbook for them to publish as a fund raiser. But your husband thinks that if you are going to write a book you should send it to Doubleday to be published and "really make some money."

There you are, with about half your best recipes neatly copied and filed on index cards, and the other half smeared and turning brown around the ragged edges of the scraps of paper they're written on, crammed into an old shoe box that once held the kids' art supplies. When you dump everything out, you know you'll find crayon crumbs stuck to the tomato-paste spots on all three of your lasagna recipes. How do you get those recipes from the disorder of the shoe box into a book? Where do you start?

You start by asking why you want to write a cookbook, and for whom. Keep your answers firmly in mind as you read and learn how the cookbook-publishing world works, and you will begin to see where *your* book fits into the scheme. Then you will be able to decide which form of publishing suits you best, and the chapters on how to manage the kind of publishing you choose will guide you step by step from there. The chapters on writing and illustrating your book will tell you what to do with your materials once you have worked out your decisions about publishing.

You'll find it easier to think about all this if you understand some of the ways to classify all cookbooks, whether they are published commercially or privately. Cookbooks fall into at least six different categories: thematic, single-subject, ethnic and regional, general, hybrids, and gimmick. (So many cookbooks on health and nutrition have appeared in recent years that you could almost make a case for listing them as a seventh category. Most of these books seem to fit into existing categories, however, so I've resisted the temptation to create an additional one.)

Classifying Cookbooks

Thematic cookbooks contain recipes selected according to a central idea or theme. Many of the new cookbooks published these days are thematic. The Dial Press, for instance, published Martha Rose Shulman's *Fast Vegetarian Feasts*. The title gives you the theme, and just in case you're a little slow to catch on, the subtitle spells it out: *Delicious Healthful Meals in Under 45 Minutes*. Because of the title, you wouldn't expect to find any recipes in the book, no matter how good they are, directing you to stir, simmer, or knead for a long time. Martha Rose Shulman has written other cookbooks, run a supper club and a catering service, and spent long hours in her kitchen creating new recipes, but her choice of theme—vegetarian meals you can prepare in less than 45 minutes, automatically excludes many of them from this book.

This is hard discipline for an enthusiastic cook. If you write a thematic cookbook, you may find yourself tempted to slip in a few recipes that you like, but that are not quite what the theme demands. In the case of this book, you might be tempted to include a recipe or two that you justify with the comment that it takes a little longer, but here it is anyhow because it's so good. A good author resists that temptation.

To develop the idea further, consider the two volumes of *The Vegetarian Epicure*, by Anna Thomas. Like Shulman's book, these feature vegetarian recipes, but the word "epicure" indicates that they are meant for gourmet tastes. Whether they take a long or short time to prepare does not govern what recipes are included, only whether they offer the subtleties of taste and texture we associate with gourmet cooking. In these books you will find recipes for making stocks that need long simmering and breads that require kneading, but because of the theme, you will not find recipes directing you to make a quick supper of leftover rice, warmed-up beans, and a couple of quickly sliced radishes.

Other examples of thematic cookbooks that stick successfullly to their themes are *No Salt, No Sugar, No Fat* from Nitty Gritty Productions, and Adelle Davis' classic *Let's Cook It Right*. Thematic cookbooks these days often deal with health, fitness, and weight, but they aren't the only topics. Martha Stewart's *Entertaining* and Lou Pappas' *Entertaining in the Light Style* and *Ready When You Are: Make Ahead Meals for Entertaining* represent variations on a theme. One deals with entertaining in a general way, the second with avoiding heavy party food, the last with preparing ahead. You shouldn't find any last-minute recipes in *Ready When You Are* or any high-calorie foods in *Entertaining in the Light Style*.

Thematic cookbooks offer wonderful opportunities for imaginative illustrations and a chance to get away from rigorously realistic art that seems to be obligatory for food articles in women's magazines. This painting by Dennis Abbe from The Picnic Gourmet *by Joan Hemingway and Connie Maricich suggests an old-time romantic view of picnics, filled with grace and glamor. The book offers more than "300 delectable recipes for every kind of picnic meal." It isn't hard for the reader browsing through the book to develop the notion that preparing some of the recipes will result in a story-book picnic. And maybe it will.*

Thematic cookbooks may be broad or narrow, and they may include more than one theme, either by definition in the title or by implication in the recipes. Such diverse books as *Fifteen-Minute Meals* and *Quick Meals with Fresh Foods* represent different approaches to speed as a theme. Consider the difference between a fast-meals book using convenience foods and these two books, both of which emphasize using fresh ingredients, though in different amounts of time. You will see how carefully a theme can be defined. In *Fifteen-Minute Meals*, the author is prohibited by theme from including some recipes using fresh ingredients, which could be included in a book such as Ortho's *30-Minute Meals*. Incidentally, the inclusion of fresh ingredients in the theme is stated explicitly in Sunset's *Quick Meals with Fresh Foods*, while you have to examine One-O-One's *Fifteen-Minute Meals* to see that it is part of the underlying theme in that book too.

The main thing to remember about thematic cookbooks is that every recipe must be consistent with the theme. Single-subject cookbooks impose similar discipline on you.

Single-subject cookbooks are easy to recognize. They tell you all you ever wanted to know (and sometimes more) about a particular ingredient—ground beef or apples or chocolate or fish or phyllo. Single-subject cookbooks often come as part of an entire set or line, such as those published by Sunset or HP Books. Often they are displayed together in a special rack to encourage customers to acquire an entire cooking encyclopedia a subject at a time. Some publishers find single-subject cookbooks an economic disaster and won't publish them, but a few subjects, such as seafood and chicken, seem to attract buyers endlessly. My own cookbook collection includes four different chicken cookbooks, and I am writing one myself, on assignment, even though common sense would suggest there can't possibly be any new ways to bake, broil, or sizzle chicken.

This brings us directly to the major problem with writing single-subject cookbooks. Trying to think up many ways of using a particular ingredient tempts you to include ridiculous recipes. Zucchini must be the best example; think of all the midsummer zucchini recipes you've seen in the newspapers. Zucchini pickles, which seemed bizarre enough the first time I saw the recipe, pale in comparison to zucchini shortcake and zucchini ice cream sundaes with chocolate sauce. (I wish I were making this up, but I'm not.) There is a demand for such books, however, because we are always looking for new ways to cook foods that are plentiful, inexpensive, or popular.

Recently I consulted with a woman who is writing a book of peach recipes. You and I may think the best thing to do with a peach is to peel it and eat it, but she's collected enough credible recipes to approach the Peach Advisory Board about subsidizing her project. Nearly every state has such boards, devoted to the promotion of products produced in the state. The same foods may also have national boards or councils.

Food producers and processors of all kinds offer consumer booklets and pamphlets to encourage customers to use their products. These organizations can be a good outlet for your writing if you become expert in cooking with their products.

There are more of them than I could possibly list, from the Alaska Seafood Marketing Institute, the South Carolina Egg Council, and the California Artichoke Advisory Board to the Washington State Potato Commission. Three directories in your public library list these organizations: the *Encyclopedia of Associations;* the *National Directory of State Agencies;* and *Trade and Professional Associations of the United States.* Some of the organizations you find listed will be good places to sell a single-subject cookbook devoted to their product. I would begin with the state-level associations rather than the national ones, on the theory that national organizations are more likely to have money to hire big advertising agencies for their development programs, while smaller ones are more likely to turn to freelancers for single-subject cookbooks.

Another version of the single-subject cookbook reflects the technology of the times. Appliance books sell well if they are any good, and sometimes even if they're not. Think of how many books you've seen devoted to slow cookers, microwave ovens, blenders, convection ovens, outdoor grills, food processors, pressure cookers, and clay pots. The problem in writing these books is similar to the problem in writing single-ingredient books; you end up trying to make the device do something it really isn't suited for. I'm reminded here of the old line about the dancing elephant. The remarkable thing isn't that it dances well, but that it dances at all. Maybe it's remarkable that one *can* bake potatoes in a slow cooker; surely it's a tribute to ingenuity that anyone thought to try, but once you've tasted the potatoes you know that's not what slow cookers are good for. Recipes for microwaved roast beef, pressure-cooked vegetables, food-processor cole slaw mush, and crockery-pot cakes are dancing elephants. I think producing them hurts your reputation.

If you look back over this list of appliances and their corresponding books, you see no mention of electric skillets. This demonstrates another problem with single-*appliance* cookbooks. They become obsolete as soon as the public loses interest in the new appliance. When was the last time you used your electric-skillet cookbook? For that matter, where *is* your electric skillet? Or your automatic egg cooker?

The positive side of single-appliance cookbooks is that while an appliance is in vogue, books for using it are in tremendous demand. Usually new appliances are sold with little booklets that contain a few recipes; big books of one hundred or more recipes generally come from trade publishers. Because such single-subject books stimulate sales of the appliance about which they're written, publishers who specialize in cookbooks are very likely to want books about each new appliance as it comes along. The publishers then sell the books not only to bookstores but also to gourmet shops, hardware stores, and housewares divisions of department stores, where enterprising merchandisers often arrange displays that combine the new appliance with cookbooks for using it. While the appliance is new and many people are buying it, they will also buy the books for using it. As interest in the appliance dies down, book sales will fall off too. The popularity of some appliances lasts longer than others. Nitty Gritty Cookbooks' entire line began with one appliance book, the *Fondue Cookbook*, during the fondue-pot craze when the smell of burning sterno permeated the land. The book sold in tremendous numbers for a long time. Owlswood Productions began with a cookbook for Bundt cakes when Susan Herbert couldn't get Nitty Gritty to publish her book to go with Bundt cake pans. If it is possible to build an entire cookbook line around a cake pan, nothing is impossible; if *you* like your idea, do it.

Ethnic cookbooks are easy to identify, and it's hard to find a cookbook publisher who doesn't have at least a few, maybe to represent the origins of the office staff: *The French Cookbook, Italian Cooking, The Chinese Cookbook,* and so on, except that often the names are gussied up a little: *Secrets of Chinese Cooking, Let's Cook Hungarian!, Mastering the Art of French Cooking.*

Such cookbooks come in great variety. In Chinese cooking, for instance, the possibilities range from *Dim Sum & Other Chinese Street Food* to *Chinese Cooking for Two.* And you know that *Don't Lick the Chopsticks* must differ substantially from *The Classic Chinese Cookbook.* If you are lucky enough to have a strong ethnic background that included a lot of good cooking, you have at hand almost limitless possibilities for writing cookbooks no one has thought of yet.

Remember, though, that not all ethnic cuisines have equal appeal to the cookbook-buying public. This fact could influence your decision whether to approach a trade publisher or to publish privately, and it could influence the number of copies you decide to publish if you self-publish. The foods of some countries seem to have almost unlimited appeal in America. If you look at the number of Chinese cookbooks available in the bookstores, for instance, you wonder why chopsticks have not replaced forks. But Vietnamese cookbooks are relatively hard to find. Apparently the American public has not yet developed so much interest in cooking Vietnamese meals at home as they have in Chinese, although more and more Vietnamese restaurants are opening around the country. The same is true of Indian cooking. You can find Indian restaurants in any major city, but the number of Indian cookbooks in the bookstores is comparatively few. Strange as it sounds, one way to gauge the appeal of an ethnic cuisine to the cookbook market is to see what has already been published. If you find many books for a particular cuisine you can safely assume that it's popular with the buying public.

If you publish another ethnic cookbook in an already crowded area, your challenge will be to find a new approach or to offer previously unknown recipes. One way to accomplish this would be to develop subthemes within the ethnic book. Some examples of this are *Jewish Cooking for Weight Watchers, Italian Meatless Cooking,* and *Viennese Desserts Made Easy.* The Jewish theme has low-calorie recipes as a subtheme; vegetarianism is the subtheme in the Italian book; and the Viennese book is narrowed not just to desserts, but to *easy* desserts.

But what if your expertise leads you to publish a book of ethnic recipes in one of the less popular areas? My background is English on my mother's side, and I have my English recipes, but the world is not beating down my door to get them. (My daughter who lives in England says she can see why.) If I wanted to publish my recipes to prove how good English cooking can be, I would probably have trouble convincing a trade publisher that the market for an English cookbook was strong enough to warrant the project. I might consider self-publishing, but decide that not enough people were interested in English cooking in the markets I had access to. Personally publishing a few of the recipes might be the best thing to do with an English family cookbook.

If you narrowed the focus in an English cookbook to something like *Entertaining with Prince Charles and Lady Di*, you'd have a book that might do very well as a trade book in England, where it wouldn't be considered ethnic at all. And if you narrowed the focus to *London Favorites*, the book would be considered regional.

Regional cookbooks could come under a separate category, but essentially they are like ethnic cookbooks in that they too emphasize the food eaten by a particular group of people. *The California Cookbook, The Colorado Cookbook,* and *Two Hundred Years of Charleston Cooking* give you the idea. Regional cookbooks also lend themselves to a variety of treatments.

The other extreme from these highly specialized ethnic and regional books is the **general** or **all-purpose** cookbook, which purports to tell you how to cook everything. Rombauer and Becker's *Joy of Cooking* still finds its way into the kitchens of most brides, bachelors, and kids on their own. The recently revised *Fanny Farmer Cookbook* is another strong contender in the all-purpose field. I remember that my mother's standard was the *American Woman Cookbook,* and many of my friends used *Betty Crocker's Cookbook.* Although these are what most of us think of when people talk about cookbooks, they are not the best kind to try to write. Most of us want only one or two such all-encompassing books in our cookbook collections, and those have been done already by well-known experts, sometimes even by teams of experts. Moreover, writing a truly competitive encyclopedic cookbook would be an overwhelming project for a beginner. The knowledge and research that would go into one such book can produce instead several more modest and manageable books.

All the cookbooks I have written are spun off from the big general one I envisioned before I discovered the realities of cookbook publishing. I wanted to write *Cooking from Scratch* for all the people I knew who could prepare a block of frozen green peas from the grocery store but hadn't the faintest idea what to do with a sack of fresh peas in the pod

What can you do with a regional cookbook to keep it from being straightlaced and too much like all the others? The Junior League of Orlando-Winter Park in Florida used these cute little critters drawn by Jeni Bassett to illustrate their book Sunsational. *The drawings make good-humored fun of the fantasies we have about the pleasures of living in Florida, the state of frogs and alligators.*

donated from a neighbor's garden.

I submitted a proposal with an introduction and a couple of sample chapters to Chilton Books, and their editor encouraged me to develop the project further. But a few months later, with the book in process, Chilton decided to go out of the cookbook business because the market was too competitive. They returned what they had of my manuscript, all carefully edited and full of comments in the margins.

I used the comments to revise the material and sent it to Stephen Greene Press. They sent it right back with a standard printed "doesn't fit our plans" form. I bought another brown envelope, retyped the first page, and sent the proposal and sample chapters to Garden Way Publishers. They sent it back with a letter saying that it didn't fit their plans either, but that they liked my work and wondered if I would like to write a different book for them on assignment.

I was so excited you could have scraped me off the ceiling with a butter knife. *Cooking from Scratch* was forgotten as I delved into the mysteries of sourdough, dried beans, whole grains, poultry, and (for another publisher) jams, jellies, pickles, and preserves. If you were to gather these little books all together and study them, you would see that *Cooking from Scratch*, though fragmented, lives on.

Cooking from Scratch came close to what I call a **hybrid** cookbook. A hybrid fits no category exactly, but combines the characteristics of several. Had it come to fruition as I planned it, *Cooking from Scratch* would have combined the features of a general cookbook with those of a thematic one. Some hybrid books that succeeded are *Laurel's Kitchen*, a general cookbook written around the theme of mastering the nutritional principles of vegetarian cooking, and *Fast Italian Meals*, a hybrid of thematic and ethnic recipes.

It is only a short hop from hybrid cookbooks to **gimmick** cookbooks. You might as well know that I have a personal bias against gimmick books, but honesty compels me to admit that they are very popular, not only with consumers and publishers, but also with authors' agents. One New York agent, who said she would sprinkle my pilaf with ground glass if I used her name, told me that the only kind of cookbook she would even consider representing was one written by a celebrity or with a strong gimmick. If someone actually wrote the Prince Charles and Lady Di book, in England it would be a celebrity gimmick. Maybe in America too! I think *What's Cooking in Congress*, featuring Daniel Patrick Moynihan's Curried Cauliflower and Tip O'Neill Jr.'s Beer Roast is a gimmick. So is *Tofu Fantasies*, billed as an X-rated cookbook with real recipes. I'm not sure what to make of books like the *Nancy Drew Cookbook for Children*, but as I remember, Nancy Drew was too busy running around in her little blue "roadster," chasing Ned, and solving murders to spend much time in the kitchen. I think I'd have to classify that one as a gimmick too.

I remember a book called *Cooking Out of This World*, a collection of recipes that the editor solicited from science-fiction writers. A few of the recipes were fair; more of them were nonrecipes of the pour-a-bottle-of-A-1-Sauce-over-cream-cheese variety. That's the real problem with most gimmick cookbooks, I think. The recipes are not serious enough to stand on their own. The only reason anybody thinks you can create an appetizer by pouring something on cream cheese is that the idea came from a well-known science-fiction writer. This approach to cookbooks reflects not love of food but infatuation with fads, celebrities, and a quick buck. If you're looking for ways of talking about good foods, *Best Recipes from the Backs of Boxes, Bottles, Cans, and Jars* is hard to take seriously.

Similarly, it's hard to take seriously the *Presley Family Cookbook*, featuring favorites of Elvis, although the volume contains some real, down-home Southern recipes. Somehow a rock-and-roll star seems a peculiar subject around which to organize a collection of recipes. And I still haven't decided whether I think such books as the *Runner's World* cookbooks are gimmicks.

At this point, honesty compels me to acknowledge that my unwillingness to take gimmick cookbooks seriously is not reflected in the marketplace. Witness *More Recipes from the Backs of Boxes, Bottles, Cans, and Jars,* and then (can you believe it?) *Even More Recipes from the Backs, Bottles, Cans, and Jars.* All three books were written by Ceil Dyer (who is undoubtedly a good deal richer than I am right now), and published by McGraw-Hill. So, if you cook for a celebrity or have a thousand recipes for marathon runners or a month's worth of menus to serve on the space shuttle, ignore my disdain for gimmick cookbooks. You will probably find a publisher and make some money. I never thought much of Coca-Cola either. A word of warning: if your idea for a gimmick is timely, related to a person or event likely to pass from the scene quickly, get to a publisher as fast as you can. This is a situation in which simultaneous submissions, which are discussed in detail in the chapter on trade publication, may be a good idea for saving time and getting the book out while the foundation for the gimmick is still hot. *Recipes to Cook Standing on Your Head* might be a success as long as the fitness craze and interest in yoga last, but if you want to do a book about what John MacEnroe eats before Wimbledon, you'd better do it before people are saying, "John who?" If you don't get your idea out while it is still timely, you're left with those saddest words of tongue or pen, "It might have been."

What's Your Purpose?

By the time you have thought through all the different kinds of cookbooks you might write, you should have a good idea which one is right for you. If you still are debating, go back to the questions, "Why do I want to write a cookbook? For whom?" If your answer to the first question is "I want to make a lot of money," I refer you to my comments on gimmick cookbooks or suggest that you look into printing money instead of books. But if you want to share your enjoyment of food with particular people, ask yourself a few more questions to refine your cookbook plans.

What is your intended audience like? Are they experienced cooks or beginners? Do they cook for fun or from necessity? What matters most to them, the sensual pleasure of food or its nutritional value? Are their eating habits restricted by health problems? Do they prefer to use fresh or prepared ingredients?

You should also ask questions about your recipes. Are the recipes old family treasures or did you make them up? Are they for basic daily fare or for special occasions? Do they take a long time to prepare or are they for fast meals?

Looking back over these questions, let's see how your answers might influence your planning. If your audience is your children and their friends, all of whom are just about to leave home (halleujah!) to live on their own, you may decide they need a cookbook with directions for fundamental cooking processes. The recipes they want might be the family favorites they grew up with. But since they are young and busy, they won't want to spend as long making a Brunswick stew as you do. So you'll work out a quick variation on the old favorite, substituting some prepared ingredients where the original recipe used fresh.

I don't want to belabor this example. You can see how it works. Write down as many questions as you can think of about why you want to write a cookbook and for whom; then answer them. Your answers will help you understand clearly what you should and should not try. When you think you have asked and answered every question you can possibly dream up, try one more: how do you want your readers to think and feel and behave as a result of reading your cookbook? Write your response as a declarative sentence. For example, *I want my readers to be able to cook daily meals that taste good, take no more than an hour, and supply the nutrients of the basic four food groups. I want them to feel that it is so easy and pleasant to cook at home that they will not want to go to Burger King every night.* In the beginning you may have had in mind a simple compilation of the recipes you used over the years, but your answers to the questions may have led you to a cookbook that includes suggested menus for complete meals, with recipes adapted to make them faster and easier to prepare.

You can see how your intended audience guides your decisions, but your personal interests are something else again. Suppose, for instance, that over the years you've marveled at all the interesting dishes you can make with peanuts; you've collected and created hundreds of peanut recipes and would like to share with other cooks the unappreciated possibilities beyond mixed nuts. You want to write a single-subject cookbook.

In my own case, when I was writing *Cooking from Scratch*, what I really wanted was to get more people to cook and eat their food in something closer to its natural state than Twinkies and Co-Co Puffs. My first thought had been to do that with a general, all-purpose cookbook that emphasized natural ingredients, but Garden Way's invitation to write about whole grains offered me the same opportunity through a single-subject cookbook. (Here you can see how the classifications break down. If "whole grains" is a single subject, what is "wheat"? A fraction of the whole? Don't take classifications too seriously because they are static, while life moves. The only purpose for classifications of things like cookbooks is to hold them still long enough for us to think about them.)

Looking at another family example, suppose you want to leave your children and grandchildren a record of cooking that has become traditional in your family so that they can continue the tradition through future generations. You will have to write a kind of all-purpose cookbook with an underlying theme that says, "Here's how we have done it in our family."

Your underlying purpose is important. Knowing clearly what it is and staying focused on it make your book special. In her introduction to *The Calculating Cook*, Jeanne Jones explains how that process works for her. She had prided herself on dinner parties which ranged from simple to extravagant; then she learned she had diabetes. Her doctor instructed her to follow an exchange diet that emphasized weighing and measuring to be sure of eating exactly the right foods in the right quantities at each meal. At first she thought she would have to give up gourmet dinner parties. Instead she decided to work out recipes in which she knew how much of every ingredient was in each portion. The process of creating balanced recipes in which ingredients could be calculated by the portion led her to write *The Calculating Cook*, a gourmet cookbook for diabetics which is equally good for everyone else who wants a well-balanced diet. Her underlying purpose was to create recipes for diabetics which would please gourmet tastes as well. Since then she has also written *Diet for a Happy Heart, Secrets of Salt-Free Cooking, The Fabulous Fiber Cookbook,* and *Fitness First—A 14-Day Diet and Exercise Program.* "In each case," she told me, "I was proposing to meet a special diet need." Her steady focus on meeting that need keeps each of her books internally consistent.

Your purpose may not be quite as demanding as Jeanne Jones', but it should be so well defined that it guides you in deciding what kind of cookbook to write, whether to do it alone or with collaborators, and how to publish it.

Publishing Possibilities

The most obvious place to start is the commercial, or trade book publisher. Nevertheless, bundling up your recipes and sending them to a familiar publishing house is only one of several options, and not always the best one at that. Self-publishing, in which you handle everything yourself, from finding the printer to selling the finished book, has long been the preferred way for all kinds of church groups and women's organizations looking for ways to raise money. There is even an annual directory of the best cookbooks published by volunteer groups all over the country, called *The Collection: Classic Community Cookbooks.* It lists nearly 150 self-published cookbooks good enough to warrant nationwide attention from booksellers. (The Collection, Inc., P.O. Box 11465, Memphis, TN 38111.)

For publishing on a smaller scale, personal publishing—that is, creating just enough books for family and friends without concern for making money through sales—enjoys increasing popularity.

The following chapters describe in detail how to go about each of these kinds of publishing. Since collaborating and working with groups are most frequent in the cookbook projects of organizations that self-publish, you will find a lengthy discussion of collaboration in that chapter, although the same advice would certainly pertain if you were collaborating on a personal or trade project.

To see how the kind of publishing you choose will affect your book, let's go back to the make-believe Italian cookbook. If you let your husband talk you into looking for a trade publisher and (you hope) a national readership, you'll have to be careful not to duplicate too many recipes found in existing cookbooks; you must also decide on a theme and a focus that appeal to cooks across the country. Titles such as *Italian Cooking for Appalachians* won't have a broad enough appeal. Moreover, you'll need to make sure the ingredients specified in your recipes are available across the country, or you will have to suggest substitutes. If you decide to use all the nice little family stories about your recipes, you will have to do so in a way that makes interesting reading even for people who never knew your family.

If you choose to do this book as a self-published fund raiser for a local woman's club, you will have a bit more leeway. If the club's intended market is mainly Cleveland, for example, you might work out a title identifying that market, such as *Italian Cooking Comes to Cleveland.* You must be sure that all the ingredients are available in Cleveland—never mind about Kansas. If your Italian family is well known in Cleveland's restaurant circles, you might want to include some stories about the restaurants where recipes originated or were frequently served, or some other details to keep the Cleveland slant strong.

Suppose, though, that you want to publish something to give your kids and all your relatives who love your Italian food and want your recipes. Then you are looking at personal publishing. You would need a title along the lines of *Mama's Family Recipes* or *The Pitzers Cook Italian.*

And since some of the people in your family may live far away, you should tell them what to substitute for the ingredients they can't buy in Anchorage, Alaska. When you introduce the recipes, you have at your disposal every memory you can conjure up, as well as all the old family stories you fear will disappear before the younger generations can learn them.

You can see from these somewhat exaggerated hypotheses that your cookbook would be substantially different in each of the three modes of publication, even if you used identical recipes.

As you read on, try to develop your own ideas of what you want from a cookbook. You will find that those ideas are shaped by the things you value. My inclination toward natural foods, for instance, leads me to prefer cookbooks that do not use canned soups, powdered mixes, or Jello. But a cook who relies on those kinds of ingredients will appreciate a book that shows her new and interesting ways to use them. For her, that will be a good cookbook. As much as our individual tastes affect our judgment, however, people who work constantly with cookbooks have developed some fairly uniform standards for judging their quality.

What's in a Cookbook?

David Strymish founded a cookbook distributing company called Jessica's Biscuit, which specializes in creating cookbook catalogs for home consumers. He supplements the catalogs with newsletters about the latest cookbooks. (Jessica's Biscuit, Box 301, Newtonville, MA 02160). Strymish knows cookbooks; in two and a half years, Jessica's Biscuit attracted more than 40,000 customers.

When Strymish evaluates cookbooks, he does it with those customers in mind:

I'm really looking for value. I ask myself if the book is really worth its price. I look at the quality of the recipes, the graphics, and whether or not the book is easy to use. I look to see if it offers something different. And I consider each book in terms of two different markets, the "down-home" people who want a down-to-earth cookbook, and the sophisticate market that is looking for the "gourmet" approach. I just look at each book and try to think if this is something people would want.

Judith Jones, cookbook editor at Alfred A. Knopf and collaborator with her husband on *The Book of Bread*, is probably one of the most influential people in the cookbook world today. In an interview for *The Cook's Magazine*, she said that before buying a cookbook you should check recipes to decide how much they really teach about how the dishes should look and taste. She suggests checking a few recipes for foods whose preparation you know, to see how the book's directions stack up against your own knowledge. Like Strymish, she likes to find originality and new ideas in cookbooks.

Susan Herbert, who is editor and publisher of the Owlswood cookbooks, is also a partner with her husband in distributing equipment wholesale to gourmet and cooking shops. In her view, the most important thing about a cookbook is that its recipes work and that their results taste good. "I think illustrations make a difference in the appeal of a cookbook, too," she said, "but mainly, when you look at a recipe, its method should make sense."

Karen Hess, who has specialized in food history and reviews cookbooks for many periodicals, including the *New York Times,* is especially sensitive to the honesty of recipes in cookbooks. "A recipe should deliver what it promises," she said. "And if a particular recipe needs very fresh organically-grown vegetables and real cream to turn out properly, the cook has a right to know that."

Sheila Lowenstein, associate editor of *Cook's* magazine, said that for her the important thing about a cookbook is how well its parameters are defined and how well it conforms to them—in other words, how well it does what it set out to do.

Perhaps the best-known evaluators of cookbooks are the people who select the books to receive the Tastemaker Award for outstanding cookbooks, given each year by the R.T. French Company. To be nominated for the award, a book must be copyrighted and must be original. Recipes must make up at least 50 percent of the text, and must list ingredients in the order in which they're used. Each recipe must be printed on a single page, avoiding continuations to following pages. (See the Appendix of this book for a list of winners.)

Publishers usually nominate books for the competition. The judging panels, made up of authors, editors, and publishers, consider the nominees for the quality of recipes and text, the usefulness of the book, the quality of its presentation in layout and design, and the book's originality. As you can see, the question underlying these considerations is, as Ms. Lowenstein suggested, "How well does the book accomplish what it set out to do?"

Just as you look at cookbooks with these various criteria in mind, so people who know about cookbooks will look at yours. One more time, then, make sure you have thought carefully about those two questions:

> Why do I want to write a cookbook?
> For whom?

Let the answers to these questions and the criteria sketched out in the preceding paragraphs guide you from here. At this point it is a good idea to sit down with your pen or typewriter and expand on the the answers you wrote earlier to these questions, along with any new ideas that come to you about what you want to include in your cookbook. Thus you might write "I want to write a cookbook to give to my children and their friends as they go off to start their own homes because they have all told me so often that they liked 'Sara-food.' I will include recipes that I remember they enjoyed in my house, but I will not use any complicated recipes because they are probably novices in the kitchen. I will make my directions very simple and give them a step at a time. And just for the pleasure I think it will give them, I will introduce each recipe with a little story about when one of the kids first ate it at my house."

As you continue this way, you will probably eliminate trade publishing as an option. You might also decide that self-publishing for money is not what you want, but that personal publishing, as described in Chapter Five, would be just right. As you read the chapters and write down the results of your brainstorming and the answers to your questions, you will find that you have mapped out a course of action for yourself, covering everything from how to organize your book to how to illustrate it. You may find that the justifications for your decisions and the explanations of what you are doing can be used as part of the introduction to your cookbook. Even if you eventually write a different introduction, this brainstorming on paper will help you conquer the urge to procrastinate often elicited by the sight of white paper waiting for words.

CHAPTER 2

Finding and Testing Recipes

*A*s moments of truth go, it was one of the worst. My daughter was on the telephone long distance, saying "Mom, I'm trying to bake this honey-oat bread in your book. When you say to let the yeast mixture stand until frothy, how frothy is frothy?"

I described froth for her, sounding more confident than I felt, and hung up with a thousand worries in my belly. My kid was out there teaching herself to cook out of *my* cookbook. Early failures might turn her off altogether and make her feel like a failure herself. Was that recipe *right*? Did it really work? Did I get the instructions clear enough?

Turned out it was, it did, and I had. Her bread was better than any I had ever made from the recipe, she reported.

This episode points up a reality: people *use* cookbooks. They buy the ingredients you list, apportion them in the quantities you specify, and assemble them in the ways you direct. Certainly, many of us collect cookbooks compulsively and read them more than we cook out of them, but you can never assume that nobody will try a recipe, no matter how complicated or bizarre. I've had cookbooks I didn't use for years, and then on impulse some idle afternoon tried out the recipe for an exotic dessert I remembered reading in the book. This means that any recipe you put into a cookbook has to be something that a cook *could* use, even if you consider it unlikely and included the recipe mainly as a curiosity.

Where Do Recipes Come From?

Everywhere. We get recipes from other cooks; we make them up; we change existing recipes; we ferret them out of historical sources; we collect them from family files. And a few of us, I am sorry to say, just plain steal them.

I still remember a conversation I overheard at a writers' conference between a woman who wanted to write a cookbook and another woman who already had.

"What do you do," the inexperienced writer asked, "if you want to use a recipe that's already in another book?"

"Change a little something," the second writer said.

It goes on. Think of all the recipes you've seen for, let's say, Crab Imperial. Haul out a bunch of books with seafood recipes. You encounter Crab Imperial with wine and Crab Imperial without wine, with mayonnaise and without mayonnaise, with sour cream, with green pepper, and with wheat germ topping—a lot of recipes that differ from one another in small ways but offer nothing really new.

You've probably heard the saying that there are no truly new recipes. I don't believe it. But I think it seems true because of the abandon with which cookbook writers have borrowed from one another without acknowledgment. Some of the most borrowed-from publications are *Gourmet* magazine and the various books by Julia Child, James Beard, and Craig Claiborne. Experienced editors and publishers recognize their influence when it's too strong, so no matter how much you like their recipes, find others for your book.

One newspaper food columnist said that whenever she wanted to "borrow" a recipe she just added a fourth-cup chopped parsley to it. Somehow I've never imagined that the practice raised her chocolate brownies to the level of those made famous by Alice B. Toklas.

When I asked an editor, who has obviously seen one too many borrowed recipes in her time, what she would like me to include in a book for would-be cookbook authors, she replied, "Define plagiarism."

Legally a recipe cannot be copyrighted, but its presentation can. This means that you can use the ingredients and proportions of a recipe already in print, but you must give the instructions for assembling and cooking in your own words, not in the words of the original writer of the recipe.

There's an exception to this rule: if you decide for some reason that you must use a recipe from an existing book exactly as it is written, you can write to the publisher and request permission to print the recipe, explaining briefly how and where you intend to use it.

If the publisher's full address is not given in the front of the book from which you want to use a recipe, check *Writer's Market* or *Literary Market Place* listings under "book publishers." You will find a complete address and often the name of the person to whom you should direct a request for permission to use quoted material. If a publisher does not list anyone to contact for permissions, simply mark your envelope "Attention—permissions editor."

In your letter, give the name and page number of the recipe you want to use, followed by the title and author of the book in which it appears. Explain that you wish to reprint the recipe in a book you are writing, and give the title, publisher, and probable publication date. If the book is to be self-published rather than published by a trade house, say so. If permission is granted (and it usually is, sometimes for free and sometimes for a specified sum called a "permissions fee," which may be about $50), you can include the recipe in your book. The publisher who granted you permission to reproduce the recipe will tell you what to say in giving credit to the source.

A more common approach is to use the recipe, possibly changed a little and expressed in your own words, with some explanation to the effect that the recipe is based on one from Julia Child or similar to one from James Beard. I have used this technique in creating recipes using whole-grain flour, based on versions that called originally for white flour. But if, in contemplating your book, you find yourself "borrowing" many recipes, maybe you aren't ready yet to write a cookbook to sell. I can't think of any reason why the world needs another rehash of existing gourmet recipes.

It's a different story if you're creating a personally published book to share only with your family and friends. Technically you still can't offer word-for-word copies, but recipients will understand that the recipes in your book come from a variety of sources and that you are offering them because they please you and because you think they would please the people to whom you are giving the book.

However you publish, if you are offering a collection of old recipes, famous recipes, or recipes from celebrities, you ought to give credit to your sources, not only to be fair, but also for the added interest. At first the line between collecting and borrowing recipes may seem fuzzy, but the difference lies mainly in what you are collecting. If you are collecting recipes of the Old South, for instance, you might gather them everywhere, from old handwritten family manuscripts to the slick pages of *Southern Living* magazine. They would warrant being reproduced as a new book, first, because they don't exist all together anywhere else, and second, because you are making no claim that you originated them. The implication in "borrowed" recipes not attributed to their sources is that the author created them and that they differ significantly from those already in print. A collection makes no such claim.

Recipes as Collectibles

Most of us are recipe collectors. Anybody who habitually clips recipes from newspapers and magazines, or who consistently badgers restaurant chefs for recipes, or who can't leave a dinner party without getting the dessert recipe from the hostess, is a collector. Our growing interest in our history and heritage has made collections of old recipes especially popular lately, but you can collect any kind of recipe: family favorites, ethnic dishes, celebrities' specialties, or historical classics. Many of us have collections which are probably large enough to become books. For years I have collected cheesecake recipes and recipes using chocolate. A man with whom I work has eased the boredom of almost constant travel by cultivating an interest in local chili—the chili served as a specialty in all the eating places in all the cities he visits. He has a huge stack of chili recipes, including one calling for possum meat which I don't believe he has ever tasted.

Probably neither his collection nor mine will ever become books because they've been done so often already. I can't imagine what I could do to offer something more enticing than Mabel Hoffman's HP book, *Chocolate Cookery,* which contains more than 225 recipes using chocolate, or what I might include in a book to compete with *The Joy of Chocolate,* by Judith Olney and Ruth Klingel, which made the Book-of-the-Month Club catalog. The world doesn't seem to need another chocolate cookbook. And though Ken's chili recipes vary in quantity, making anywhere from a quart to fifty gallons, and in some of their ingredients, they all seem too similar to each other to make a very interesting book, even for chili lovers. Besides, Frank X. Tolbert has already written the definitive chili book, *A Bowl of Red,* complete with anecdotes.

In collecting recipes for a book, the important thing is to have a strong theme to serve as your guiding and organizing principle and make your book unique. Recently I talked with some women who want to publish a book of recipes from the wives of the South Carolina state legislators. They liked the idea of calling it *The Kitchen Cabinet.* No telling how that project will eventually turn out, but we discussed the fact that simply being wives of legislators wouldn't add up to a good or interesting cookbook; they needed a secondary theme. In South Carolina some possible secondary themes are seafood recipes, since South Carolina is a coastal state; or barbecue recipes, since the area is famous for its barbecue; or recipes for entertaining, since politicians do so much of it; or picnic recipes, since political stumping at picnics is part of the summer tradition. Then the resulting book might be something like *Best South Carolina Barbecue Recipes,* by the wives of state legislators, or maybe *Kitchen Cabinet Picnics.* A collection defined in this way would not only make a better book, but would have a better chance of selling.

A book that has used an interesting title to emphasize its theme is *Chicken Foot Soup (And Other Recipes from the Pine Barrens),* edited by

Arlene Martin Ridgway. The recipes all come from the New Jersey Pine Barrens, but beyond that they have nothing in common. Some are old; some are new. Some are from local people; others are the editor's. Some reflect the ethnic influence of the American Indians who once lived in the area; others do not. But they are all from the Pine Barrens. Ms. Ridgway amplified the theme in her introduction, saying that the common element in all the recipes is ingredients that are "readily available in the Pine Barrens—berries, seafood, vegetables, and game. The remaining ingredients are low-cost items." And so the book emphasizes simple, inexpensive recipes, which means that even if she has some splendid gourmet recipes from elsewhere for shrimp (and I'm sure she does), Ms. Ridgway had to leave them out. Her title emphasizes the theme further; as she explains, "It is appropriate to single out this title because it serves as a reminder that little is wasted in the Pine Barrens." Not only do they use chicken feet, they also use the food from the shore, the woods, and the swamps. Also, that organizing theme makes it reasonable for her to include recipes for cranberry wine, clam bisque, and roast wild goose, all in the same book.

In this kind of collection, the "author" may work more as an editor, gathering and organizing the recipes but using them essentially as they were given to her, except to make whatever changes are necessary for clarity, accuracy, and consistency. In such collections, the author-editor usually writes an introduction and whatever text is necessary to connect the recipes.

Another approach is to collect the recipes and rewrite them all in your own style. Either way, the trick to assembling a good collection-type cookbook is in finding recipes that are not already available in a dozen other books or in last month's *Good Housekeeping* magazine.

Another source of recipes, in addition to your own family, is other cooks. People who like to cook exchange recipes almost as a matter of course. Most of us take pride in being asked for our recipes. I still boast about the woman who once told me that my Marinated Garden Relish "haunted" her, although I never heard from her again after I sent her the recipe. As it happens, a neighbor had given me the recipe years earlier. I don't know where she got it.

That brings us to a caution in publishing recipes given to us by other people. How can you be sure you got the recipe from its original creator? I have received many recipes nicely typed on "from-the-kitchen-of" cards and believed the recipes were created by the person who gave them to me, only to be disillusioned later when I found the same recipe in a popular cookbook.

It can happen to anyone. Last Thanksgiving the staff for *All Things*

Considered on National Public Radio made a huge production of correcting a mistake they made with a recipe the year before. They had given listeners a recipe for an unusual cranberry relish containing sour cream. They attributed it to a staff member's sister-in-law, who said it was her mother's. A year later they confessed that when the sister-in-law's mother heard the recipe attributed to her, she said she had taken it from an old Craig Claiborne book. As part of their second-year correction, *All Things Considered* called Craig Claiborne to apologize for what had happened to his recipe. Fortunately, Craig had forgotten it. He had gone on to new ideas and entertained the radio audience with a description of what he planned to serve for Thanksgiving this year. The story might not have ended so well.

One way to avoid publishing as original recipes already used in cookbooks is to trace a recipe to its originator by asking the person who gives it to you where she got it, then checking with whoever gave it to her, as far back as you can. Also, the more familiar you are with other cookbooks, especially the more popular ones such as those by Claiborne, Beard, and Child, the more likely you will be to recognize a recipe from a book, even if it comes to you handwritten on the back of a telephone bill.

You can also get interesting ideas from restaurants whose food you like, and sometimes from the little booklets offered by various manufacturers. I respond to almost all those "write for free recipes" offers, even though I use very few of their recipes.

You may find good ideas in the brochures and newsletters put on by county extension agents, utility companies, food boards, and the various organizations with which you are affiliated. The best cookie recipe in the world, for Pumpkin Spice Cookies, came to me one Halloween in a monthly consumer bulletin written by a home economist on the public-relations staff of an electric company. Oh—those cookies! They baked up tender and just a little puffy, like tiny cakes; not too sweet, with a faint caramel taste. The pumpkin turned them a delicate shade of orange and the cinnamon and clove in them hinted at pumpkin pie. After I tasted the first cookie, I would have gone out and bought an electric stove if the recipe had said they had to be baked in an electric oven and I hadn't had one. Not all recipes from such sources are so successful. Home economists don't write them all, and smaller publications from local organizations may not test recipes at all, so before you try any of them, check carefully to see if proportions, ingredients, and cooking times look right.

Yet another possibility is what I call the "rescuing from obscurity" approach. This involves tracking down *very* old recipes and presenting them to the reader in one of several ways. Rick Harwell did this with a recipe that means a lot to all true Southerners: for years he collected recipes for mint juleps. Being an historian, he collected at the same time stories about the origins of each recipe, and eventually published them in a little book entitled *The Mint Julep,* with each recipe written as it had been by its originator.

In 1933 Harriet Ross Colquitt collected old recipes (which she called "receipts") from the black cooks in and around Savannah, Georgia, who were expert at preparing the old traditional dishes of the area. Other recipes in her book came from old notebooks in which mothers and grandmothers and great-grandmothers had kept their favorites. Mrs. Colquitt then did what was necessary to translate these recipes into contemporary (by 1930s standards) cooking languages, explaining anything interesting or unusual about each recipe as she presented it. The resulting book, *The Savannah Cookbook: A Collection of Old Fashioned Receipts from Colonial Kitchens,* rescued from probable extinction the food customs of an entire region.

In Charleston, South Carolina, Helen Woodward rescued the old Charleston recipes that friends had given to Blanche Salley Rhett. Lettie Gay, the editor of the New York Herald Institute, tested the recipes in her laboratory test kitchen and tried to standardize measurements and methods. The book, *Charleston Cooking,* was published in 1930. Many of the recipes came from unpublished or out-of-print collections which had been saved through generations in plantation kitchens. In 1976 the book was reprinted with a new introduction and explanatory matter by Elizabeth Hamilton. This elaborate collaboration over time and distance rescued the cooking traditions of another region from obscurity.

In the examples I have mentioned so far, you will notice that the balance is tipped heavily toward historical collections. That's because there are so many of them and because public interest in them continues to run high. In a similar vein, regional recipes are also a popular choice for collections. Peanut Butter Publishing offers *Dining in Philadelphia,* gourmet recipes from chefs in twenty-one of Philadelphia's best-known restaurants. The same publisher offers similar books for other major cities, including Pittsburgh, Pennsylvania, an area I never specifically associated with fine dining.

For an example that is neither specifically regional nor historical, another, even more unlikely, book from Pittsburgh is the *Super Steeler Cookbook.* This collection of recipes from members of the Steeler football team includes favorites they have picked up in restaurants when they are playing away from home. The Sarasota Opera Society published

The Prima Diner, recipes from opera stars and music personalities and William Faulkner's granddaughter compiled *The Great American Writers' Cookbook.* Or how about *Dave Maynard's Tried and True All Night Radio Secret Family Recipe Cookbook?* Clearly, almost anything can be the subject for a collection of recipes.

The regional collections, celebrity collections, modernized historical collections, and so on are intended for entertainment as well as for cooking. Some of the books that emphasize the history of recipes and give them in their original form may be tricky to actually execute, but they make great reading.

Reasonable Facsimiles

Instead of collecting individual recipes, some authors concentrate on entire old books. The food writer Karen Hess specializes in tracking down classic cookbooks. She has her publishers make a photographic reproduction (called a facsimile reproduction) of the original book and then provides commentary, including historical background and explanation of terms no longer used, so that the original makes sense to the modern reader. In commentary for *The Martha Washington Book of Cookery* and *The Virginia Housewife,* Ms. Hess explains old cooking methods and equipment, showing how they would have affected the recipes in these old books and often commenting tartly on how much better the food would have tasted if prepared in that way. She defines old words and strangely spelled names for ingredients. William Woys Weaver has done much the same with *A Quaker Woman's Cookbook,* Anna Rutledge with *The Carolina Housewife,* and Marie Kimball with *Thomas Jefferson's Cook Book.* The last is a collection, not a facsimile reproduction of the recipes, which is to say that the recipes have been set in new type, not photographed from the original book.

If you have an interest in history and in old approaches to food, you may choose to collect old recipes, testing them and publishing them as they stand; to find an old, out-of-print cookbook of uncommon interest and publish a facsimile edition of it with your commentary; or to create your own new recipes from the ideas you find in these old sources.

In addition to historical interest, old sources are great inspiration for creating something not commonly found in today's cookbooks. I found a recipe in *The Savannah Cookbook* for a meatless bean soup containing turnips and rutabagas. The instructions were not too specific about quantities, but the recipe sounded as if it would make a huge amount, so I cut down on the quantity of beans. Then I added a few ingredients like carrots and celery, which were not in the original recipe, and ended up with a luscious soup which was neither an old recipe nor, to be honest, an entirely new one. Having checked and recorded my measurements, I will eventually use that recipe in a book I'm planning for vegetarian meals that don't taste too exotic for kids or for most American tastes. I will credit the source of the old recipe on which my own is based.

Old Recipes to New

Even so, adapting recipes goes far beyond modernizing historic sources. Entire cookbooks are built around adaptations of popular recipes. In many "health food" recipes, for example, honey or fructose is substituted for sugar, herbs for salt, stock for fat, yogurt for sour cream, carob for chocolate, and so on. Such variations require extensive testing because of the differences in the way the substituted ingredients may behave. Honey is sweeter than the same amount of sugar, and so on. Vegetarian cooking often adapts recipes that originally contained meat to use meat substitutes. Tofu may replace meat in lasagna; beans may replace lamb in Shepherd's Pie.

Necessity has forced adaptation, too, both today and in the past. Some canny cook made mincemeat from green tomatoes when she couldn't get beef or venison. Another old recipe makes "corn oysters" from fresh sweet corn cut off the cob, shaped, breaded, and fried like oysters. The classic "appleless pie" substitutes Ritz crackers for apples and relies on the cinnamon, sugar, and cloves to convey the aura of real apple pie. (I've always wondered where it was easier to get Ritz crackers than apples.) Zucchini pickles are an adaptation of classic recipes for bread-and-butter pickles, and I would bet my last dollar that they were created by a cook whose cucumber vines were overrun by her zucchini plants.

Professional cookbook authors seem to adapt recipes in two very different ways. One group attempts to retain the essential character of the original recipes; the other proceeds according to the notion that anything goes.

In adapting some classic ethnic recipes for the *Moosewood Cookbook* and the *Enchanted Broccoli Forest*, Mollie Katzen said that she tried to retain the "ethnic purity" of classic dishes, even though she adapted them to be made without meat. "I would never make a Chinese stir-fry dish and put cottage cheese in it," she said. As she explained it, a country's traditional styles of cooking reflect the ingredients commonly used and available in that country. In Chinese cooking, milk products are virtually never used, and cottage cheese certainly has no long and venerable history in China. Similarly, she said, "Tofu isn't Mexican, so

I would never write a recipe that used tofu in enchiladas."

While I don't want to give tofu a bad name, the anything-goes school does seem to be at its worst in trying to find ways to use it. Nobody's going to convince me that tofu can replace ice cream in a chocolate milk shake.

This unfettered approach does seem to make sense, though, when you're using the techniques of substitution and adaptation not to create another version of a classic dish, but to create an entirely new recipe. When I want to make up a new yeast bread recipe, for example, I begin with a standard recipe for basic white bread, which gives me the proportions for flour, liquids, fat, and yeast. In the basic recipe the liquid is water. I may substitute milk or stock or even diluted sour cream. Instead of white flour, perhaps I will use ground oats and whole wheat flour. Then I may have to increase the amount of liquid because I've learned that the bran in whole wheat flour soaks up liquid faster than ordinary white flour. And so I will continue, adjusting each ingredient as it seems necessary and writing it all down as I go until I have essentially a new recipe for bread, adapted from a simple basic recipe.

Andrea Chesman, a cookbook author and editor who studied at the Cornell Cooking School and subsequently spent seven years cooking to support her writing habit, describes a similar way of using adaptation to create new recipes. "I look at a recipe for something like carrot soup," she said, "and instead of thinking of all the things I could add to carrot soup to make it different, I think of what would happen if I substituted green beans for the carrots to make an entirely new soup."

Lou Seibert Pappas, whose HP book *Vegetables* won a Tastemaker Award, says many of her recipes came from ideas she gets while traveling and eating in restaurants. She said, "I can go home and duplicate what I have eaten."

This kind of adapting has a creative edge that leads you more and more into inventing recipes on your own, without relying on any that already exist. Developing recipes from scratch is fun because it's not entirely predictable.

People who create recipes work in several ways. One is first to create on paper, then to go into the kitchen to verify and adjust the results. Imagine yourself sitting down at the desk, thinking, "Let's see. I'll start with a cup of tomatoes and a cup of ground chicken. Then I'll add . . . ," and writing it all down as you dream it up.

Then, in your verification stage, you go into the kitchen and actually do what you wrote down. The mixture comes out a bit soupy and a little bland, so you throw in a cup of chopped onions and thicken the tomatoes with a tablespoon of cornstarch dissolved in two tablespoons of cold water. That makes it just right. In the process, your verification phase has moved into the adjustment stage. If you are so familiar with food and ingredients that you know automatically how thick a tablespoon of cornstarch will make a cup of liquid, this is a very rational and scientific way to proceed. If you have the ability to imagine how various combinations of ingredients will probably taste, you can develop some genuinely delicious and distinctive recipes.

The Mother of Invention

One recipe I developed in this manner for my book on whole grains was for rye berries with parsnips. I honestly don't think anybody in the world before me had ever thought to combine rye berries and parsnips. Nor does one usually hang around the kitchen fiddling with either ingredient, so the combination was not likely to come about by chance. Still, I needed another recipe for my chapter on rye.

I had read in another cookbook that rye berries tasted terrible and that you couldn't do much with them. I disagreed. In fact, I had discovered that rye berries had a pleasant, chewy, almost sweet flavor, which I thought would combine nicely with some vegetable that had a soft texture for contrast and its own hint of sweetness to blend in. But what vegetable?

Sweet potatoes? Too mushy and too sweet.

Green peas? Too similar in texture because of the skins.

Carrots? Right texture but too bland.

Parsnips? Good texture, distinctive, near-sweet flavor—might work.

I tried it and the combination was delicious, but the dish seemed incomplete. I didn't like those loose rye berries and little pieces of parsnip chasing each other around on the plate. Also I wanted something to balance the protein of the grain so the dish would be more nutritious.

Melt cheese on everything? Too gooey.

Put the rye and parsnips in milk and call it soup? Too bland.

How about a light cheese sauce, not thick enough to be gooey, not strong enough to mask the other flavors? Perfect.

I mean it. Perfect.

I've served this dish at buffets and seen people go back for seconds, provided they tasted it first and learned what was in it later. Because—admit it—when I say, "rye and parsnips," you don't immediately think, "Ah, wonderful," do you? You think, "Weird," which brings us to the main difficulty of creating recipes in your head. Old stereotypes about what goes with what may keep you from trying some splendid new combinations. If your head tends to react too rigidly to words and names, according to old preconceptions, you may be better off getting away from the desk and creating at the stove.

Improvisational Cookery

Most of us cook this way often, but we don't make it into cookbooks because we aren't paying enough attention to what we do to write it all down. *The Moosewood Cookbook* grew out of this kind of cooking. A group of people ran an eating place in Ithaca, New York called the Moosewood Restaurant. It was back in the 1970s, when many of us were just beginning to flirt with the idea of eating less red meat, using more whole grains, and preparing meals from natural rather than convenience foods. The people who cooked at the Moosewood Restaurant all brought recipes and traditions from their own backgrounds, but, as Mollie puts it, "We took turns cooking and we just cooked what we felt like." The problem was that the restaurant's customers took a fancy to some of the results, ordered the same thing again, and sometimes went so far as to request the recipes. And there weren't any recipes.

Mollie began to stand around the kitchen with a notebook, writing down what each cook did and attempting to standardize the recipes so that they could be cooked by someone other than their creators. Of course, a lot of experimenting and attempts at duplication came between those first notes and the book finally published by Ten Speed Press. But if you know that such an outstanding book originated from an approach to cooking that we all use from time to time, you should feel free to experiment in the kitchen as much as you want to—taking notes all the while.

You can make faster progress with this method of creating recipes if you remember a few culinary basics. Contrasts appeal to the palate. Bland flavors need to be balanced by piquant ones. Crisp textures contrast pleasingly with soft ingredients. Sweet and sour combinations work so well that you find them not only in such Oriental recipes as Sweet and Sour Pork, but also in the traditional Pennsylvania Dutch "Seven Sweets and Seven Sours," which includes the perfect balance of vinegar and sugar in pickled beets and pepper cabbage. And don't forget that the appearance of food affects our perceptions of how it tastes. If you've ever seen a child look at a plate of food and say, "Yuck," you know how important eye appeal is. Even grown-ups, with the best will in the world, have trouble with meals of boiled potatoes, cauliflower, and sliced chicken breast. Instinct alone instructs us to add some brussels sprouts and cranberries to perk up the plate.

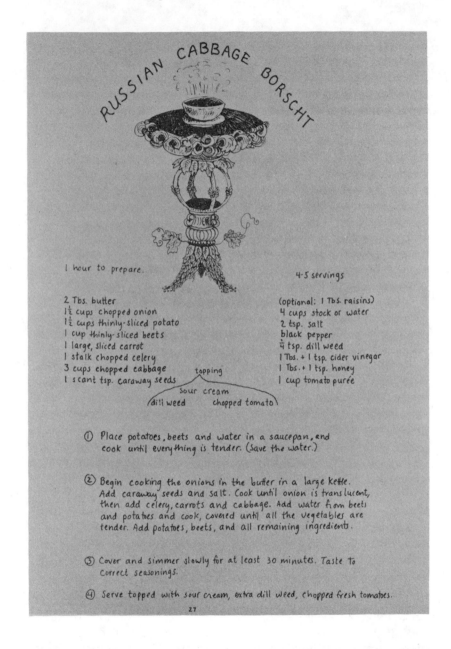

RUSSIAN CABBAGE BORSCHT

1 hour to prepare.   4·5 servings

2 Tbs. butter   (optional: 1 Tbs. raisins)
1½ cups chopped onion   4 cups stock or water
1½ cups thinly-sliced potato   2 tsp. salt
1 cup thinly-sliced beets   black pepper
1 large, sliced carrot   ⅛ tsp. dill weed
1 stalk chopped celery   1 Tbs. + 1 tsp. cider vinegar
3 cups chopped cabbage   topping   1 Tbs. + 1 tsp. honey
1 scant tsp. caraway seeds   1 cup tomato purée
                    sour cream
              dill weed   chopped tomato

① Place potatoes, beets and water in a saucepan, and
   cook until everything is tender. (Save the water.)

② Begin cooking the onions in the butter in a large kettle.
   Add caraway seeds and salt. Cook until onion is translucent,
   then add celery, carrots and cabbage. Add water from beets
   and potatoes and cook, covered until all the vegetables are
   tender. Add potatoes, beets, and all remaining ingredients.

③ Cover and simmer slowly for at least 30 minutes. Taste to
   correct seasonings.

④ Serve topped with sour cream, extra dill weed, chopped fresh tomatoes.

27

*Who ever bothers to write down recipes for soup? This recipe for Russian Cabbage
Borscht probably would have been lost forever if Mollie Katzen hadn't stood around
behind the cooks in the Moosewood Restaurant taking notes as they improvised.
(From* Moosewood Cookbook *by Mollie Katzen)*

You can do exactly the same thing in creating recipes. Let's use mashed potatoes as an example. As you know, I think that almost nothing tastes better, but their smooth texture, bland flavor, and white color call for contrasts to keep them from seeming like what we called "hospital food" when we were kids.

Now let's go to the kitchen and run through the process of turning mashed potatoes into a recipe. First, what quantity of mashed potatoes are we starting with? And how many raw peeled potatoes did it take to make them? When I did this last week I used five large Idaho baking potatoes to make four cups of mashed potatoes, whipped with 1/2 cup milk and one tablespoon of butter. *4-5 potatoes, cooked and mashed with 1/2 cup milk* to make four cups of mashed potatoes. That's where the recipe should start.

Next I wanted something crisp and colorful to break the white smoothness. I thought snow peas would work, but I didn't have any. Then I remembered an Irish concoction called "Colcannon," which combines white potatoes and cabbage. But the kids don't like cooked cabbage much, and I thought it would be too limp anyway. Broccoli is in the cabbage family and has a nice bright green color, and the florets have an interesting texture if you don't overcook them. I didn't want this dish to be all potatoes, so I used plenty of broccoli. *2 cups raw broccoli florets, steamed about 2 minutes.*

At that point I had mashed pototoes and slightly cooked broccoli florets and I knew I was going to mix them together, but the flavor of the two together would still be pretty dull. How about onions? Should I chop an onion and sauté it in butter? No, I didn't want any more butter in the recipe, and the onion would be limp and pale. A green onion. Better yet, two green onions! *Chop 2 green onions, tops and all.*

Now I had all these things ready to mix together. What next? If I had wanted an accompaniment for roast fowl, I would have mixed what I had, made sure everything was hot, and served it in a fancy bowl. But I wanted something for a nice light supper with nothing more than a salad. I needed to get some protein into this combination. *Beat 4 eggs until frothy and stir into the mashed potato mixture.* (Good idea, but next time, dummy, whip in the beaten eggs before you add the broccoli. It'll be easier.) *Season lightly with salt and pepper to taste.* I never specify quantities of salt for seasoning anymore because so many people are trying to cut down.

By now people were standing around waiting to eat. I had thought I would bake the mixture in a casserole, but I figured it would take at least forty-five minutes in a 350° F. oven to heat it all the way through, and the crowd was beginning to look impatient. So I dropped the potato combination by half-cupsful onto a lightly greased griddle, browned one side, turned the potato-broccoli cakes, and browned the other side. I thought about serving them with a cheese sauce but decided it would be too gooey. Instead, I topped each potato cake with a small spoonful of plain yogurt. It was nice because in addition to all the other contrasts, the cold yogurt stood out against the hot potatoes. I added more chopped green onion for garnish.

Here's how the recipe looked in the notes I made as I went along:

```
5 potatoes          (4c. mashed)
peal, boil, mash
       (1/2 cup milk)
2c. broc. flor.
    steam 2 min.
2 green onion
            chop
4 eggs beat
grease griddle
            brown
+ yogurt
+ green onions
```

Here's how it might look in print:

BROCCOLI-POTATO CAKES

4-5 large baking potatoes
water
1/2 cup milk
1 tablespoon butter
4 eggs, beaten

2 cups broccoli florets cut in 1/2 inch
  slices
2 green onions, chopped, tops and
  all
salt and pepper to taste
yogurt
chopped green onion

Peel the potatoes, cut them up, and put in a large saucepan. Cover with cold water, bring to a boil, and simmer until very tender. Drain and mash the potatoes with the milk and butter. Beat in the eggs. Steam the broccoli 2 minutes, until not quite tender. Mix the broccoli and chopped onions into the potatoes. Add salt and pepper. Ladle the mixture onto a lightly greased, heated griddle and brown 7 to 10 minutes on each side, or until the cakes are crisp on the outside and cooked through. Serve topped with yogurt and more chopped green onion. Serves 4-6.

Would that recipe ever make it into one of my books? I don't know. It might. Or maybe I would prefer to fool around with it some more, add more onion, put in a few lightly steamed carrots for color contrast, and figure out some kind of a light sauce to serve with it. Because I got the first attempt down on paper, all the options for change will be easy to try.

Over a Hot Stove

Creating in the kitchen is simply a matter of pulling all the ingredients you've been meaning to use out of the refrigerator and peeling, slicing, and steaming away, putting things together as impulse guides you and tasting as you go.

The trouble is that cooking itself is such an expansive, inventive, see-what-happens sort of activity that good cooks have trouble switching from the fun part to the painstaking notation, writing, and proofing necessary to transmit the original impulses to other cooks. Moreover, the concept of highly specific recipes that give exact amounts of ingredients and explicit instructions for combining them is still relatively new. In the old tradition, good food was the product of a good cook, not of a good recipe.

Mrs. Laurie Fuller Kurtz told this story in her *Gone With the Wind* series, printed in the *Atlanta Constitution*. In the installment printed May 7, 1939, she wrote:

This reminds me of an instance in our home once when we had a Northern visitor. She had enjoyed the waffles which we had for breakfast so much that she asked my mother for the recipe. Mother called our cook, Liza, in to tell this lady just how she made the waffles.

"Well," said Liza, "I take two aigs, flour cordin' ter de crowd, milk cordin' ter de flour, soda cordin' ter de milk, and den shorten' cordin ter all."

Even more recently, in my grandmother's time, exact notation was

47

not yet a uniform part of cooking. For years Mother tried to duplicate the pancakes for which Grandma Dietrick was famous, using the recipe Grandma had sent her.

Grandma's pancakes were astonishing. Unlike big fat "dinner pancakes," these were very thin, like crepes, with a pronounced buttery taste even before you spread fresh butter on them. And they weren't just dull round flapjacks, either. Grandma baked them right on the surface of her wood-burning stove, in the shape of roosters and rabbits and pussycats. Once you got one of the critters on your plate, you had to fold over ears and legs and tails to make sure they were buttered and dipped into the molasses. They were so tender you could cut them with the faintest pressure of a fork. Chewing seemed unnecessary, but we chewed anyway, trying to make each bite last as long as we could.

Mother tried. She really did. She found a big griddle for the electric stove and she learned to pour roosters, rabbits, and pussycats like Grandma, but the pancakes still weren't Grandma's. My mother, however, is not a woman to be defeated by a pancake. She stood by the counter watching every step as Grandma mixed up her batter and discovered that "butter the size of a walnut" was more nearly "butter the size of a teacup." After that, Mother's pancakes were a match for Grandma's any day.

In more recent times, I can think of a young artist who lives in an old church. She cooks in the basement kitchen with one leg up on the stainless steel counter as though it were a ballet bar, tossing odds and ends of ingredients into the pot to see what she can "genius out for dinner."

How do you get that kind of creativity down on paper? Obviously, if you are not trying to write a cookbook, you don't even try. Otherwise, disciplining yourself to keep notes on what you are doing is all it takes.

Make all your notations in standard measures, because the current vogue in cookbook writing is for precision almost to the point of silliness. We have gone from the casualness of "boil the chicken until done" and "add enough flour to make a thick sauce" to instructions as specific as the directions in a chemistry experiment, partly because it's now possible. Modern stoves can be heated to more precise temperature than old wood-burning cookstoves; every household has a set of standard measuring cups and spoons instead of a chipped teacup and a few pieces of silverware. Also, today's cooks are often self-taught. They learn from books rather than from repeated sessions in the kitchen with Mother or Grandmother. Without that knowledgeable companion to say, "There, that looks about right. That's enough milk," today's inexperienced cook has no choice but to rely on the precision of her recipes. So if you want to write a cookbook appropriate to today's culture, you have to learn to transcribe your instructions in exact terms. You can do it, even if you cook with the pinch-of-this, handful-of-that approach. If you habitually meaure salt by pouring it into the palm of your hand, stop long enough to scoop the salt into a measuring spoon so that you know how much the little puddle in your hand comes to. Figure out in fractions of a cup how much a handful of flour is in standard measure. And then, while you cook, simply write down the amount of each ingredient in standard terms as you use it. If you try to write them down later out of your head, you're bound to forget proportions or cooking temperatures, or to leave out some ingredient that's vital for taste or texture. Write it down as you go. Most of my recipes are on the backs of old brown mailing wrappers from the *New Yorker* because I cook on Saturdays, the same day the magazine arrives, and most of the time that brown paper is the only piece of paper I can lay my hands on in a hurry. This make-it-up-as-you-go approach to accumulating recipes requires not only faithful note taking, but also strong feet and plenty of patience for the experiments that require long cooking and still don't turn out as you like.

In time you may arrive at the creative technique Mollie Katzen says she eventually developed—a combination of working the recipe out first on paper and inventing it in the kitchen as you go along. She recommends thinking through a recipe, trying to envision how it will turn out, and listing the ingredients on paper. Then she suggests assembling all those ingredients, "looking at the pot," and using your experience and instinct to determine how much of each ingredient to use, writing down the quantities as you go. Mollie says that if you work this way the secret to success is, "Stop when it tastes good, even if you haven't added all the ingredients you planned." In working out her own recipes, Mollie has evolved a philosophy with which many good cooks agree: "I used to think the more ingredients a recipe had the better it was. Now I think just the opposite. The fewer the better."

Put It to the Test

No matter how many or how few ingredients you have put into your recipe, your next step is to test the recipe again to make sure it works the second time, and then to give it to someone else to make sure it works when prepared by another person. In fact, all but the simplest recipes should be tested several times over.

I don't know for sure that Rick Harwell tested all those Mint Julep recipes, since he says he drinks only about one a year and that one "ceremonially." And even though she's a cooking expert, I don't imagine that Karen Hess has tested the old recipes for preparing a calf's head. Still, those books are intended more as history than as user's guides. Most of us, however, want to produce a book that is usable as well as fun to read. To do that you can't escape testing. Even the self-published collections put together by church groups and clubs, where each member provides a favorite recipe, must contain only tested recipes. The only difference between such books and any single-author or commercial cookbook is in who does the testing. With group cookbooks, the contributors are often expected to do their own testing, but even then you need an editor with a sharp eye and experience in the kitchen to catch the glitches in recipes that turn souffles into soups.

I wasn't always aware of this and I'm not proud of the way I learned how crucial testing is.

In my youth, which would probably seem callow to me if I could remember it more clearly, I had a radio program called "The Wife Saver." It comprised all kinds of tips and talk about cooking, aimed at housewives at home in the late morning.

At that time, my enthusiasm for cooking exceeded my experience. I soon became so desperate for ideas to use on the show that I began to invent them. One of my better ones, I thought, was to suggest that cooks mold gelatin salads and desserts in cupcake papers placed in muffin tins. To serve the gelatin concoctions, all they would have to do was peel off the papers. No more struggling with alternate baths of hot water and ice to unmold without excessive melting. Neat idea.

A few weeks after I offered it to the listening audience of Central Pennsylvania radioland, I tried it myself. It didn't work. The gelatin clung to the cupcake papers with a tenacity that put Crazy Glue to shame. The only way I could have served that gelatin was with spoon for digging the stuff out of the cupcake papers. How many ladies' luncheons do you suppose I ruined? How many kids' birthday parties?

After that I never told anybody to do anything without trying it first myself.

Large cookbook publishers such as Sunset have elaborate test kitchens, in which they work over all recipes they use. So do all the major women's homemaking magazines. Some smaller publishers, like Nitty Gritty, have testing programs in which members of the staff take home copies of recipes to try and then fill out test sheets to report how the recipe worked. In very small publishing houses, like Owlswood, the publisher or editor will try the recipe herself. But before that step, the author—that's you—should have tested every recipe to make sure it works as given.

How do you test a recipe, exactly?

Once you have developed your recipe and written down the ingredients and procedure, you simply follow it exactly as written, as though it where someone else's, to make sure that following it will produce the results you expect. You should check especially to be sure measurements and cooking times and temperatures are correct. To be sure your oven temperatures are accurate, use an oven thermometer. If it doesn't agree with the oven thermostat on your stove, adjust your recipes to the standard temperatures as measured by the thermometer. (You can buy oven thermometers in the hardware store.) And if you have any doubt whether your instructions are clear, give a copy to someone else and have them test the recipe too. When you have a recipe whose results seem just right to you and can be duplicated from your notes every try (once or twice for simple recipes, three times for complicated ones), you can stop.

Sometimes you get it on the first try; sometimes you have an idea that never does work quite the way you thought it would. I once "invented" a chicken loaf made with brown rice, celery, onion, and chopped cooked chicken, with eggs to bind everything together. Technically the recipe worked. It baked into a nice-looking loaf I could unmold and slice. It smelled good. And it didn't taste bad, just boring. Nothing I could think of to do perked up that darned loaf, and eventually I gave up on it and threw the recipe (and part of the test results) away.

This brings us to a real problem. Testing produces a lot of food. What do you do with it all? Perhaps you've noticed how many cookbooks begin with thanks to the author's family "for eating the research," to the author's friends "for offering honest criticism," and to everyone in the world for being patient while the author ignored them because she was fooling around in the kitchen for hours at a time. Christie Williams' book for using the Cuisinart food processor, *What's Cookin'?*, opens with a photograph of her son and her husband matching bare and very big bellies with a fat stone Buddha in the park. Her caption is "To my boys, who ate it all!"

With equal honesty, Linda West Eckhard describes her months of testing for *The Only Texas Cookbook:*

> For months the pots and pans flew. My daughter made numberless trips to the grocery store. My sons washed a million dishes. My husband had to have the button on his pants set over. We cooked and ate and criticized.

When the family agreed that a recipe was good, she typed it up and sent it along with a batch of other recipes to the office of the *Texas Monthly* magazine, for which she was writing the book. Volunteers on the *Texas Monthly* staff took the recipes home and tested them again. All the testers and eaters recorded their impressions on an evaluation sheet.

You, too, will need to make up a test sheet form to keep volunteer testers' responses uniform. You can arrange it in any way you please as long as it elicits all the information you need. And even though you have devised it for other testers, you will find it useful for yourself as you work through recipes in repeat tests. (See Recipe Test Sheet, page 53.)

Creating your own recipes requires only a light heart and a dash of daring. Karl Stuecklen captures the excitement of improvisational cooking in this illustration from Beard on Pasta.

RECIPE TEST SHEET

Manuscript: _____

Recipe tested: _____

    Number of servings: _____   Cost: _____

Did you have difficulty finding the ingredients called for? _____
    If so, which ones?

Were the directions clearly written? _____ If not, please explain:

Was the oven temperature called for, correct? _____
    If not, please explain:

Was the cooking or baking time called for, correct? _____
    If not, please explain:

Was the finished dish attractive? _____ Please comment:

Did you like the recipe? _____ If yes, please comment:

If you did not like the recipe, please explain:

Were the servings, as suggested, adequate? _____ Comments:

Do you consider this recipe:
    Very Easy _____ Easy _____ Average _____ Difficult _____
Other comments or suggestions:

                                           Thank you very much.

Jeanne Jones, whose books include *Diet for a Happy Heart* and a number of other health-oriented books that require rigorous portion and ingredient measurement, described her testing for me in this way:

Testing is a tedious process in some respects and not so much in others, where the discoveries are serendipitous; i.e., when a creation which was a lousy souffle turns out to be a delightful mousse—or when something that is left in the oven longer than planned turns out to be better than it would have in the prescribed time.

She types up a double-spaced draft of the recipe she is trying in duplicate and takes the carbon copy to the kitchen for testing. Then, "If it flies, that's it. If not, the carbon is marked up and the original recipe scrapped or modified, sometimes several times."

Coralie Ayers described testing for her soup book: "I'd fix soups, three or four different kinds in small quantities, for breakfast, lunch, and dinner. And have people over to judge and suggest." (That is a good technique for soups, salads, and other simple recipes, but cakes, breads, and highly seasoned foods should be tested in the quantities to be used in your book.)

Buying food in sufficient quantity for recipes tests (six servings is the standard recipe size) can be expensive. A long time ago I read a description of Julia Child's decision to perfect a brioche recipe. The account was written by someone who lived either in the same apartment or the one underneath hers; I can't recall exactly. I do remember reading how Julia went into the kitchen with grocery bags full of "pounds and pounds of butter." She baked batch after batch of brioche, and the writer said that the weekend was punctuated with the thumps of one unsuccessful attempt after another being tossed into the garbage can. Recently I've wondered whether Julia would ever have perfected her brioche if she had tried to do it after the price of butter rose to nearly two dollars a pound.

You can get some relief from the cost of testing if you keep careful records of the ingredients you used, their cost, and your receipts for purchasing them. Even if you eventually feed most of what you cooked to the family, testing recipes is a business expense for a cookbook writer, and the cost can be deducted from your gross income at tax time.

As I've said, testing recipes produces a great deal of food, which needs to be eaten—by somebody. Coralie solved the problem of testing for her book *Hors D'Oeuvre, Etc.* simply: "Giant cocktail buffet parties."

Throughout her book, *The Vegetarian Epicure*, Anna Thomas talks about the many dinner parties at which she served her experiments, often to guests who were skeptical at first about vegetarian meals but ended up vociferous in their praise.

For many years I used a similar device to turn my testing into fun. I belonged to a group of three couples who met regularly at my house for the "experimental dinner club." I wasn't the only one who experimented back then; the other two women in the group did too. Our ground rules were that everybody taste everything but that nobody had to eat anything they didn't like. And everybody had to be honest in saying what he or she thought of the food. Occasionally I had to be reminded that these were *my* rules, because when one of the group would say, "I don't care for the cod," I tended to snap back, "Don't eat it then."

Later we moved to the country, and those little gatherings were harder to arrange. I did my heavy cooking on Saturdays and Sundays, and it was consumed, sometimes before I could even get it out of the pans, by my daughters' teenaged boyfriends.

Sometimes I had to remind myself that their eating was a service I needed. I particularly remember the day a young man circled the kitchen, lifting the lids on all the pots—including the stockpot, in which I was simmering vegetable scraps, chicken bones, and eggshells (for the calcium). I thought he dropped the lid too quickly. A minute later he pulled my daughter into another room, and I heard him ask her, "How come your mother boils the garbage?"

These days I give away a lot of my tests. And I've been a favorite with all the kids in the neighborhood here in South Carolina ever since the day I tested watermelon pickle recipes, which required me to scoop out and give away the meat of two huge watermelons so I could use the rind. Then at Christmas I pleased the kids' mommies with jars of the pickle.

I think it's important to have a lot of people taste your recipes to make sure they have general appeal and suit tastes less idiosyncratic than your own. Inevitably, when someone other than a teenaged boy likes something you cook, they ask for your recipe. And that brings us to a hard truth: no matter how fine a collection of recipes you've gathered or devised, you don't have a cookbook until you write them out.

Your next step is to take the notes and the cryptic instructions you've been working with and write them into real recipes. In the following chapter we'll talk in detail about how to do that. But before we do, let me mention briefly the issue of food safety.

The more we learn about the conditions under which foods spoil, the more convinced I become that many of the illnesses doctors used to diagnose as the grippe were actually food poisoning. The dangers of some process have been known for a long time. In one of John Steinbeck's novels, one of the characters killed a woman by sprinkling poison on her green-bean salad. Because canned beans were notorious for developing botulism, everyone assumed that the poor woman had been the victim of a jar of canned beans gone bad.

Other hazards have come to light more recently: the dangers of stuffing a turkey larger than twenty pounds with a dressing that contains egg, for instance, or the realization that sealing jelly with paraffin does not always prevent dangerous molds from growing on the jelly during long storage.

In light of this, you have an especially strong responsibility during the development and testing stage for seeing that your recipes and practices are consistent with *current* food science. Recipes have changed over the past quarter-century. In preserving and canning, processing times have increased and the importance of vinegar with a reliable acid content have been accentuated. So has the importance of cooking poultry and meats and foods that contain eggs.

If you have any doubt about whether your expertise is up to date, ask your extension agent or any home economist for the current bulletins on food science. You may find that you should change some of your procedures, especially if you are adapting old family recipes.

CHAPTER 3

Time to Write

Someone once said that writing is very simple; all you have to do is sit in front of your typewriter until little drops of blood form on your forehead. This observation explains a phenomenon noted by science-fiction writer Phil Klass, who spent a number of frustrating years teaching writing classes at Penn State. "Everybody's interested in writing either in prospect or in retrospect. Nobody wants to sit down and do it now," said Klass. And no wonder. It's hard to start and hard to sit still long enough to keep on writing. I've been struggling with it for years.

My technique for getting started is to sit down at the typewriter in the morning with my coffee before I'm fully awake. By the time I've come to, I'm several pages into whatever I'm working on simply from typing mechanically, and I have been too numb to suffer the pangs of beginning. Sometimes I have to scrap the first couple of pages, but that's okay. If I didn't do it that way, I wouldn't have any pages at all.

As for sitting still, that's tougher. I have avoidance behavior down to a fine art. When I write I eat pretzels, which make me thirsty, which makes me drink water, which makes me have to go to the bathroom, and then while I'm up I grab a handful of pretzels, which makes me thirsty. . . .

What makes it so hard for all of us, I think, is our fear that what we write won't work. It will sound dumb or it won't make sense or it will be less than perfect. Mercifully, though, whatever we get down on paper that first time through (I call it "brutalizing a rough draft") doesn't have to be the final product. In my view, getting something—anything—down on paper gives you something to fix, and fixing is a lot easier than the initial writing. The pros call it "rewriting" rather than "fixing," but that's still what it is. Most good writers I know, except for newspaper reporters, expect to rewrite a piece two or even three times before they are satisfied with it. Newspaper reporters don't have this luxury because of their time limits and deadlines, but now that most of them work on video display terminals (which are really just word processors), even they have the opportunity to make changes and corrections. The point is that as long as you know you have the opportunity to change what you have written, you take a lot of pressure off yourself to get it perfect the first time, and the words come more easily.

Miriam Ungerer, the food columnist, says she thinks writing a cookbook is easier for writers who cook than for cooks who try to write. Perhaps so, but I don't share her belief that the best answer for a nonprofessional is to get a collaborator to handle the writing. I hate to see you miss the fun of doing it yourself. If you can read, talk coherently, and follow directions, you can write your own cookbook.

What follows is a step-by-step guide for getting everything down on paper and for rewriting it into a finished manuscript. It should be easier because you are really not starting from scratch. Whatever you have written already in the process of testing and developing your recipes is a beginning. So, with the knowledge that you have the luxury of rewriting and polishing your first draft later, you can concentrate this first time through on what you want to communicate and to whom. The first step, as a professor of mine used to say, is to *sit down and begin*.

Before You Begin

If you have done some brainstorming on paper, as I suggested in Chapter One, to answer the questions about why you want to write a cookbook and for whom, you have already taken the first step. Thinking through the organization of your cookbook will also help you get started. Some writers say they prefer simply to begin writing and let the form emerge, rather than imposing structure on their work before they know exactly what they will be saying.

When it comes to cookbooks, this is not a good way to begin. You are apt to find yourself spinning your wheels, dashing off a dessert recipe and then a soup recipe and then perhaps some advice on taking care of kitchen knives. You need to know the broad shape of your book and to have some idea of the order in which you will present your subjects before you try to write out chapter introductions and explanatory material for recipes. Otherwise you may spend a lot of time on recipes you ultimately don't use at all. Let's return to the make-believe Italian cookbook for a moment. If you spend a weekend on recipes for Italian candies and then build a book based on main-dish recipes, you will either try to squeeze the candy recipes in where they don't legitimately fit or you will be annoyed with yourself for wasting a weekend.

Most cookbooks are organized in the same order as we serve a meal, beginning with appetizers and ending with desserts, but many other arrangements are possible. *Beard on Food* uses categories, such as "My Ways with Meat," "A Good Catch," "Sweet and Soothing Drinks," and "Holidays, Parties, and Picnics." There seems to be no particular reason for one category to come before or after any other.

Marlene Ann Bumgarner's *Book of Whole Grains* presents recipes for each grain in a separate chapter, beginning with "Wheat," working through "Triticale," "Buckwheat," and "Barley," and ending with "Nuts and Seeds," and "Dried Peas and Beans." Presumably the grain chapters appear in order of familiarity. I think that the nuts, seeds, dried beans, and peas, however desirable they might be in one's diet, are inconsistent with the theme and title of the book, but placing them at the end rather than somewhere in the middle or at the beginning implies an "oh-by-the-way" attitude that makes them fit a little better. Miriam Ungerer's *Country Food*, subtitled "A Seasonal Journal," is organized by season, with each chapter devoted to recipes for the foods that are plentiful in spring, summer, fall, and winter.

In a sense, the material that you choose *does* suggest the form you should or should not give it. If you have all dessert recipes, for example, you certainly can't write a book that begins with appetizers and ends with desserts. Certainly you shouldn't just sit down and start writing before you have a structure for your book, but you can let your material guide you.

Who Is Your Audience?

First gather all your recipes, however they are written down. Depending on the kind of book you plan, you need anywhere from twenty-five to several hundred. When I'm at this stage, my recipes are mostly scribbled out on the back of those old *New Yorker* wrappers I mentioned, but some cookbook writers proceed more efficiently, working from typed copies of their recipes with changes penciled in. The pages may even be organized in categories in a binder. Now, no matter how you have kept your recipes, think back to your answers to the first questions in the first chapter before you begin to write them in final form. Why do you want to write a cookbook? For whom? Do you want to teach a beginner how to cook? Do you want to preserve old recipes? Is the book for your closest friends or for the crowds who hang around bookstores looking for the latest in cooking novelty?

Knowing your audience and your purpose will help you know how to write the instructions, what recipes to include, and what tone to take in your writing. If you are peddling novelty, for instance, don't make your introductory remarks nostalgic.

Jacob's Cattle	Navy or Seafarer	Black Turtle	Bush Lima
Christmas Lima	Pink	Yellow Soybean	Canada Red
Mexican Red	Pinto	Yellow Eye	Fava
Soldier	Great Northern	Chick-pea	Black-eyed or Cowpea
Red Kidney	Scarlet Runner	Dixie Speckled Butter	Light Red Kidney

When you are instructing your readers about ingredients that may be unfamiliar to them, illustrations such as these complement the text. Although not detailed, or in color, these drawings from the Garden Way bulletin Cooking with Dried Beans *help a reader recognize the beans in the grocery store.*

As I have mentioned, getting this judgment right is tremendously important. Sheila Lowenstein of *Cook's Magazine,* who sees hundreds of cookbooks a year, says that one of her most important criteria for judging each one is how well it fulfills what it set out to do for its defined audience. Knowing for whom you are writing determines not only how detailed your instructions must be, but also how many of your terms need to be explained somewhere in the book. If you are writing a book for accomplished cooks, you certainly have less explaining to do than if you are writing a book for beginners. If you tell a long-time cook to fold in the egg whites, you can assume that he or she will know how; if you write it for a beginner, you'll have to tell how to do it. One reason that many of us have so much trouble with old recipes from earlier times is that they seem so cryptic. They were written on the assumption that they would either be used by a knowledgeable cook or passed on with person-to-person instruction.

Most new cookbooks these days assume only a modicum of experience on the part of their readers. This is probably wise, especially as we venture into the cooking techniques of various ethnic groups whose practices are not familiar to us, and try to learn how to cook in greater and greater variety.

Simplified line drawings by Mike Nelson demonstrate how a Chinese steamer works, what it looks like, and how to use it. It would be virtually impossible to describe this in words so that a cook could tell exactly what you were talking about. (From Wok: A Chinese Cookbook *by Gary Lee)*

French cooking traditionally presents us with our first humbling experiences in interpreting recipes, even if we have been cooking for a while. I still remember how annoyed I was the first time I turned to a recipe that began, "Make a blond roux." I had been cooking for several years, but that was new to me. I stomped around the kitchen muttering, "A blond what? Is a blond roux anything like a brunette roué?" In my own writing, I will probably always prefer to give the simple instructions for such processes as cooking melted butter and flour together, even though I know it means I'll never get to use classy words like "roux."

On the other hand, I think you can also err in the direction of simplicity. You have to give even the beginning cook credit for some sense. In one editorial meeting I recall, we were discussing a book for beginners, and we argued for twenty minutes about whether or not it was necessary to tell the reader to take the pit out of an avocado. My vote was to let anybody dumb enough to swallow it go ahead and see what happened.

Form Follows Function

Once you have determined the level of your audience and your goal in writing for that audience, you should decide next on the format for your recipes. It must be consistent from one recipe to the next. Almost all the cookbooks published these days give a few brief introductory remarks to a recipe, followed by a listing of the ingredients in the order in which they will be used and then the instructions for assembling those ingredients. Editors insist that you list the ingredients as they will be used.

My early instincts were to write down ingredients in what I considered their order of importance. If the recipe was for shrimp bisque, I thought, surely the shrimp, which cost the most and was the main ingredient, should be listed before the tablespoon of butter and the chopped shallot sautéd in the butter, to which the shrimp were then added. I must have worked with some kind editors, because when they sent me revised copy to check, I observed that they had moved the ingredients around in the list. Then I would make the same dumb mistake again the next time, but no one ever complained to me. Finally I caught on, and I still remember the jubilant little note I got from Roger Griffith, who was with *Garden Way*. "Looks great, and you're even listing ingredients in the order they're used. Nice job!"

Information on length of preparation time, how many servings the recipe makes, and whether or not to preheat the oven usually goes somewhere near the listing of ingredients. It doesn't matter too much where, as long as the information is easy to find and is in the same place every time. This is especially true for things like preheating the oven, preparing a pan, and the size of the pan. Imagine getting everything ready for a soufflé and then discovering at the end of the recipe that it must be baked immediately and you haven't preheated the oven, or that you don't have the right-sized baking dish. True, a good cook should read through the directions before beginning, but honestly, friends, do you always do that?

Give your instructions step by step, telling the cook exactly what to do with each ingredient in the order the ingredients are listed. If you tell readers to beat or mix, tell them how long to do it or how the mixture should look when they are done.

None of this sounds like a big deal, but a surprising number of recipes in published books fail at it. The classic example is the recipe that begins, "Measure 1/2 cup brown sugar and set aside." After the cake is baked, the brown sugar is still sitting in the cup on the counter because the instructions never told the cook what to do with it.

Learning the Hard Way

When I first started to write food columns for newspapers I relied largely on recipes from my husband's family and my own. Readers liked them, but I got letters from time to time that suggested I hadn't paid enough attention to detail. I remember especially a response to Grandma Dietrick's recipe for soft molasses cookies. I'd been lyrical in introducing that recipe in my column because, in fact, they are the best cookies I've ever eaten. The letter said, "Who goofed, you or your grandma? You tell us to cream the shortening but you never say how much or what kind. Is that because the shortening is lard and you don't want to admit it?"

Well, the shortening was vegetable shortening, one-third cup of it; I'd skipped it in typing the recipe, and in my hurry to meet a deadline, I missed the omission in my proofreading. That episode taught me to be careful.

The lesson was clinched by the story of a friend who had tried a recipe for nut bread from my column. I had somehow omitted the sugar, and she baked the bread following my sugarless recipe. Her husband ate it and complained that it lacked sweetness.

"Jack, it's bread, not cake." she said. "It's not supposed to be sweet."

Poor Jack dutifully dry-mouthed his way through an entire loaf of pasty nut bread, believing that it had to be that way because it was bread, not cake, when in truth I had messed up.

Mistakes can creep in even when you are careful. Once while I was working at the newspaper, a Craig Claiborne column came in over the wire machine with a chili recipe that called for thirty-two cups of chopped onion. No correction ever clattered over the teletype with greater urgency!

Even as meticulously prepared a publication as *Cook's Magazine* suffers occasionally from gremlins. Once a rich dessert that called for more than a dozen eggs and almost a dozen packages of cream cheese ended up in print calling for just one package of cream cheese. And this correction notice appeared one January in *Friends Magazine:*

> In our December issue appeared a recipe for "Chicken-Fried Steaks with Pan Gravy." Inadvertently an extra two cups of flour slipped into the gravy providing a lumpy surprise for any trusting cook.

Experienced cooks can spot such discrepancies, but the novice could end up with a pot of chilied onions, a cheeseless cheesecake, or fried steak in wallpaper paste before figuring out that something was wrong. The only way to keep errors down to a minimum is by paying meticulous attention to detail at every step, from making your first note in the kitchen through proofing the finished pages of the manuscript and its later typeset stages.

Be Specific

Your instructions should be specific. It's surprising how the little details that seem perfectly obvious to you will remain a mystery to the cook who is trying a recipe for the first time. In a recent issue of *Cook's Magazine*, which I consider one of the most carefully edited cooking magazines published, I read a recipe for melon soup. The instructions said to purée the honeydew and watermelon meat in a blender and then to strain the pulp through a fine sieve into a large bowl, pressing with a wooden spoon to get as much juice as possible. Next, the recipe said, add cream and white wine. But was I supposed to add those things to the melon pulp or to the melon juice? Probably to the juice, I decided, since the recipe made a point of telling me to put it into a large bowl. Someone who had made melon soup before would probably know automatically, but I never had, and I'm still wondering.

Also be sure to tell your reader how the food is supposed to look or taste or feel along the way. The old-time cookbooks often say to roast something until it is done, for example, but if you have never cooked a goose before, how do you know when it is done? Or when a cake is fin-

When you are giving step-by-step instructions, how-to photographs help the reader understand exactly what you mean. In these photographs from the American Egg Board, the first two photographs don't really illustrate much. We see no action. The following photographs are more helpful because they show how the crepes should look at various stages in their preparation. Another interesting aspect of these photos is that although they are several years old they look contemporary because there are no appliances or once-fashionably-dressed people in the pictures to date them.

ished? Or when pudding is "thick enough"? You need to give your instructions in ways that let the cook visualize the end result—"roast the goose about an hour per pound, or until it is dark brown and the legs move loosely in their joints"; "bake the cake until a toothpick inserted in the middle comes out clean"; "cook the pudding until it is as thick as heavy cream." Since stoves, pans, and cooks differ so much, it's good to give an approximate length of cooking time and a physical description.

Some physical descriptions are easier to visualize than others. I remember my daughter's phone call, when she asked me how frothy was "frothy" in proofing yeast. And I recall the instruction that always confounded me: "Knead until smooth and elastic." Eventually I dealt with my confusion by kneading until I got tired of kneading, but I still haven't found a better way to express how the dough looks and feels when it has been kneaded sufficiently.

To this day I'm confused by recipes for jellies and candies. The instructions often suggest cooking to a certain temperature on the candy thermometer or until the syrup falls from a metal spoon in a sheet. I have been cooking for twenty years and I have yet to see a sheet fall from a metal spoon.

In another recipe I was instructed to "sauté the eggplant in the butter until golden." I am here to tell you that eggplant doesn't *get* golden. It gets greenish and then the edges get dark brown and then the butter burns and everything gets black. But of course you can't write cookbooks telling people to sauté the eggplant until just before the butter burns and everything gets black, so I confess that I've done my share of telling cooks to sauté things until golden. My apologies. The point here is that the best cookbook writers learn to observe and report exactly what food looks like in its various stages of preparation.

Measure for Measure

In putting together the entire book, you must decide how you will give measurements and amounts, and remain consistent from one recipe to the next.

Are you going to say:

Three carrots, peeled and chopped
or
Three peeled and chopped carrots?

Do you see the difference between:

One cup chopped radishes
and
One cup radishes, chopped?

Which is more:

One celery *stalk*, diced
or
One celery *rib*, diced?

Is it better to say:

Two medium onions, chopped
or
One cup chopped onions?

The point is that these statements sound similar, but they mean different things. A cup of chopped radishes will be more radishes than a cup of radishes which you then chop. A stalk of celery, if you ask a gardener, is the whole plant; a rib is one section of the plant. And whether you specify two medium onions chopped or one cup of chopped onions depends on how crucial it is to have an exact quantity of onions in the recipe. One cup is a more exact quantity than two medium onions.

To complicate matters further, the terms we use for cooking processes may not mean the same thing to everyone. If I tell you to chop the celery and dice the onion, presumably you know that I mean for the onion to be cut in smaller pieces than the celery. Or is it the other way around? And is finely chopped raw potato finer than diced raw potato? Again, cooks in earlier times knew what size the pieces of a carrot or turnip or onion should be in a particular dish because they had watched other cooks prepare it. But today, when so many of us venture into unfamiliar foreign cuisines with only a cookbook to guide us, even experienced cooks need to be told what to do as specifically as possible. Rather than relying on words such as "dice" or "chop" to convey your meaning, try tell your reader how the food should look. Write "Dice into quarter-inch squares" or "Chop until very fine." The important thing is that the same word must mean the same thing each time you use it. And if you begin a cookbook by giving measurements in cups ("1/2 cup chopped turnip"), don't be inconsistent and switch to giving the measurements in other measures ("one medium turnip, chopped") halfway through the book.

You have leeway in these kinds of choices as long as you are sure you are saying what you mean, but once you have picked a format, stick to it for each recipe in your book.

You also need to be consistent in the way you write your quantities. Although you sometimes see "cups" abbreviated as "C." and "teaspoon" and "tablespoon" abbreviated as "t." and "T.," I think it is best to spell these things out. It takes very little more space and eliminates the possibility of confusion.

Differences among systems of weights and measures in other countries don't make writing cookbooks any easier these days, either. Despite the efforts of scientists and other mathematically inclined people to convert America to the metric system, we have clung to our comfortable quarts and pints. Who cares how other countries count? We like decimals. Even the wine and liquor industry's conversion to liters and milliliters hasn't swayed us. Perhaps you have seen a cookbook written with the measurements given twice, once in metrics and once in the decimal system. To me, this takes the fun out of cooking and turns a session in the kitchen into something reminiscent of those high-school algebra classes which you were supposed to figure the rate of a river's flow against the rate of a canoe going upstream and calculate when you could paddle into Milwaukee. I suggest that you write your recipes in whatever weights and measures are most familiar to you and then get help later in making conversions if you decide your audience will need them.

If you look at many foreign cookbooks, you will also notice that in some countries dry ingredients, such as flour, are measured by weight (pounds and ounces) rather than by volume (cups). Before the days of standard measuring cups and spoons, this method was more accurate. But today, measuring dry ingredients by cup is faster and easier than weighing them, and has become the preferred method in America. (Weight Watchers and diabetics, however, use weight as a measure in portioning meals.)

I could go on. In my *Jewish Cooking for Pleasure*, written in Israel by journalist Molly Lyons Bar-David and published in London, an entire page is devoted to explaining weights and measures. It says that weights are given in pounds and ounces but capacity measures are in imperial pints. For American readers, cup measurements have been given to the nearest U.S. standard cup, but spoon measures follow the British Standards Institution specification. To complicate matters further, American measuring spoons hold less than British standard measuring spoons. If the book were written in French, my confusion would be total. This example shows that if we try to be too accommodating we can create more problems than we solve. Work in the weights and measures you have come to know as standard. Get help with conversions if conversions seem necessary. As long as you are consistent within the recipe, someone else can always translate it.

Consistency from recipe to recipe is also important in giving warnings and special advice. In my books, for example, in the recipes that use a porous clay pot, I caution the cook to open the lid away from his or her body to avoid being scalded by a burst of escaping steam. But once I've said it in three or four recipes, I tend to get bored with the repetition and leave it out of subsequent recipes. Fortunately, good editors put it in for me, because I can't assume that the reader has read all the other recipes before trying one where I've omitted those instructions. As Sheila Lowenstein of *Cook's Magazine* said, "Every recipe in a book should be able to stand on its own."

When you think about it, that makes sense. People don't always read recipe books front to back, beginning to end, as we do novels. Often they skip around. A cook would risk missing an important caution or direction if it appeared only sporadically. This advice applies not only to major cautions about hot steam, but to the little things as well. The last line in every recipe in Jeannette Seaver's book, *Soups*, tells you how to serve that particular soup.

This brings us to another detail in writing recipes: telling the reader you're done. Somebody once did some research in communication, which demonstrated that human beings need "closure." That is, they need to know that a process they've begun has a formal ending, even in something like reading recipes. Here's how an editor explained it to me, when I hadn't been doing it. "Recipes need a final sentence. Something, as simple as 'Serve hot,' 'Serve cold,' 'Serve immediately,' or 'Be careful not to overcook' will do, to let the cook know that the recipe has ended and the typesetter hasn't stopped in midrecipe." This is a good place to suggest garnishes and accompaniments, too.

If you've read many cookbooks lately, you've probably noticed a lot of these little closing lines. If the books are older, you may also have noticed that not all the recipes are written with the ingredients listed first, followed by the instructions. For a while home economists advocated writing recipes in what I call "story style," a kind of narrative in which the ingredients were worked right into the instructions.

Brown *two pounds* of *beef cubes* in *one tablespoon butter* and place them in a porous clay pot which has been soaked in cold water for fifteen minutes. Cut up *two onions*, sauté until golden in *one tablespoon butter*, and place on top of the beef cubes.

I have been told that the idea behind this treatment was to make a cook read all the directions before beginning to prepare the recipe, but the story format is much harder to read, and almost always requires that ingredients and measurements be italicized or underlined so that they will stand out from the narrative. And as far as I'm concerned, enough people in this world are already trying to force me to do things I don't want to do without a cookbook making me read clear though a recipe before I break an egg. I suspect that most people share my attitude, which is why you rarely see cookbooks written in story style these days.

The one contemporary exception I can think of is the text in *James Beard on Food*, a book based on some of his newspaper columns. The ingredients are printed in ink of a contrasting color to make them stand out from the narrative. James Beard gets away with it because he's famous and amusingly chatty, but those recipes are hard to cook from. I always go through and list the ingredients separately in the margins to keep track of what I'm doing. By far the better format these days is the listing followed by instructions, to which we've become accustomed.

Clarity, Consistency, Accuracy

In telling the cook what to do, how-to writing is like poetry in some ways. It compresses a lot of meaning into a few words. But it differs from poetry in that a poet makes you work to figure out all the layers of meaning, while how-to writing tries to make the meaning so clear that no one can possibly misunderstand.

This is not so hard as you might suppose. Back in 1919 Will Strunk, a cantankerous, opinionated professor of English, wrote *The Elements of Style*, a little book telling people how to write so that they could be understood. His rules survive to this day as an almost universal guide for writing clear prose. I have adapted them into a short list of tips for writing recipes that will get you through the process almost painlessly, because even if you can't practice them as you sketch out your first draft, you can apply them in rewriting. Here they are in all their simplicity:

1. Use simple words.
2. Use short sentences.
3. Use the active voice.
4. Use strong verbs.
5. Arrange words in sentences—*subject, verb, object*—with nothing between them unless you have a good reason for deviating from this pattern.

Let's see how well this works.

Use simple words. You don't see it too often these days, but in past years cookbook writers would sometimes spin off into such flights of literary fancy that you almost felt you couldn't cook without a dictionary to interpret your cookbook. The example that sticks in my mind is an old cake recipe with instructions to "incorporate" the sugar into the eggs a little at a time. Incorporation is for General Motors and Litton Industries; for eggs and sugar I think "mix in" says it better. Not only do unnecessarily big words make you sound silly and archaic, but reading them slows down the cook, who is looking for instructions, not literature.

Use short sentences. If you have an ear for prose, you may be disturbed by a series of short declarative sentences unbroken by longer graceful ones. "Beat the eggs. Sift the flour and stir it in. Knead until smooth and elastic." It does sound abrupt, but write it this way anyhow because it's much easier for a cook to follow instructions written in this style than if you write, "After beating in the eggs, stir in the flour, which has been sifted, and knead until smooth and elastic." The latter sentence may be more interesting from a literary point of view, but it requires too much thinking to figure out the order of the instructions. For function and for ease in understanding, short sentences work better.

Use the active voice. If you learned your grammar after 1950, the lessons may not have included anything about the active voice or how it differs from the passive voice. I nearly drove myself nuts trying to explain it to a writing class, so instead of finishing myself off by trying to explain it to you in the abstract, I'll give you some examples.

ACTIVE VOICE	PASSIVE VOICE
My family enjoyed the casserole.	The casserole was enjoyed by my family.
Be careful not to open the pressure cooker before the steam escapes.	Care should be taken not to open the pressure cooker before the steam escapes.
Sift the flour.	The flour should be sifted.
Don't forget the salt.	Salt should not be forgotten.

The first thing you notice is that it takes longer to say things in the passive voice. Confusion can easily creep into a passive construction. In the passive voice something *is done to* the subject of the sentence. Flour is sifted, care is taken, the casserole is enjoyed. In the active voice, however, the words are turned around so that the subject of the sentence *does* something. In sentences that give directions the subject is often the implied *you*. *You* sift the flour; *you* don't forget the salt. One reason you hear so much passive voice in committee meeting reports and corporate memos is that it's never quite clear who is doing the acting. (Care should be taken. By whom?) Politicians and executives often want it that way. But even if you're a corporate executive who's hiding the doers of dubious deeds at other times, now you are writing a cookbook. You need to be clear about who does what, so write in the active voice. It makes more interesting and readable writing.

Use strong verbs. In writing a cookbook, strong verbs come naturally because cooking is a vigorous activity and you are directing the reader to do many different things. Always try to use the verb that describes most specifically what you want the reader to do. For instance, don't say, "Put the eggs into the simmering water" if "Drop the eggs into the simmering water" is more accurate. Be aware of the differences between such verbs as "stir," "sauté," "fry," "beat," "mix," "fold," and "whisk." Choose the one you really mean.

Use subject, verb, object in that order. As I've already said, the subject in how-to writing is almost always an implied *you*. You (subject) do something (verb) to something (object). We talk and think in this order, but sometimes when we start to write we get carried away and our sentences grow convoluted. A cook who's trying to follow your recipe will do better if you can keep your instructions sounding just about as they would if you were speaking to someone in your kitchen and telling them what to do.

When I wrote food columns for newspapers, the greatest compliment I received was from people who said, "I feel like you're standing right there beside me, telling me what to do." I think this ability has done me more good as a food writer than my ability to think up novel recipes. I know how to do it because I grew up with a father who taught us in meticulous detail how to do everything one step at a time. If you're not good at this you can borrow my father; sometimes he drives Mom crazy. Or you can simply learn to think of yourself as teaching your reader to go through a cooking process one step after another.

When you have trouble writing, ask yourself what you're trying to say, answer the question out loud, and then write down what you just said. It nearly always works.

To illustrate by example, here is what I consider a badly written recipe, followed by the same recipe written better.

SCALLOPED MUSHROOMS

4 T. butter	*1 can mushrooms*
6 T. flour	*4 hard-cooked eggs*
2 C. milk and juice of mushrooms	*2 T. chopped pimiento*
1 t. salt	*2 T. chopped green pepper*

Make a thick white sauce with butter, flour, salt, and milk to which you add mushrooms cut in halves, incorporate the chopped eggs, peppers, and pimiento. Blanket the surface with bread crumbs and bake in moderate oven about 35 minutes.

SCALLOPED MUSHROOMS

4 tablespoons butter	*4 hard-cooked eggs, peeled and chopped*
6 tablespoons flour	
1 8-ounce can whole mushrooms, drained	*2 tablespoons chopped pimiento*
milk and mushroom juice to equal 2 cups	*2 tablespoons chopped green pepper*
1 teaspoon salt	*1 cup fresh bread crumbs*

Grease a 4-cup baking dish.
Preheat oven to 350° F.
Preparation time: 50 minutes—1 hour
Yield: 4 servings

In a small saucepan, melt the butter and stir in the flour. Cook and stir the mixture over medium heat until the flour begins to brown slightly, about 5 minutes. Gradually beat in the milk and mushroom juice with a whisk, stirring constantly to avoid lumps. Remove sauce from heat as soon as it thickens, in about 10 minutes. Add the salt. Cut the mushrooms in half and put them into the greased dish with the chopped eggs, pimiento, and chopped pepper. Pour the mushroom-milk sauce over the ingredients in the dish and stir just enough to coat them with the sauce. Cover the top with the bread crumbs. Bake in a 350° F. preheated oven about 30 minutes, or until the mixture is heated through and bubbling and slightly brown on top. Serve immediately.

Start Writing

Up to this point I've made it sound as if you simply sit down one day and start to write out your recipes. In reality, you've probably been alternating between writing and testing, so that eventually you end up with a stack of typed or handwritten recipes in essentially final form. For me, a rhythm develops between periods of testing and making notes and periods of writing and polishing.

Actually, my feet and my fanny guide me. I cook until my feet hurt too much to stand on them anymore; then I gather my notes and write until I can't sit still any longer. By then my feet are better, so I start cooking again. You will find your own rhythms too, and eventually you will reach the point where you have written all your recipes. It's a good idea then to have someone else read them to be sure they are clear.

The next thing you need to do is write whatever introduction and connecting material you want. You may use the rough draft you wrote during your brainstorming period or you may decide on an entirely new introduction. The introduction is usually where you state your intentions and define the scope and the subject of your book. It shouldn't be too long, but it should include whatever explanation a reader needs to understand the book as a whole—what it is and what it is not.

Putting some specifics in the introduction saves you from having to repeat them in every recipe. In the introduction to my book on whole grains and my book on poultry, for instance, I said that nearly all the recipes could be made successfully without salt, but I added that in any recipe where I thought a specific amount of salt was necessary to make the dish taste right, I said so. That statement left me free to write "salt to taste" in the recipes and let it go at that, except for those few cases I mentioned in the introduction. Jeannette Seaver includes almost two pages of general tips in her introduction to *Soups*, to avoid saying over and over that fresh herbs are better than dried, that sandy greens should be carefully washed several times, and that hot soups should be served very hot.

Of course, the introduction is the place to woo your subject. This is good fun, in which most cookbook writers indulge to excess. What bread book doesn't talk about the joy of kneading and the pitiful quality of store bread? What soup book doesn't elaborate on the superior aroma, nutrition, economy, and flavor of homemade soups—usually with a dash of nostalgia thrown in? What author doesn't assure you that using his or her book will be great fun?

I especially enjoy all those great family-oriented introductions, which I am prone to write myself because I like to link us with our past in such an elemental way. A splendid example of this kind of introduction is found in *To All My Grandchildren: Lessons in Indonesian Cooking*, by Leonie Samuel-Hool. Referring to lessons she learned as an apprentice in her own grandmother's kitchen before she reached the age of nine, she writes, "When I was very young I wanted to cook more than I wanted toys or dolls, but before I was even allowed to touch uncooked food, I had to learn respect for the many spirits that lived in Grandma's kitchen." She develops the mood further as she describes the area, Depok, which was out in the country where there was no running water. This leads her to describe how her family drew drinking water from the well and kept it covered with cheesecloth outdoors overnight to be "enhanced by the night dew." Then, with totally engaging dry humor, Leonie recalls, "Grandma said that in order to be a cook I would have to learn to boil water and to do this I would first have to learn how to start a fire in the stove."

All this seems to set the tone perfectly for the exotic recipes that follow: Telur Pindang (spiced eggs, which of course are boiled first in water); Bumbu Kagang (peanut sauce); and Gado Gado (Indonesian salad).

Writing to Inspire

I think introductions are important. Your introduction should be to the rest of your cookbook what all those books on running, golf, and tennis are to would-be athletes—motivation to get out there and *do* it. You know you have read a really good cookbook introduction when your next impulse is to see whether you have all the ingredients needed to try one of the recipes. Your goal in writing your own introduction should be to affect readers the same way.

Your introduction is closely related to whatever material you write to connect the recipes. Whether this is short or long depends on the cookbook and whether it emphasizes history, nostalgia, atmosphere, or the actual recipes. The trend these days seems to be toward brief comments, which appear mainly at the beginning of chapters or the individual recipes.

Bert Greene is effective in handling the relationship between his introduction and the connecting material in *Honest American Fare*. He begins by recalling the daily meals all our grandmothers cooked from scratch (where would cookbooks be without grandmothers?) and mourns the near replacement of these meals with convenience foods after World War II, followed more recently by the ubiquitous influence of "ethnic gourmet" cooking:". . . *French* yesterday; *Italian* today, and *Greek, Indonesian,* or *Coptic* tomorrow." Bert's mission as a food writer, he says, is "to preserve the option of . . . honest American fare."

His introduction, which includes some mouth-watering descriptions of Kate's Biscuits, Clara's Ham Loaf, and a Pennsylvania Funeral Pie, moves smoothly into connecting material for the recipes, which talks about the origins of each recipe, the people who created, cooked, and ate them, and the regional sources of their basic ingredients. The result is marvelous reading, good cooking if you like homey old-time American food, and a huge helping of nostalgia that unifies the cookbook. His recipes for "Depression Meatloaf," for instance, came from a "grandmotherly lady who lives in Omaha." It got its name because of the large quantity of raw rolled oats added to stretch the meat. She called it "Mr. Roosevelt's Roast" until, as Bert puts it, "succeeding presidents made fiscal insecurity generic!" Such writing, along with his claim that he has never failed in making meatloaf, is almost enough to make you like meatloaf.

Timothy Firnstahl wrote an exuberant little book called *Jake O' Shaughnessey's Sourdough Book*, to resurrect the spirit and preserve the sourdough recipes that were part of a boisterous Seattle saloon in the 1800s. Firnstahl's descriptions of the lore and flavors of sourdough are evocative of the life from which they emerged. At the same time, his recipes for Jack O'Shaughnessey's breads and flapjacks and biscuits provide minute detail about what to do when, with what ingredients, in what quantities. I use the book. If you do what Firnstahl tells you I think it would be impossible to fail. And while you are carefully measuring and timing, you are enjoying yourself because of the vigor of his presentation. As I stand at the kitchen counter beating the batter for his Billycan Bread with a wooden spoon, I can "invent" the running jokes and complaints of the Gold Rush prospectors who used to throw it together for supper. If Firnstahl can make that happen with a topic as capricious as sourdough, surely the rest of us can manage to do it with the foods we love and cook well.

Regional and ethnic cookbooks also invite this kind of literary enthusiasm because we have so much to say about how the food fits in with the place and its people. For the reader, the combination of your words and your recipes can evoke a mood that goes far beyond appetite.

Trim the Fat

How much you indulge in this kind of evocative prose depends on the theme of your book, your audience, the preference of your publisher (or limitations of space, if you are self-publishing), and your skill as a writer. The easiest way I know to handle both the composition and the space problems of writing the introduction and connecting material, especially if you are not a professional writer, is to let yourself go and say everything you want to say, without worrying at all about length or style or wording. Then go back over the material, or have someone else do it for you, and trim out the excesses by applying the simple-word, short-sentence formula. You can get all kinds of ideas and help by looking at the introductions and connecting material in the cookbooks you like best. Not that you want to copy them, but they will help you understand more clearly what style appeals to you and what you can write with genuine enthusiasm.

If you are reading with a pencil in your hand, please go back and underline the word "enthusiasm." Underline it twice, because even though grammar, spelling, and sentence structure matter, they won't make a good book if you don't feel enthusiastic about what you are doing. Now and then I read an article that tells how you can make money writing about food even if you are not much interested in cooking. Horsefeathers! That's like trying to paint a seascape when you hate the ocean and the sand. So if you love cooking and food, don't worry about being a little short on writing skills; if you really know and like what you are writing about, those details can be managed. Now go back and read that last clause: "those details can be managed." It's in the passive voice. The details are going to have something *done to them.* Passive. I told you to avoid the passive voice, so why have I used it here? Because if I had used the active voice, I would have said, "You can manage the details," making *you* the subject, and that's not what I wanted to say. I wanted you to understand that if you can get the basic knowledge and enthusiasm down on paper, the details can be handled by your or by someone else—a professional writer, an editor, a friend, your spouse.

Coralie Ayers collaborated on *The Art of Cooking for Two, Country Cookery, Hors D'Oeuvre Etc.,* and *Real Bread: A Fearless Guide to Making It,* with a different person for each book. She had no formal collaborator for her book *Soup,* but says that her former husband did the actual writing on it and on the history in *Country Cooking of Many Lands.* "Really, my efforts go to the recipes," she said. "The introductions and actual writing are difficult for me. I must make notes and work with my editor."

One way to find out if you can collaborate in cooking and writing with someone is to cook with them several times just for fun. Over the years I've cooked with many people, but I wouldn't want to collaborate with any of them. Janet Fleming may be the best cook I know, but she moves like a bat out of hell. The way I move could have inspired the old epithet "slow as molasses in January." I love to eat what Janet cooks, but I can't cook with her. I can't keep up. Another old friend likes to have company when she cooks, but somehow everything she tries goes wrong. The bottom of her bread burns; her jelly turns to tar; she gets distracted and salts her homemade catsup twice. The truth is, she likes to eat but doesn't really like to cook. I can't cook with her either. After the first hour or so I find I'm making the same mistakes she is. And then there's Twink. She's probably my best friend in the world. (I'd tell you how she got such a dippy nickname, but then she wouldn't be my friend anymore.) Twink is a wonderful cook who, like me, writes about food. She approaches recipes with awe-inspiring irreverence. "Oh, well. I don't have any Worcestershire sauce. Let's try a tablespoon of Tabasco." I admire her style but I can't keep track of it in writing. For creating and writing recipes, I can't cook with her any more than I can with my other friends. And since nobody writes to suit me either, collaboration doesn't seem to be an option. If you want to collaborate you must find someone whose strengths complement your weaknesses and whose mode of operation fits comfortably with your own.

Collaboration can help you manage the parts of writing a cookbook that you find difficult, but it doesn't always work. Coralie says that she had problems with at least one coauthor because they disagreed about using convenience foods. And sometimes a coauthor isn't around when you need him or her, or wants to proceed faster or slower than you find comfortable, so even if you decide that this is the best way for you to work, don't expect it to be problem-free.

Polish the writing as much as you can, but don't worry about it so much that it keeps you from going ahead with your cookbook. I know many writers, including some often-published ones who probably will be just as pleased if I don't mention their names, who routinely turn their writing over to someone else—to a wordsmith, let's say—for final polishing.

Manuscript Mechanics

This brings us to the final manuscript and its preparation. Writers have all kinds of feelings about preparing a final manuscript. The teacher and writer I admired most in college advised me to type my own manuscripts because the final typing was a good opportunity to make a few last-minute improvements. I have always done it that way, partly because I have come to agree with him and partly because I hate to pay a typist. Unfortunately I've never had a wife whom I could thank for typing my pages.

If you plan to submit the manuscript to a trade publisher, it *must* be typed. When I first started to write I read everything I could find about what a finished manuscript should look like. What confusion! Some books said to leave a one-inch margin on both sides and at the bottom of the page; some said the margins should be one-and-a-half inches, which didn't seem to leave much room on the page for words. Some said you needed a cover page with nothing but the title and your name and address; some said that information belonged on the top of the first page of the manuscript. I read different versions of how to number pages and how to label them. Eventually I put away all the books, and did what I thought made sense and would be clear to anyone looking at the manuscript.

In fact, there is no one correct way to prepare a manuscript as long as it can be easily read, edited, and typeset. The only absolute rules for commercial publishing are that the manuscript must be typed, double-spaced, on one side only of good-quality white paper. Do not use erasable paper; it's slippery and it smudges all over editors' hands and makes them grouchy, and if it's handled too much the words come off altogether. Double space everything, including blocks of quoted material that you would indent and single space in term papers and the like. In this way the editors will have room to make whatever marks are necessary.

Leave enough margin on all sides for more editorial instructions to typesetters. I try to leave at least an inch all around; sometimes if I'm feeling artsy and in the mood for lots of white space, I leave larger margins just for the aesthetic pleasure it gives me.

Number every page and make sure your last name is on every page. How you do this doesn't matter too much as long as your system is clear and consistent. I put the title, or part of it, on every page, as well as the number of the chapter. I prefer to number pages within the chapter, beginning with "1" for each new chapter, rather than running the numbers all the way from Chapter One to the end. The numbers will be changed in the book, of course, but my system seems easier if you have to move chapters around while making revisions. Here how the top of one of my manuscript pages looks:

Pitzer   jams-jellies 5-1

Some publishers prefer specific formats, but no one ever rejected a manuscript because the numbering didn't fit their format. The worst that could happen would be that you'd have to go back over the manuscript to change the numbers. It's a good idea to begin each new recipe on a new page so that the recipes can be moved around in designing the book, if necessary.

Your final draft doesn't have to be absolutely flawless. Minor handwritten corrections are perfectly acceptable, as long as they are neat and clear. In fact, some editors like to see them because it's a sign that the manuscript has been proofread.

I can't think of any place where proofreading is more important than in cookbooks, unless it's in books about atomic formulas or income tax returns. Your proofreading should be done against your original copy, and you or your proofreader should take special care to verify that all measurements and cooking times are correct. Remember poor old Craig Claiborne's thirty-two cups of chopped onions.

If you are self-publishing, the rules are just about the same. You are not trying to impress a publisher, but your manuscript must still be clean enough to be read by a typesetter. If you decide to have your book set directly from typescript, you'll have to have letter-perfect copy, but more about that in Chapter Four.

If you're working on a personal book, perhaps you have decided not to typewrite at all. Your alternatives include calligraphy and writing each recipe out in your own handwriting. In these cases, I think proofreading is more important than ever. It's one thing to have some anonymous cook somewhere trying to make your chili recipe with thirty-two cups of onions, but the idea that one of your very own friends is doing it from a recipe in your handwriting is downright horrifying.

In fact, handling your book as if it were going to be a personal gift to a good friend is a perfect approach, no matter how you decide to publish. After all, you are communicating with people about something that is important to virtually all of us—the food we eat. The cookbook you write for others deserves the same careful attention to detail that you would give to a dinner you were serving them.

CHAPTER *4*

Self-Publishing

T he number of cookbooks that people publish on their own, without the help of trade publishers, boggles the mind. So does the popularity of these books. It would be virtually impossible to tabulate all the self-published cookbooks in the country or to tally all the money they would make (and lose).

Inevitably, when someone tries to write about self-published cookbooks, the stories deteriorate into hyperbole filled with dollar signs, exclamation points, and an excess of adjectives. Even the *New York Times* got carried away in a story by Bryan Miller, which describes the phenomenon of self-published regional cookbooks in 1982. The article began with an anecdote about the choir members at St. Nicholas Church in Palisades Park, New Jersey, who wanted to earn a little money to replace the stairway to their choir loft. They did that and then moved on to other renovations, on the proceeds from a simple little book called *Favorite Recipes from Our Best Cooks*. Then the story went on with starry-eyed astonishment to tell about the money earned by a variety of well-known self-published cookbooks: the Baton Rouge Junior League book, *River Road Recipes*, earns profits of $100,000 to $150,000 a year. The sequel, *River Road Recipes—a Second Helping*, netted over $100,000 in 1980. But when Miller quoted a trade publisher, saying that they often pick up these cookbooks and republish them because "they have a *very* large sales potential," you realize that he was impressed, because as a rule, journalists avoid using the word *very*, even in quotes, as rigorously as the rest of us avoid kissing people with communicable diseases.

Of course it's true. Mollie Katzen's now-famous *Moosewood Cookbook*, from Ten Speed Press, was self-published. Even the Bobbs-Merrill classic, *Joy of Cooking*, started out in 1931 as a project of the First Unitarian Women's Alliance in St. Louis.

Sky Magazine has been dazzled too. In an article entitled "Cook-

28 CURRIED SHRIMP

Serves 6

*Preparation
15 minutes*

This is a mild but very flavorful curry dish, making it ideal for a brunch or luncheon and lovely chafing dish fare for large groups. You may prepare the sauce a day ahead.

½ cup minced onion
5 tablespoons butter
5 tablespoons flour
1 teaspoon curry powder
1 teaspoon dry mustard
¼ teaspoon pepper
½ cup chicken broth
½ cup water
2 teaspoons catsup
2 cups milk
3 cups cooked shrimp (crab or chicken may be substituted)

Cook onion in butter until tender. Combine dry ingredients and stir into onion and butter with a whisk. Add broth, water, and catsup, stirring over low heat until warm. Add milk while stirring and cook until smooth and thickened.

Just short of serving time, reheat the sauce and add the shrimp to heat through but do not boil. Provide the following condiments in separate dishes:

1 cup shredded coconut
1 cup toasted whole almonds
1 cup CHUTNEY
1 bunch green onions, chopped
¾ pound bacon, cut in slivers and fried until crisp

For a very pretty buffet, feature a big bowl of fluffy, white rice that has been tossed with butter and chopped parsley, PARTY ROLLS, and a large platter of butter lettuce leaves topped with slices of pink grapefruit and avocados and a celery seed dressing. SUMMER LEMON SOUFFLÉ is just the right ending.

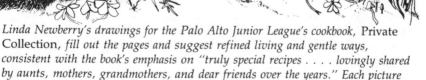

Linda Newberry's drawings for the Palo Alto Junior League's cookbook, Private Collection, *fill out the pages and suggest refined living and gentle ways, consistent with the book's emphasis on "truly special recipes . . . . lovingly shared by aunts, mothers, grandmothers, and dear friends over the years." Each picture appears several times through the book.*

books with A Cause," Barbara Kate Kinick examined the world of self-published cookbooks and reported that in Washington, D.C., the Congressional Club (wives of government officials) earns $75,000 a year for its publication of continuing editions of *The Congressional Club Cook Book*. And in 1981, three California teenagers earned enough money to get to the Boy Scouts of America Jamboree in Virginia by writing and selling a sixty-eight-page cookbook for kids, entitled *How to Survive When Mom's Away*. Junior Leagues that belong to the Association of Junior Leagues, Inc. raised $1,670,798 by publishing and selling cookbooks, most of them regional.

Looking at other self-published cookbooks, Linick found additional success stories. Atlas Van Lines published a book of recipes from world leaders and famous personalities; the employees of Texaco published *Taste Treats from Texaco* to foster morale in the company; and the Daughters of the American Revolution attracted notice with *A DAR Sampler: Dining with the Decorative Arts* to help publicize the DAR Museum in Washington, D.C.

In McKeesport, Pennsylvania, Bob Dvorchak filed a story with the Associated Press about a group of women who ran a food bank for laid-off steel workers; they earned $18,000 with two printings of a 122-page booklet called *Cooking on Extended Benefits: The Unemployed Cookbook*. The book was designed to help people cook with the government-issue foods available from the food bank and to get maximum use of their purchased ingredients as well.

I am trying to introduce a note of restraint into these accounts, but not because the stories are too good to be true. They are true. But I've told you only a few of them because I don't want you to slam this book shut, leap from your chair, and rush down to the club to start the cookbook that will earn you a quarter of a million dollars and allow you to join the camaraderie of successful self-publishers, standing arm in arm in a huge circle singing, "Let Us Break Bread Together." As Paul Harvey would remind us, you need to know the rest of the story.

More than Just Good Cooks—Or Good Books

Self-published cookbooks that succeed do so for a variety of reasons, only one of which is the quality of the book. As indicated in the articles I mentioned, the quality of the successful books differs in sophistication and professionalism. Some have recipes tested three times by teams of home economists. Some are simply compilations of recipes scribbled by donors on the backs of old envelopes, for which the only testing is a call from the compiler to the donor if something about the

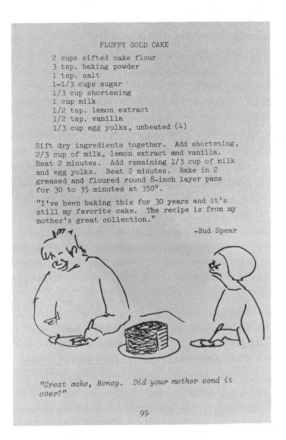

The cartoons in this book function mainly to fill and enliven the pages. Their relationship to the recipes is not through the actual cooking, but in the attitudes and stereotypes we have about cooks. (From the Unitarian Cookbook *self-published by the Unitarian Fellowship, State College, PA.)*

recipe doesn't look right. If your project is to succeed, you need to understand a great deal more than what makes a good recipe.

Let's ease into that understanding with a letter written to me by a friend about her church group's experience in publishing their own cookbook in 1975. I've always thought it was a nice little book; I cook from it, and on occasion I've used some of its recipes, with credit, in my various food columns and cookbooks. Because I like the book so much, I have always assumed that it did well and that the church group made some money from it.

Thinking it would be useful to tell you the story of a successful project, I wrote to the editor to ask for her recollections of the project. Her response dumbfounded me:

Dear Sara,

That cookbook was a long time ago and my memories about it are very fuzzy, so I checked with two other women who were also involved in the project. We came up with a few things that might help.

To my mind, a cookbook is just like a PTA meeting bake sale. The same people who bake the cake go to the meeting, make the coffee, buy a slice of cake, and buy the leftovers to take home. You don't make money except from yourselves, and it takes a lot of work and time to achieve very little.

Because I didn't understand this at the time, we didn't make money. As you know, it costs more per copy to print a few books than to print many. We had a small group—about fifty people willing to contribute recipes. Each of them bought a couple of books, of course. We sold the books for $3, and we could have paid our printing costs and made a little cash if we'd had 150 or 200 printed, even if the cost was $2.50 or $2.75 a copy. By buying quantity, however, I got 700 for $1.30 each. (I think we'd planned on 500, which still would have been way too many. We'd have gotten those for something under $2.) Anyhow, we had way more than we could sell and that cut into the profit. We sold 100 right off the bat; we got another 100 sold with difficulty in the next year; eventually we broke even and cut the price on the remainder to $1.30 and then to $1. Now, eight years later, we still have a box or two.

Another thing I didn't understand: a cookbook is a vanity project. I was therefore absolutely the wrong editor. Committees drive me stark raving mad; inconsistency leaps out of the page and smites me; inefficiency bothers me. The recipes were terribly complicated—whether to peel the potato from right to left or vice versa and how to level the sugar in the spoon. I edited them to basics and, in doing so, I'm sure I must have ruined grandmother's recipe for many a donor. I dismissed the group who offered to help edit after seeing the mishmash of the first afternoon. When someone suggested that each person hand-write or type her own recipe, I found another person just like me to type the entire manuscript. As a result we had a two-person project instead of a fifty-person committee project. I think a different leader could have worked out an acceptable compromise on looks and efficiency versus group fun.

Because of the way we operated, I have no little anecdotes. The other volunteer and I baked a lot of cakes for the PTA, so to speak; a few people worked their tails off to try to get the "leftovers" sold elsewhere; a few contented folks saw their recipes in print and enjoyed the compliments of their friends; the church didn't lose money on it. I won't demand anonymity, but this is not one of the things in my life I'm proud of or that I think I did even reasonably well. On the other hand, even if I'd done it well I'd rather have just donated $5 and stayed home.

Best wishes,
Fran

Disillusioning. But in Fran's story, at least, a good cookbook did get published, and even if the church didn't make any money, neither did they lose any. Unfortunately, for every story that turns out as well as that of St. Nicholas Church, the Baton Rouge Little League, or even Fran's church, there are uncounted numbers of aborted projects, where collections of recipes languish in various states of readiness; projects that lost money and had to be repaid out of the pockets of their once-hopeful perpetrators; and projects that never got off the ground at all. The rest of this chapter is devoted to helping you keep your cookbook in the category that gets newspaper and magazine writers all dewy-eyed, and out of the category of those who wish they had just donated $5 and stayed home.

Vanity of Vanities?

The first step in self-publishing is to understand exactly what it is—and what it is not. It is not what is sometimes called "vanity publishing." You see advertisements for vanity publishers in writers' magazines and other publications likely to be read by would-be writers. These publishers take your manuscript and your money and give you in return an agreed-upon number of printed, bound books. Generally, these books are looked at a bit sideways in the publishing industry, and books published by vanity publishers, who prefer to call themselves "subsidy publishers," seldom receive much serious attention from booksellers, book buyers, or book reviewers, although a few people have earned fame and money this way. I have never seen a cookbook published by a subsidy publisher, though a few must lurk somewhere in basements and garages.

In self-publishing, you or your organization play the role of publisher, from conceiving the project and editing the manuscript to designing the book, arranging for the printing, and distributing it. In contrast to trade publishing, you make all the decisions. Whether this is an advantage or a disadvantage depends on your situation and your nature. For all the heroines whose success stories we have marveled at, it was clearly an advantage. For the nameless thousands whose efforts have gone unpublished, unenriched, and unappreciated, it was a disadvantage. To make self-publishing work, you must understand before you begin not only how *it* works, but also how *you* work, as clearly as my friend Fran had come to understand those things at the end of her project.

Pros and Cons of Do-It-Yourself Publishing

The obvious advantages to self-publishing are that you can make money at it and that you can do things your way. Another advantage is that it's a way to publish a cookbook you couldn't sell to a trade publisher. The disadvantages are simply the flip side: if the possibilities of profit and the freedom of decision belong to you alone, so do the risks and the extra work. No writing and forgetting. You will have to monitor quality control, production, distribution, and financing.

If that sounds like a lot of work, you haven't heard the half of it. Somebody will have to contact the bookstores and libraries, pack the books, arrange for shipping, keep track of the orders, handle the billing and accounts payable, write the advertising and buy space for it to keep interest alive, and pound the pavements in search of new customers once the first spurt of sales has passed. Notice that these are all things someone has to do after the book has been written, designed, and printed.

The best advice is "Don't try to do it alone." The most common self-publishing teams are organizational groups or committees and husband-wife teams, but small groups of friends and two or three family members also work together frequently in this kind of publishing. Working with others is a good idea not only to lessen the labor, but also for the improved insights and creativity you get by mixing personalities and talents. A publisher I know once excused a squabble among his small staff on the grounds that their diverse attitudes were necessary: "I would expect my marketing manager to be impatient and have fire in the belly; I would expect my business manager to be watching the ground and stooping to pick up pennies; I would expect our authors to be developing grandiose ideas; and I would expect my editors to be honing them down to reality."

Sharing Responsibilities

To bring a project like a cookbook to successful fruition, a group needs a strong leader with the ability to direct volunteers. It also needs someone who knows and understands foods, cooking, and recipes, someone with a mastery of writing skills, and others with good business sense and an understanding of how to sell.

If I have just listed more traits than you have workers, don't worry. Many people have more than one of these skills. The person who is good at organizing volunteers may also be good at business; someone with a knack for selling may also be knowledgeable and enthusiastic about food and cooking. What matters is that each role or required function be filled and that someone be firmly in charge, with all workers understanding exactly who is responsible for what.

You also need the balance for perspective on how well you are working. During the years I taught communication in the College of Business Administration at Penn State, we used to divide the classes into small groups and assign them huge presentations to be prepared and presented within a tight time schedule. Inevitably some groups performed brilliantly, some were okay, and some got everything so totally wrong that we, as their teachers, were embarrassed. When we tried to understand how they could have worked together and come up with such a mess, we always concluded that they had sat around "feeding each other poison." We meant that no one in the group could see or would say that things had gone off course; or if someone tried, no one else in the group would listen. To be a successful publishing group, you need members who will speak up if they sense something wrong and you need members who will listen to each other's warnings.

Communication Is the Key

Listening is a learned art; so is speaking up without being obnoxious. You learn those two skills only through practice and sensitivity to what is happening in the group. Talking things over with each other and offering positive suggestions, not criticisms or reasons why ideas won't work, is the best beginning. And middle. And end.

Several things will assure an effective group. First, get together and discuss the kinds of personalities you need. Then decide whether or not you already have likely candidates for each function in the group—people with enough impatience to be good at sales, people with enough love of detail to be good at editing, and so on. If you don't, you can recruit the missing types as volunteers or consultants or extra help. Be frank about why you need them. Then, if your group still feels shy of the necessary personalities or roles, each of you can try to move in and fill the gaps as you are able. Maybe you are usually patience personified, but if your group needs someone to get a little impatient in pushing sales for the book, try it on, like a part in a play. At home you can't keep up with the checkbook, but the group needs someone to track expenses and control spending. Why not you? You've probably been told often enough how to do it. Play the part.

Clarifying Goals

In working with a group, remember that not all groups are formed for the same reasons and that the way a group should function depends on its purpose. From time to time most of us belong to three different kinds of groups: working groups, therapy groups, and social groups. Working groups include all kinds of committees (including cookbook committees), task forces, and planning groups. Their main purpose is to get a job done. Groups such as Weight Watchers, exercise clubs, and Alcoholics Anonymous are therapy groups. They exist to help each individual through mutual support. Bridge clubs, travel groups, gourmet clubs, and the like are social groups. People join them mainly to have a good time.

Working groups often get into trouble when they try to act like social groups or therapy groups. Often people who volunteer to work on something like a cookbook have had little experience with work groups and tend to behave as they would in their social or therapy groups. For instance, a person who hesitates to reject unacceptable recipes or reorganize a business plan for fear of hurting the volunteers' feelings is operating by standards that would prevail in a social or therapy group, but which must be subordinate in a work group. The same is true of the person who spends much meeting time in high good humor, joking and distracting attention from the work at hand. On the other hand, volunteers and people in partnerships join the group because they enjoy the camaraderie of working with others. You can't use so rigid an approach that they feel transported to the ninth floor of corporate America. Consider also that people who spend all their time in high-powered work groups are often lousy in social groups. Who hasn't met the man who gets into the picnic-softball club and says, "Let's get this thing organized," and then watched all the fun drain away?

In working with a committee to publish a cookbook, spend a few minutes in an early organizational session to discuss the kind of group you are and how each of you feels about the balance of work and play. It could head off problems later on if you can figure out ahead of time how to balance the work and the social aspects of your group.

To get a sense of how this might work, look back at my friend Fran's letter and speculate on how she might have handled the situation after receiving a "mishmash" of differently edited recipes at the end of the group's first afternoon of editing, instead of simply dismissing everyone and doing the work herself. If you are inclined to do as she did in such a situation, assign the managing of volunteers to someone else and put yourself in a position where your work doesn't require direct involvement with them. Many organizations avoid this particular problem by giving recipe donors a master format sheet and a style sheet or list of rules to follow in writing recipes. These instructions help keep recipes consistent with each other from the start. To learn more about the different steps involved in editing, see Chapter 6, "Looking at Trade Publishing." In producing a self-published book you will have to follow the same procedures and divide the editing responsibilities accordingly.

Once you have established your operating routines, settle down to the decisions about the kind of book, the audience, the theme, and the defined purposes, exactly as if you were planning a book for commercial publication, according to the guidelines in Chapter One. This will involve discussions—lots of them. If you find that you disagree, you are operating just like every trade publisher I've ever seen in action. And you'll have to settle the differences either by compromise or edict, just like every trade publisher.

Here's a line I stole from somewhere: "You pick your battles." Any group that tries to work together to publish a book will generate different and sometimes conflicting ideas about what the book should be like and how to go about creating it. People, especially volunteers, tend to pout if a dictator takes over and says, "Okay, this is what we're doing. Discussion closed"; a group would do well to learn the same kind of give-and-take that the professionals in trade publishing must practice. Try to figure out which points matter so much to you that you are willing to fight for them. Concede the rest. You may be surprised at how few things anybody feels strongly enough about to fight for, when presented with the differences in that way. Your fight and somebody else's concession may match perfectly. This works astonishingly often if all the members of the group understand the concept.

Book Specifications

As you and your partners or volunteers assemble and test the recipes for the book, organizing it according to some coherent scheme and deciding exactly how it should look, you must consider what image you want the book to project and how to project it. Some major considerations are trim size and format (size and shape), use of illustrations and color, binding, kind of paper, and dust jacket. All these factors affect the appearance of the finished book and hence its personality.

Sunset and HP, for example, have become so widely associated with paperback books measuring 8 1/2 by 11 inches and illustrated with many color photographs that anybody else who uses the format (as several other publishers do) risks being confused with Sunset and HP. The large pages have the advantage of offering plenty of room for illustrations and the possibility of fitting several recipes onto a page. On the other hand, a book like this will be slender and have a thin spine. To attract sales in bookstores it will have to be displayed face out, which booksellers often refuse to do because face-out displays take up more

95

room than spine-out. Publishers sometimes try to circumvent this problem by creating racks or spinner display units for their books—more cost—but most bookstores resist putting in publishers' racks because they take up floor space. In self-publishing you almost certainly want to avoid racks, which means that you should carefully weigh all the other pros and cons before going to a Sunset-type format. The same considerations hold true for the 8 1/2-by-5 1/4-inch shape favored by such publishers as Nitty Gritty and Owlswood, and of the 8 1/2-inch-square format typically used by 101 Productions. If you are not planning to sell your books in bookstores, size and shape need not concern you. Otherwise, consider the more standard book sizes, 5 1/2 by 8 1/2 inches or 6 by 9. Odd shapes and sizes are not only usually more expensive to print, but for booksellers to shelve and display.

You will also have to decide on the binding and the cover for your book. Cookbooks are often spiral-bound. A "perfect binding," in which the signatures (groups of pages) are glued into the cases with a flexible glue, allows the opened book to lie flat on the counter. For smaller books a saddle-stitch binding, which sews or staples the pages together through their folded centers, works well. And finally, the cover, if your book is paperback or has a washable vinyl cover, or the dust jacket, if you decide to use a jacket over a hard cover, must be designed to clearly reflect the contents of your book.

Every one of these choices involves money. In all probability, doing the book exactly as you would like will cost too much, forcing you to charge so much for it that it would be priced out of the market. You will have to make some compromises: smaller page ("trim") size, perhaps, or fewer pages and fewer illustrations. Maybe you'll decide to use only two colors instead of four, or print on a less expensive paper. In these compromises, you will need all your skills in interpersonal communication to deal with the people who have donated recipes to the book and with those who are working on it; quarrels may arise not only from the decisions about the appearance of the book, but also about the content.

Suppose, for instance, that something you learn from the printer makes it clear that you have to cut fifty recipes from the book. Whose do you cut? How do you tell them? Or suppose your setup is such that all recipes are supposed to be tested before they are given to the cookbook committee for compiling and typing, and the editor thinks she sees something wrong with a recipe. How does she check and correct the problem?

Years ago my own family nearly came unglued over a recipe when the Women's Auxiliary of the First Presbyterian Church in Strouds-

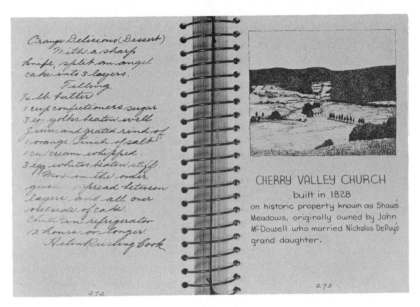

Local scenes are sometimes used to illustrate regional cookbooks, especially self-published ones. In this case, a dessert and a picture of a historic property just happen to come side-by-side. Each recipe in this book is reproduced in the handwriting of the person who contributed the recipe. This is an older book, as you can tell by the wire spiral binding. (From Secrets from Pocono Kitchens, *self-published by the Women's Auxiliary of the First Presbyterian Church of Stroudsburg, PA)*

burg, Pennsylvania, put together *Secrets of Pocono Kitchens*, a handwritten collection published to raise funds. My Grandmother Dietrick was on the committee that created the book, and she not only donated a good many of her own recipes, but also helped edit the donations of others. She was a wild, creative cook who was always trying something new, like adding vanilla to apple pie so that it would taste as if it had ice cream on it, and then forgetting to write the ingredient into the recipe. My Grandmother Pennington, on the other hand, was very precise and could tell you to the last quarter-teaspoon exactly what went into the foods she cooked. She donated the Pennington family recipe for English steamed plum pudding.

Grandmother Dietrick looked at the recipe and decided that all that suet and flour boiling in a muslin bag for three hours would turn out too dense. Mrs. Pennington must have forgotten to mention the baking powder, the kind of mistake Grandmother D. made in writing all the time. Well, I don't know who called whom or what happened in what order, except that Grandma Pennington, ordinarily a peaceable

97

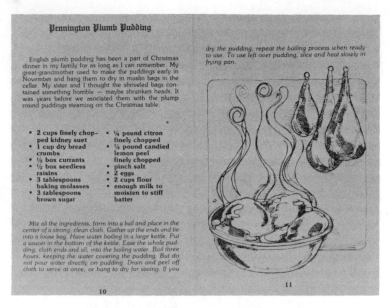

The artist for Christmas at Our House *did an uncommonly good job of capturing the spirit of the holiday and the tone of the individual recipes. In addition to enhancing the mood of the book and its recipes, the art helped fill pages. The title of the recipe is an outstandingly good example of mistakes that creep in when you work too fast and under pressure. The Pennington pudding was* plum, *not* plumb. *(From the premium cookbook,* Christmas at Our House, *commissioned and distributed by Drake-Chenault Enterprises, Inc.)*

woman, finally got on the phone and said in stentorian tones that *under no circumstances* was anyone to put baking powder in the recipe for plum pudding. The two ladies were notably cool toward one another for a long time afterwards.

If so much passion can be generated within a family by a teaspoonful of baking powder, you can see the importance of putting a diplomat who knows cooking in charge of compiling, culling, and criticizing recipes. This is important not only to keep peace among volunteers for the sake of general goodwill, but also because you will need all those people to help you with marketing your book.

Common-Sense Market Research

Like a trade publisher, you must consider market possibilities for your book as you make your decisions. To give a simple but clear example, if you lived in Salt Lake City where a significant portion of the population is Mormon and eschews the use of alcohol, coffee, tea, and (to some degree) excesses of red meat, you would have to look closely at who would remain to buy your book there before you published a collection of cocktail recipes or a single-subject book like *The Coffee Cookbook*. On the other hand, you could expect a good market for a book on how to use whole grains, since practicing Mormons store a year's worth of grain in their homes. The local market is usually the beginning place for self-published cookbooks, and the tastes of the local population should guide you in shaping your cookbook. As I have suggested, certain subjects may be inappropriate for people in a given location, but if you can hit upon a popular subject, you'll probably do all right even if it has already been done.

Consider the romance that people have with the seaport town of Charleston, South Carolina. Even though a number of Charleston cookbooks already grace the shelves of bookstores in that area, each new one that comes along seems welcome. The classic *Charleston Receipts*, created by an ambitious Junior League more than thirty years ago, continues to be a best-seller; the new *Caterin' to Charleston*, by a mother-daughter team whose recipes come from years of entertaining in that city, is finding an equally receptive market, even though the book is sold from the family garage. For these books the audience includes not only the myriad tourists who buy their way through Charleston, but also the natives, who enjoy reading about themselves, and people throughout the rest of the South who have succumbed to the Charleston mystique.

If you don't have the magic of Charleston going for you, you may have trouble deciding whether or not an idea has enough romance to make it in an already crowded market. If you live in Cody and somebody's already published a successful *Cooking in Cody*, don't try to borrow on its success by publishing *Cooking in Cody Revisited*. Instead, look for a new angle—maybe *Cooking Game, Cody Style*. And if you knew Cody, you'd know what a good idea that is. It would be the right book in the right place at the right time.

Find a Need—And Fill It!

Another example of a self-published book which was in exactly the right place at exactly the right time is *Simply Scrumptious*, by Mary Ann Feuchter Robinson, Rosemary Dunn Stancil, and Lorela Nichols Wilkins. The three had been home economists at the University of Georgia until they left to raise families. Then they began to do freelance work for the Litton company, consulting and running cooking classes.

In dealing with the hundreds and hundreds of people who buy microwave ovens and then can't figure out what to do with them except heat up leftovers, the women saw a need for a cookbook that would tell people how to make the most of their microwave ovens. As Ms. Robinson said, "That's an expensive piece of equipment, and people kept telling us they didn't really know what to do with it. We could see the need for a microwave cookbook, but we knew it would have to be different and better than any of those already around."

As they tried to create a "better and different" microwave cookbook, they developed "cooking from scratch" recipes to combine the value of basic ingredients with the convenience of the microwave oven; they included recipes for using the clay pot in a microwave oven, and they included chapters of recipes for jams, jellies, and other foods not usually cooked in a microwave. Finally, they added a chapter on nonfood uses, such as drying flowers and making modeling clay for children. No matter how you feel about microwave ovens, you can't help admiring the perceptiveness that led these author-publishers to spot a market niche and fill it with a book unlike any others available.

Once they had written their book, they incorporated themselves and began to sell it. They meet once a week to make sure each of them knows what is going on and that everything that needs to be done is being done. And there's plenty to do; they even package and ship their orders themselves.

No glamour here. But there is success. The *Simply Scrumptious* microwave cookbook sold 27,000 in its first year. The authors worked virtually full time to create new markets to get the books out. It was an ambitious book, with more than 500 recipes, and they dared to print 10,000 in the first printing. To sell it they travel to promote it at gourmet shows and booksellers' meetings.

You may decide that a smaller-scale project is more appropriate. Your decisions about the number of recipes, pages, and illustrations, as well as your decisions about design and format, should be determined by the size and skill of your work force, the amount of money you are prepared to invest in the project, and the number of books you think you can sell in a year. And that's hard to calculate. Trade publishers with long years of experience have trouble with it; that's what those tables in the bookstores, full of last year's best-sellers priced as "bargain books," are all about. As an amateur in the business, you may have trouble with such projections too, but booksellers report that the self-published cookbooks they stock regularly, especially regional ones, never need to be discounted.

You don't have to print a year's supply of books in the first printing. For one thing, the total cost of printing a year's supply may be more than you can pay in one lump sum. You may find it more practical to print a smaller quantity the first time. The cost per book will be higher but the total cost will be less, and you can use money from the sales of the first printing to pay for subsequent printings. Your decision should be based not only on how many books you think you can sell, but also on the price breaks in the printer's rate schedule. For example, it might cost you three dollars per book to print five hundred. At seven hundred, the cost may drop to two dollars per book. At a thousand, the cost may drop dramatically. But you may not feel you can afford the overall cost of printing a thousand at once, and you may be afraid that five hundred books will sell out too quickly. In that case the middle choice, seven hundred books at a lower rate but not the cheapest rate, would be most reasonable.

Tips on Storage

If you have published a book that is not appropriate for bookstores, and rely entirely on a local market, the extras may end up in someone's garage or in the church basement. Even if you plan so skillfully that you have no extras, be sure to think about where you will store your inventory. Let's say you decide to begin with one thousand books. They come from the bindery packed twenty to a box. That's fifty boxes of books—too many for the hall closet. And space isn't the only consideration in storing boxes. They must also be kept someplace fairly free of dust and moisture, which rules out the garage and probably the attic, too. Basically, books need about the same environmental conditions as people. In parts of the country with very high humidity, warehouses for books are usually air-conditioned to keep the humidity down and prevent mildew.

I can give you a hard and fast rule about warehousing books anywhere. If the roof is going to spring a new leak, it will be over the area where you store your books. Moreover, if you have boxes of old, worthless books, and boxes of new, salable ones, the roof will leak on the new books. So wherever you find a cool, dry, dust-free place for your books, protect them further by keeping a plastic cover over all the boxes.

Too Many or Not Enough

I still blush to recall that back in the days when I was planning to self-publish *Cooking from Scratch* in partnership with a newspaper for which I wrote food columns, I let a printer convince me that we should run 25,000 copies to get the lowest possible unit cost. What a huge number of books! The university press where I work now has never printed that many of *anything* at one time. The publishers for whom I write, though larger operations, seldom print that many books at a time. Yet in my enthusiasm and ignorance, I honestly thought I could advertise in the newspapers for which I wrote food columns, take the books to the state fair, visit a few bookstores, and sell all 25,000—in a year or less! By myself! Such faith must have been what parted the Red Sea.

I know now that even faith could not have sold 25,000 copies of a cookbook based on a practice not in vogue among the busy, overcommitted women who cook these days, as long as I was limited to what I could sell in the central Pennsylvania area where I was known. And—supposing I could have sold them—who was going to pack up and ship 25,000 cookbooks?

In Rebersburg, Pennsylvania, at the other extreme, the women of the Ladies' Aid of the St. Peter's Lutheran Church published a little book of about a hundred pages, crammed with old family recipes, modern information about the protein and caloric content of foods, household tips, suggested menus, and quantity recipes. In a community proud of its cooking, where housekeeping skills are still valued and nearly all the residents have large families that live outside the immediate area, a generous market for the book seemed obvious. But because they were conservative by nature and inexperienced in publishing, they began cautiously by printing just 250 copies. These were all sold at $5 each even before all the members of the church could get copies. The ladies ordered two more printings for a total of 500 books, and they're still sold out, while people (including me) are trying to get a copy. The book is rapidly becoming a local collector's item.

Finding the balance between too few and too many books for your situation requires study. Some of the factors that trade publishers examine in trying to get it right include built-in or automatic markets, easy secondary markets, and additional possibilities through enterprising sales efforts.

The built-in markets comprise all those people who will buy the book no matter what. They are what Fran referred to as "the PTA meeting bake sale." The people who contribute to a cookbook can usually be considered a built-in market. If one hundred people contributed recipes, you can safely assume one hundred-plus guaranteed sales. In a community where people maintain close contact with friends and relatives, you can safely assume another hundred sales, figuring that each contributor will want a book for herself and another for a friend or relative. If you're publishing the book for an organization in which not all

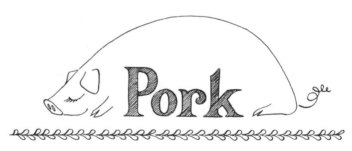

A little whimsy at the beginning of these chapters helps the reader make light of knowing that lamb, veal, and pork come from real live (formerly) animals. The drawings are from a self-published book called Forum Feasts, *"favorite recipes from friends of the Forum School in North Jersey." The theme of the book is Roman, in keeping with the school's name. The drawings by Anne S. Samson have the balance and structural formality that suggest Roman style art.*

the members contributed recipes, you can assume that at least two-thirds of those members will also buy a book. (But don't forget to deduct those members who contributed recipes. You've already got them figured for two books each.)

The easy secondary markets are those people who will buy a book if they know about it and find it easily accessible—the people in a small community who are not involved in the publishing organization, but would pick up a copy if it were on the counter of a local store, for example. And the enterprise markets are those you find if you expend extra energy and take the book where it might otherwise never be seen. In my Rebersburg example, I think that the Grange fair, a week-long event at which people come from all over the country and camp in tents and trailers near the midway, would be a place to sell the cookbooks for years to come.

All too often, when groups (especially small ones) publish their own cookbooks, the marketing stops with the built-in sales. But if the book is any good at all, it doesn't have to stop there. Depending on the cost, among other things, you should be able to place your book in local gift shops and bookstores as well as selling it directly to individual buyers. Cost, marketability, size, and quantity all lock into an unbreakable circle; the decision you make about each depends partly on the decisions you make about the others. Let's look at these other factors, then, before we return to a fuller consideration of marketing later in this chapter.

Consult Your Printer

In determining quantities and setting prices, your printer's advice is essential. Take your tentative plans to a printer whose reputation you know and ask for price breakdowns on printing various quantities of your book. The printer will be able to show you prices for various bindings, papers, and cover materials. As you make first choices on size, format, binding, and paper, the printer will tell you how much he or she would charge you for the resulting book in quantities of 100, 500, 1,000, 5,000, or more. The greater the quantity, the smaller the price per book, but the greater the total cost of the job.

The confusing part of all this is that different printers will charge different prices for doing the same job. You should ask more than one to bid on the job according to your specifications. A printer who handles only large commercial jobs may not be interested in bidding at all; a moderately busy printer who would welcome the work but is not hungry for it would quote you a moderate to high price for doing the job; while a printer who is looking for work would make a bid almost as low as his own cost. This means that your specifications must include a time schedule, since printers' work loads vary from month to month.

One decision the printer will discuss with you is whether you should have your manuscript typeset or reproduced from camera-ready copy produced by a superior typist on a good electric typewriter. "Camera-ready" means that the page will be reproduced just as it is. It may be reduced in size but nothing further will be done to it. Some printers have typesetters on the staff; others will recommend typesetters who do nothing else. Either way, typesetting is a cost to be figured in addition to the actual printing, and you should get bids on it just as you do on the printing. Typesetting produces a more professional-looking book, but it costs enough to make typewriter copy worth considering. If you decide to use a typewriter, remember that leaving margins of one inch or even more will make the pages look neater and more attractive.

If you decide to use typewriter copy, the typing must be done on an office-size electric typewriter, such as an IBM, with film ribbon. Each finished page must be perfect because that page, reduced, is exactly how the page in your book will look. If you decide on typesetting, your printer's recommendation about reliable typesetters will be valuable. Try to find a typesetter who has had experience with cookbooks. You may get a temptingly low bid from a typesetter who is new or looking for jobs, but if others who have worked with this typesetter advise against him or her, listen.

I wish I could write this advice in letters two feet high. Even the language traditionally attributed to sailors cannot do justice to the grief an incompetent typesetter can cause you in a project like a cookbook, where the text includes lists of ingredients, quantities given in number form, and directions that include times and temperatures. Recently I ignored my own good sense and allowed a new and untried typesetter to talk me into giving her a complicated project because she was local and bid the job about one-third lower than the other two typesetters I contacted. The resulting mess was like the fairy-tale tree that couldn't be felled because every time the woodcutter chopped out a chip, two grew back. Every time I sent back a correction in the set type, the typesetter made two new errors in correcting it. My time schedule mushroomed from the six weeks I'd planned to six months, and I don't dare count the number of people who stood around muttering, "I told you so."

An incompetent printer can give you grief, too. One who is accustomed to handling self-published cookbooks is ideal, and surprisingly, quite a few of them exist. In larger communities you should be able to choose among several; in rural areas, however, you may be lucky to have any printers at all. In such a case, you should consider taking your project to the closest area where you can find many printers to choose from. Some of the relatively new small print shops with names like

Quik-Kopy and Quikee-Print may prove adequate if you're planning to print a small quantity of books, say between 50 and 500 copies. Another option is to work with a printer who specializes in cookbooks, even though the shop is far from your location. *Literary Market Place* is a publishers' and writers' resource book that should be available in any good public or college library. It lists printers who specialize in printing small quantities of books—500 and less. Start there if you must look outside your area. The new magazine *Small Press* also carries advertisements for short-run printers (*Small Press*, 205 East 42nd St., N.Y. NY 10017). It's easier to work with someone near home, though, so I recommend the long-distance option only when you can't find anyone who suits you nearby.

In judging a printer, consider his or her cooperativeness and helpfulness. Find out if the shop has had experience with similar projects. Look at other work they have done and watch for little things, such as whether the finished product is free of smudges, ink smears, and fingerprints. Look at sample printed pages to see if the inking of the letters appears even, not so heavy that the o's and a's are filled in and not so light that the extenders (the parts of the letter above or below the line) on the y's and h's disappear. Make sure the printing on one side of the page doesn't show through on the reverse side. Finally—and this is critical—find out from others who have used the shop whether the printer is reliable in meeting deadlines.

Those of us who work often with printers have a cynical line: printers lie. And we chant their litany of lies to crack each other up when we're sitting around and sharing a libation or two:

> It's in the mail.
> It goes on press this afternoon.
> It's on the loading dock.
> It'll be ready by noon tomorrow.
> It'll be ready by noon today.

Of course, printers don't lie any more than householders who have trouble meeting the bills, or teenagers who've missed curfew, or girls who've somehow made two dates for the same night. Just getting along in this world can be complicated. Printing is a sporadic business, where most of the time there's either too much work or not enough. Printers have the same problems with staff and equipment and supplies that other service-oriented businesses have. And these problems can affect your book.

The best you can hope for is a printer who doesn't invite an undue portion of such problems, who copes with them effectively, and who will be honest about what's going on when they do happen; one who really wants to do a good job for you. Your contribution to success at this stage is to meet *your* deadlines and produce clean copy on time.

Signing on the Dotted Line

When you have agreed to work together, your printer will ask you to sign a contract. I think it's a good idea to consult a lawyer at this stage, but unless you can find one who is knowledgeable about publishing, you still need to be alert to little details that don't come immediately to mind but could affect the success of your entire operation. Two important items that you should have written into the contract are 1) that the printer supply the agreed-upon number of books on or before a given date, and 2) that after the first printing, the plates from which the work was done belong to you. If you allow the plates to continue as the printer's property, you're stuck with him forever for subsequent printings, unless you're willing to pay all over again to have new plates made. Basically this means going back to the reproductions of your set type—if you can find them.

If all goes well, you may be perfectly happy to continue with the same printer, but many things could change. You might be able to make a better deal; your sister might go into the printing business; the company you're working with might change hands. The women who published *Simply Scrumptious* fell into this situation not because of malice on anyone's part, but simply because their printer was not familiar with such arrangements. Establishing their right to the plates for that book has cost them time, energy, and money for legal advice, money they would have preferred to spend elsewhere. Write it all into the contract and avoid the possibility of a problem.

As you line up your composition, paper, printing, and binding costs (call them "manufacturing costs" if you want to sound professional) you must think about the retail price for your books. Trade publishers have complicated formulas for working out prices to allow for overhead and production costs while allowing for a given percentage return on investment. Even university presses, notoriously less concerned with profit than they might be, price by formula—most of the time. One publisher I know observed that he thought you might be able to do as well in pricing books "by spinning a coin."

In self-publishing a simple formula once used was simply to double the unit cost. (Unit cost is the total cost of producing one book.) This probably won't be enough anymore. Small trade publishers may multiply the unit cost by four or five and also figure in a percentage to allow for overhead and royalties. (Larger publishers may offer a markup of six times or even more.) That's probably a good formula for self-publishing too. And don't forget to figure in a dollar or so per book for mail orders.

What we're all trying to do is to figure out how to make as much money as we can from selling our books and still keep them priced reasonably enough for people to buy them. The best formula in the world is worthless if it prices your book out of the market. And merely multiplying your unit cost to arrive at a price won't work if it doesn't allow for such costs as advertising and distribution. In other words, don't assume that the difference between production costs and retail sales is all profit. That margin must provide what you have to spend in advertising, gas for delivering books, storage, and office supplies related to the book. And if you expect bookstores and gift shops to carry your book, remember that they will expect to buy it from you at anywhere from 20 percent to 55 percent off the retail price; 40 percent is more or less standard in bookstores.

About the best possible advice is to figure out how much each book must earn to cover *all* costs and make a modest profit; then compare that figure with the prices of comparable cookbooks. In general, small organizations tend to underestimate what people are willing to pay for a nicely done cookbook. Don't forget that cookbooks are essentially collectible items. Having one doesn't prevent a customer from buying others; if yours differs from all others in her collection, she will probably buy it—at any reasonable retail price.

Here is a checklist to help you negotiate the printing maze:

> What will be the format of the book (size and shape)?
> How many pages will it have?
> Typesetting or camera-ready typewriter copy?
> Illustrations?
> Color?
> What kind of paper?
> Type of binding?
> Jackets?
> Time schedules and deadlines?
> Own plates at the end of the job?

Before you're ready for printing you must take care of three details that are necessary if your book is to be acknowledged in the publishing industry as a real book; a copyright, a Library of Congress number, and an International Standard Book Number (ISBN). Copyrighting your cookbook will keep someone else from copying all or parts of it and peddling the work as his own. To apply for a copyright and to learn exactly how it works, write to the Copyright Office (Information and Publications Section, Library of Congress, Washington D.C. 20559). Request the pamphlet "Copyright Basics," and the Application for Copyright Registration for a Non-dramatic Literary Work (Form TX).

The ISBN number is essential if you want your book to be sold in bookstores. Write to International Standard Book Numbering, R.R. Bowker Co., 1180 Avenue of the Americas, New York NY 10036. Send the title of your book, the author's name, and the name and address of your publishing location. The number that will be assigned to your book is for that book alone; no other book will ever carry the number. This is the number by which wholesalers, retailers, and even some knowledgeable individuals will identify your book when they order it. It's important to get started on these things well before press time so that you can have all the information typeset or typed for the front matter in your book.

A Self-Publisher's Work Is Never Done

Helen Hayes is one of the founders of Hayes-Rolfes & Associates (P.O. Box 11463, Memphis, TN 38111), cookbook consultants who specialize in seminars for people who are self-publishing and distributing their cookbooks. She says that the worst mistake many people make in publishing their own cookbooks is to assume that once the book is completed and off the press, their work is done. "They don't understand that they're looking at years and years of marketing after publication. A person who is a good cook and has no business sense should find a partner to help with the marketing."

Dot Gibson of Gibson-Rees Consultants, Inc. (1603 Rainbow Drive, Waycross, GA 31501), another firm of seminar leaders and cookbook distributors, emphasizes in her sessions that promoting a cookbook involves everything from writing press releases to contacting bookstores, activities that must be handled by the publishers. In self-publishing, that means you.

People talk about marketing as though it were a big deal, but I'm a marketing manager and I don't agree with them. All marketing takes is a little ingenuity, a little nerve, and a lot of time and energy. Also, I think people confuse marketing, selling, and distributing books. I hear these words used more or less interchangeably, so let's straighten them out. Marketing means finding and creating places to sell your books. Selling means getting the people in those places (wholesalers, retailers, or individuals) to buy the books. Distributing means getting the books to those places. Such promotional activities as getting publicity, buying advertising, and giving cooking demonstrations are functions of marketing that help to generate sales.

While we're speaking of terminology, publicity is attention you get for your book through reviews, television shows, and special demonstrations and the like; advertising is display ads, radio ads, billboards, and other printed or broadcast material for which you pay. Publicity is invaluable in selling your books, but it does not replace advertising. At least one publisher I know is facing steadily declining sales after initial high profits because he refuses to pay for advertising. On the other hand, a number of Junior League cookbooks across the country are thriving because of skilled and judiciously placed advertising.

The more ambitious your project, the more you need advertising and publicity, but the way you go about getting them is remarkably the same no matter what size your operation. If you have ever worked to help promote any organizational activity, from the Girl Scouts' cookie sale to the college Spring Week fair, you already have a good idea how to promote your book. We will discuss publicity and advertising here before we get into marketing, sales, and distribution because publicity and advertising are the ways you let people know your book exists, so that they will want to buy it.

The Best Things in Life Are Free

I don't care where you live; if you publish a cookbook, you can get some free publicity for it. Talk shows, newspaper columnists, local magazines, and local clubs are hungry for interesting subjects for interviews, columns, feature articles, and speakers. And people are fascinated by cookbooks and by people who write them. All you have to do is search out and contact all these hungry people and tell them about your cookbook in a way slanted to *their* interests. Rather than developing example after example, let me pass along a saying I learned from a professor who taught persuasion. He said, "You gotta look at your audience and answer their question, 'What's it to me and Sally Ann?' " In a more epigrammatic moment he also said, "A fool gives me *his* reasons. The wise man persuades me with my own."

To amplify just a bit more, if you're trying to get a chance to talk about your cookbook to people who specialize in fund raising, offer them a speech on cookbooks as fund raisers. If you're trying to get a nutrition-oriented columnist to print a column about your book, send information about the nutrition problems you encountered and solved in your book. If a holiday is near, try for a feature article in a local publicity about cookbooks (not just yours) as gifts—and make sure the article is accompanied by a photograph in which your book is prominently displayed and identified. Get the idea?

Everything you try won't work. I estimate that about one in ten of my ideas produces results. A cynic I work with says that's a blessing to humankind. (Don't expect to be loved for your prowess as a publicist and attention getter.)

Selling Frigidaires to Eskimos

When it comes to advertising, the stuff you have to pay for, you can accomplish a great deal with small display ads in newspapers and community magazines. Classified ads are even less expensive, and work well. You may want to buy some radio spots on stations whose audiences seem suited to your book; it's no use advertising cookbooks on a teenybopper station where Clearasil is the number-one sponsor. Television is too expensive to touch. If your book is published by a group in a church or other organization, the newsletter or bulletin it circulates among its members is a perfect place for announcements about your book. I hope you noticed that I wrote announcements—plural. A single ad or announcement is not anywhere near as effective as repeated reminders. If you have to decide between paying for two big ads or four smaller ones, choose frequency over size every time.

Time all this promotion so that it begins shortly before you start to sell your book and continues indefinitely. Meanwhile, try to find and devise markets for your books. Whether to try for national or only local publicity depends on whether you honestly feel that the book has interest for anyone outside your immediate area.

The all-time most ingenious piece of marketing I have ever encountered is a sweet little caper by Triad Publishing Company. Technically, they are a trade publisher; although small, they publish books by a number of different authors and so cannot be considered self-publishers. Triad has produced a book called *The Chosen: Appetizers & Desserts,* made up of recipes from 120 different Jewish fund-raising cookbooks, and most of *them* were self-published. The built-in market here is almost beyond calculating.

Not to stop now that they have a good thing going, Triad offers another book, *Jewish Cooking Made Slim,* also created from recipes chosen from Jewish fund-raising cookbooks across the country. Not only that, the editor of this volume, Marjorie Weiner, is a counselor at Weight Watchers of North Florida, and she and her husband boast a combined weight loss of nearly 100 pounds, which they've managed to maintain. The book has built-in markets on so many fronts it's hard to visualize: all those people who contributed to Jewish fund-raising cookbooks; all those people who live in Florida; all those people who go to Weight Watchers; all those fat people who want to get thin; all those thin people who want to stay that way; all those Jewish people who just want more recipes . . . I can't go on! Study this, friends. This is marketing!

Put Energy into Your Sales Effort

When it comes to selling your books to the markets you have found and created locally or nationally or both, start thinking about energy. You have three basic categories to deal with: individual sales, retailer sales, and wholesaler sales. An individual sale is one in which you deliver a book to somebody and the somebody gives you the asking price for the book. For small organizations with small print runs, this is the most important kind of sale. Retailer sales are those you make to bookstores, gift shops, and other merchants who will resell your book. As I said earlier, they will expect to buy the book from you at a discount of anywhere from 20 percent to 55 percent to sell at your established retail price.

The way to sell your book to independent book stores, gourmet stores, and gift shops is to plan a campaign and carry it out. If you know the buyers or owners of the stores where you want to place the book, the job is slightly easier, but it's a good idea to follow these steps in any case. First, prepare a written description of the book, making it sound as appealing and salable as you can. Include the title, author, number of pages, number of illustrations, and trim size (dimensions) of the book, as well as the retail price. If the book has an ISBN number, be sure to include that too. Then, about a week before you plan to make your sales calls, phone the stores you want to visit and find out who handles the buying. Mail each buyer a copy of the book description, along with a note to say that you will be calling soon for an appointment to show him or her the book. Try to make the phone call three or four days after the buyer has received your flyer and note. Ask for an appointment and say you will need only about fifteen minutes of the buyer's time.

Before you make the sales calls, prepare a rate schedule for discounting the books. Usually the discount increases with the quantity of books purchased at once. (See sample discount schedules.) Decide whether you will bill the stores or ask them to prepay. Publishers often encourage payment by offering a substantial discount on quantities of books that would earn less discount if billed according to the schedule.

Be prepared to say whether or not you will accept returns. The usual policy is to accept returns of any books in mint condition no sooner than three months from the date of invoice and not longer than one year later. Accepting returned books is a nuisance, but many store buyers are more willing to try a new book from an unknown author if they know they won't be stuck with the books should they fail to sell.

Sample Retailer Discount Schedules

1-5 books	20%
6-25 books	40%
25-100 books	42%
100-250 books	48%
40% if prepaid	

1 book	20%
2-9 books	30%
10-24 books	40%
25-99 books	41%
100-249 books	42%
250-499 books	43%
500 or more	46%

Make yourself some sort of an order blank, with spaces for information about where to ship, whom to bill, number of books (by title) ordered, and discount earned. Be sure this form includes your name or the name under which you are publishing the book, a business address (even if it is your home address), and a telephone number.

These sales materials do not have to be typeset or elaborately printed; typing is fine, but make everything as professional and businesslike in appearance as you can. Show that you are treating your publishing venture as a business, not a hobby.

When you go to see the buyers, take along all the materials you prepared and a sample copy of the book. Show the buyer the book as soon as you can after introducing yourself, but don't just hand it over and let him or her flip the pages. Keep it in your own hands at first, while you talk about the book's outstanding features, and turn to the appropriate pages to demonstrate these points; *then* let it go. While the buyer looks through the book, explain what its main selling points are and why you think customers will buy the book. This pitch is almost as important as having a genuinely good book to sell. If you feel shaky about it, brainstorm with someone else to make sure you know and can express all the reasons the book will sell. Practice the spiel. Do not expect anybody to stock the book as a favor to you. Instead, convince them that stocking it will be good for their stores and customers. *Sell* it!

If the buyer seems interested, offer to write up the order on the spot. *Try to walk out of the store with that order in your hand.* Even professional buyers act on impulse. If a buyer asks you to leave an order form and promises to get in touch with you later, you have to think of it as a lost sale. Sometimes the order actually will come through later, but your chances are reduced significantly. The best way to get an order on the spot is to be so excited about your book that the excitement is contagious. If, for some reason, you can't get excited about your book, don't make sales calls. Get somebody who can be excited. One sales manager I know believes excitement is so important that he teaches his salespeople to jump up and down before they go into a store if they can't get turned on any other way.

If you took an order during your call, leave a copy with the buyer and take the other copy back for fulfillment. If fulfillment is as simple as carrying books in from your car, ask the buyer where you should bring them in (back door?) and keep your copy of the order for accounting. Some stores will probably ask to handle the books on consignment; you give them books to sell and eventually they give you money from sales plus the unsold books. I don't recommend this method; record keeping is a headache, and you are likely to end up with a lot of returned shopworn books.

Selling to the book chains, especially Waldenbooks and B. Dalton, works differently. These chains have central purchasing offices, and although you may be able to get a manager in a local store to request an order from the central office, you can't count on it. It won't hurt to try to make your pitch to local managers, but if you really want to get into the chain stores you need to approach the buyers in the central office. This is not much fun. The chain buyers spend most of their time listening to pitches from people who claim the books they're selling are the greatest, hottest, future bestsellers. Like anybody whose work day is spent listening to people who are trying to sell something, the buyers sometimes get hassled, cynical, bored, and just plain tired of listening to sales talks. This can make them cranky, especially if your approach is unprofessional. Your contact with these people will probably be by mail and telephone. Waldenbooks' central office is in New York City; B. Dalton is in Minneapolis. (Other chains, such as Cokesbury, buy both locally and from the central office. When you are not sure about a particular store, just call and ask.) Not everyone will agree with me, but I think that being a new self-publisher off the beaten path can work to your advantage when you deal with the chain buyers. If you are fresh and not slick, your approach and your book can be a delightful, unexpected surprise that breaks up a routine day. Of course, you have to know what you are doing and be professional in your presentation, or your contribution to some buyer's day will be comic relief—and that won't sell your book. I think the best way to proceed is to call the headquarters of the chain and find out who the buyer is for the category into which your book falls. (There are buyers for regional books, history books, general nonfiction trade books, and so on.) If you're uncertain about the proper category, you can get help by describing the book to anyone who will talk to you. Then ask for the name of the person who buys in that category. Write a letter to the person and send it along with a copy of the book and the same information you used to approach local stores. If you have any reviews of the book, send copies—the more reviews the better, even if they are from publications known only in your area. In your letter try to be realistic about whether you think the book has national appeal or is good strictly for the local market. Say that you will call in a few days to discuss an order, and do it. If you've had any contact with your local store managers, this is the time to ask them to contact the central office and say that they'd like to carry the book. If your book really deserves major bookstore attention, you'll probably make the sale.

The best advice I can offer is that you should not be intimidated by the big-time corporate patina that seems to adhere to people in these positions of power. They really want to buy good books; their reputations are built on doing it well. The best way to succeed is by offering an outstandingly good book to the right person.

Much that I have said about dealing with bookstore chains applies also to wholesalers. Wholesalers are middlemen who buy your books and distribute them to booksellers, libraries, and other merchants. Wholesalers who sell them to bookstores usually expect a discount of 50 percent to 55 percent off the retail price for handling your books, and they usually purchase in quantities of 100 or more.

Library jobbers or wholesalers generally accept a smaller discount—20 percent or less—and buy in smaller quantities. Then they provide the books to libraries at full price. A few companies, such as Baker and Taylor, sell books to libraries and to bookstores. Among bookstore wholesalers, the most important for trade books is probably Ingram Book Company, with Baker and Taylor running a close second. No single company stands out quite so strongly among the library suppliers.

If you decide to approach any of these companies, proceed as you would in approaching the chains. It would be a good idea to talk to someone in your local bookstores and library to find out which companies they deal with most frequently. In this way, at least, the company you contact will know that your part of the country exists. The people you consult can give you addresses and telephone numbers, or you can look up the information in *Literary Market Place*. You will find an almost overwhelming number of book distributors listed there. Unless you know the specialties of each, it's hard to guess which ones might be able to help you. That's why it's so helpful to consult with bookstore owners, librarians, and—if you can find them—other publishers.

Two other distributors you might find especially worth contacting are Bookpeople (2940 Seventh Street, Berkeley CA 94710) and Carolina House Publishers, Inc. (920 West Industrial Drive, Aurora IL 60506). Both have established good reputations for distributing books of bookstore quality for small trade publishers and self-publishers. In my dealings with them I have found that even when they prefer not to handle your book, they are generous with suggestions and advice about other possibilities.

How far you go with your sales efforts depends to a great extent on your book. Genia Lee Himes, a restaurateur in Gainesville, Florida, is publishing her own book, *The Cuisine of Cathay*, because, as she puts it, "No commercial publisher in his right mind would think it could make money." The book, which took her four years to prepare, has 250 pages and 380 illustrations, most of them color photographs. Its trim size is 9 by 12 inches. Even at the price of nearly $40 a copy, Genia estimates that she would have to sell 50,000 copies to break even. Her first print run is for 10,000 copies. Genia says it's okay that her book won't make money because she makes her living with her restaurant, the Cathay Tea House. She's publishing her book "for silliness."

The book is simply magnificent. Every serious collector who sees it will want a copy. And even though she says she doesn't expect to make money, Genia is treating the book like a major market product, which she can do because the quality of manufacture is better than that of most commercially published books. To reach booksellers, Genia has been exhibiting at such regional gatherings as the South Eastern Book Sellers Association's annual meeting, which is attended by bookstore owners and managers from all over the region. (Your local bookseller can tell you about these meetings. *Publishers Weekly* and *Literary Market Place* are also good sources of information.) She exhibits alongside big commercial publishers from New York, small commercial publishers from all over the country, and a few other ambitious self-publishers. Her book holds its own.

Another self-published cookbook author, Joyce LaFray, not only exhibits her *Famous Florida* cookbooks at booksellers' conventions, but also makes personal appearances at gourmet shops to demonstrate recipes from her books and appears on television as the "Florida Gourmet." She makes sure bookstores are aware of her marketing strategies and know that she also uses advertising and talk-show appearances to create a demand for her books. It would be appropriate and possible for her to use wholesalers. This aggressive approach is really commercial, though her company, LaFray Publishing Company, is technically a self-publishing company because she created it to publish and sell only her own books. She has had to go through all the do-it-yourself steps described in this chapter, which are part of any self-publishing venture at any level.

At the other end of the spectrum is an equally successful project by more modest standards. *The Best of Cook's Corner,* published by South Carolina Women Involved in Rural Electrification (WIRE), sells steadily but will never get to a professional book show. It's a different kind of book, whose marketing relies entirely on individual sales. The book was created by a committee, mainly from recipes contributed to a food column called "Cook's Corner" in a little magazine, *Living in South Carolina,* which electric cooperatives distribute to their customers. The book was edited by a home economist who worked with the committee to keep it "down home." One of the women involved in the project said, "We wanted the recipes to rely on ingredients you usually have around the house. It was okay for recipes to be a little bit different, but not too strange."

The group started out with $500 seed money from their state organization. They met regularly to decide on the format of the book, the number of pages it should have, the paper it would be printed on, and the illustrations. They bid out the job to several printers and took not the lowest bidder, but the one nearest the editor. Committee members culled recipes, retyped manuscript, read proof, and struggled to meet their deadlines. Their first print run was 7,500 copies of a 192-page book, trim size 6 by 9 inches.

While the book was being printed, they ran blurbs in their magazine to promote it, and included a coupon to order advance copies at a dollar discount (it sells now for $6). By the time the book was off the press, the group had taken in enough money in sales to pay for the printing. Coupons in the magazine continue to be the main sales device.

The South Carolina Women in Rural Electrification wanted to accomplish two things with their cookbook project: to raise money for other community work and to increase their visibility. They accomplished both goals. Their book, with no color illustrations, no elaborate marketing, and simple recipes, was a financial as well as an aesthetic

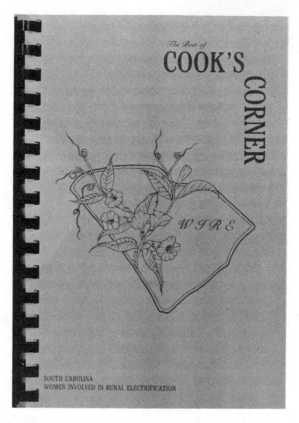

The art on the cover of the Best of Cook's Corner *is an outline of the shape of the state of South Carolina. The flower is yellow jasmine, the state flower. Both are appropriate for a book published by the South Carolina Women Involved in Rural Electrification (WIRE).*

success. I know people who would rather have a copy of *The Best of Cook's Corner* than of the elaborate *The Cuisine of Cathay* I mentioned earlier. Each book has a legitimate audience; each publisher has developed marketing strategies to sell that audience.

One more marketing device worth mentioning is mail order or direct mail. If your first thought is that mailing pieces are the "junk mail" you throw into the trash basket as soon as they come, you're right—ninety-eight out of a hundred people usually do. The other two percent take the offer if you're lucky. On a large scale, direct-mail marketing is costly, chancy, and sometimes tremendously productive. It has long been the main marketing tool for publishers of scholarly books because it is a comparatively inexpensive way to reach exactly the right people. For example, if I want to sell a new book about eighteenth-century literature, I rent a mailing list from College Marketing Group (a firm that specializes in creating, maintaining, and selling mailing lists), comprising the names of college-level teachers for the subject. The list costs me about $50 per thousand names for one-time use. Then I design a mailing piece, which may be an elaborate brochure or a simple letter, with a coupon, offering the book at a "special" price.

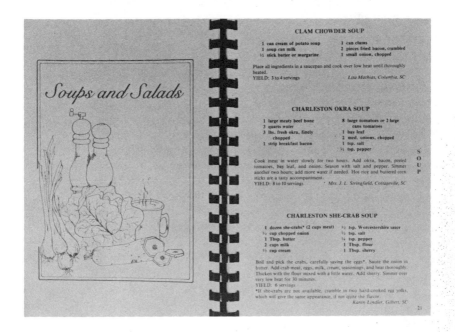

The Best of Cook's Corner, *a cookbook self-published by the Women Involved in Rural Electrification, has illustrations only to introduce chapters. Their purpose is simply to convey the theme of the chapter. Notice also in this picture the plastic spiral binding of the book. This is a popular, successful, and relatively inexpensive way to bind a self-published cookbook.*

It doesn't take much math to figure out that with a two percent return, which is considered good, a fairly high price will be needed to pay for the mailing piece, envelope, and postage, and still have something left over for profit. One way to handle the problem is to offer several books at once, with an added discount for taking them all. One of the most effective mailing pieces I ever saw was a simple single-fold sheet of orange paper. On the outside all it said was, "Here's your special offer on the three most important cookbooks in Maryland." Inside, the books were described enticingly. The cost of all three would have been $21 at regular price; if you bought all three the total price dropped to $18. I know that brochure was still pulling orders six months after it was sent out. The people to whom it was mailed were all residents of the state, and the mailing list had not been bought from anywhere. It was compiled from a number of private sources, including women's clubs, and from the names and addresses of people who cashed checks in gourmet shops.

If you decide to do more with direct mail than send out a hundred or so letters, you can purchase a bulk-mail third-class permit. This allows you to mail out letters or brochures for considerably less than the first-class postage rate. Of course you'll lose some response this way because some people automatically toss all third-class mail unopened into the wastebasket. But for large mailings, first-class postage is prohibitively expensive and likely to get worse. To find out about applying for a third-class permit, visit the post office. And for more detailed advice about designing mailing pieces and assembling or renting mailing lists, consult the *Book Marketing Handbook: Tips and Techniques for the Sale and Promotion of Scientific, Technical, Professional, and Scholarly Books and Journals*, by Nat Bodian, published by R.R. Bowker. It doesn't sound useful for selling cookbooks and, frankly, I'm not sure that anybody at Bowker would know a crêpe from a carp, but they do know bookselling, and Bodian's book offers what I consider one of the best available discussions of direct mail for the layperson and the small publisher.

If you choose to keep your direct-mail activities local, you can probably afford first-class postage provided you are careful to mail only to people you are reasonably sure will order books, because the correspondingly higher response will bring in more money.

Clearly, your choice of marketing strategies depends on the nature of your book and the intended audience.

All this brings us back to those early questions: Why do you want to write a cookbook? For whom?

Your answers to these questions will direct your marketing, sales, and distribution just as they directed your decisions about how to publish and what to include.

Perhaps you have been nodding as you read along, knowing that you do want to publish yourself, but feeling that what you care about most isn't wide distribution or making money. You want to be able to give your cookbook to good friends and people in the family who admire your cooking and ask for the recipes. The answer is self-publishing on a smaller scale. We call it "personal publishing."

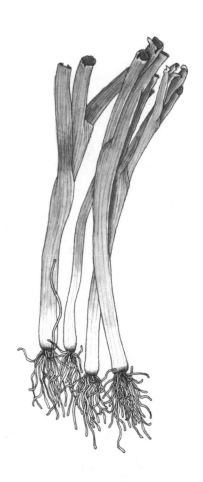

CHAPTER 5

Personal Publishing

N ot everybody has what it takes to write a good personal cookbook. You need a special love of food and a feel for how much it means to other people, the kind of sense our ancestors displayed when they wrote their recipes. Their words conveyed familiarity with ingredients and highly pesonal involvement with what they cooked. Think of some of the phrases they used. 'Knead together the usual proportions of butter, flour, salt, and parsley." "Add a few herbs and as much as you like of mace." "Make a brine with enough salt until just before you gag." "When you perceive a syrup jelly take the quinces out." "Wash the rice several times and when you think you have finished, wash it again for luck." From a recipe for sponge cake, these were the instructions for beating the egg white until stiff and dry: "The old-fashioned flat egg beater is highly recommended . . . You'll get stiff and dry before they do, but no matter . . ." "Make a nice cream sauce and cook until it is as thick as you like it."

What these instructions lacked in precision they made up in individuality. You never lose the sense that the recipes were created by people to help someone else prepare good food for other people. Certainly I've never been one to romanticize "the good old days." I know that life was hard and that many people, especially the women, wore out young. I don't advocate a return to the times when cooking took nearly all of a woman's time; nor would I give up the closely calculated specifications of modern recipes. But I hope we can find ways to retain and even increase the old sense that food is for people and that eating is not merely fueling the body, but one of life's greatest pleasures. I don't mean that the only cooking that matters is what has come to be called "gourmet cooking." Indeed, if you think back on memorable meals, I'd bet they weren't "gourmet" at all.

Of all the meals I've ever eaten, the one I remember most vividly was a casual dinner for four, prepared by a friend back when we were young and just starting families. None of us had much money to spend on exotic foods, but how we loved to eat! The main course in the meal was Russian borscht. None of us had ever tasted such a thing before, let alone cooked it. A good-sized slab of beef, cooked to falling-apart tenderness, was served in large pieces in shallow soup bowls. The broth was rich with the juices of the beef and deep, deep red from tomatoes and beets. The beets, I remember, were fresh from the garden. Sig peeled them and cut them in chunks that didn't even vaguely resemble the perfect cubes from supermarket cans. Her recipe called for five cloves of garlic, which nearly a day's simmering had mellowed to a heady perfume. Toward the end of the cooking she added coarsely sliced cabbage; it stayed firm and kept all its flavor. Equal amounts of brown sugar and cider vinegar gave the soup a faint sweet-sour taste so good it made your mouth hurt. We spooned far too much cold sour cream on each steaming serving and chewed on homemade hard rolls, washing everything down with generous sips of an inexpensive red wine. How could anybody forget a meal like that?

If you can remember with equal rapture some of the food you've eaten, you owe it to your family and friends to write a cookbook full of those personal memories and special meals. You owe them a personal cookbook.

When you think about it, the earliest and most-used cookbooks must all have been personally published; that is, the authors put them together for the people closest to them. After all, how else was there to do it in earlier times? A mother would lovingly—or dutifully—copy her collection of favorite recipes for each of her daughters, working for a while each evening. These copies crossed the ocean with the first settlers, traveled west in the wagons with the pioneers, went abroad in the hands of missionaries who were determined to take their culture with them, and even today pass from generation to generation in families where history and food are valued equally.

Modern presentations of old cookbooks almost invariably begin with an explanation about the personal nature of the original writing. In his introduction to the facsimile reproduction of *A Quaker Woman's Cookbook: The Domestic Cookery of Elizabeth Ellicott Lea*, William Woys Weaver tells us that the cookbook was a "labor of love" compiled at Elizabeth Lea's bedside with the help of her nurse and staunch friend, Rebecca Russell. Mrs. Lea felt that she had been poorly prepared for her life's work as a housewife; Weaver describes how the two women worked together to create a book to help other young women so that they would be better prepared. He also describes the work of another Quaker, Ann Aston Warder of Germantown, Pennsylvania, who in

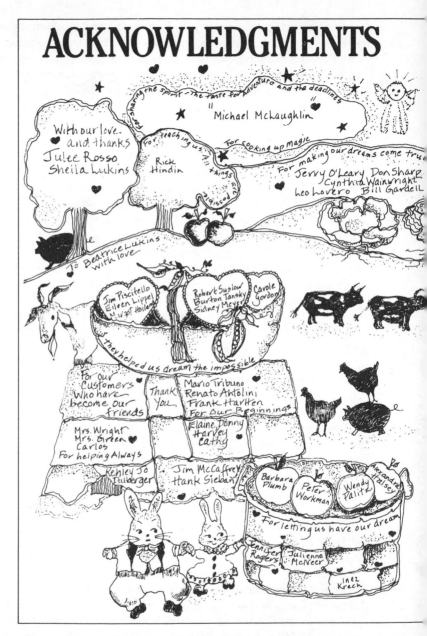

Although from a trade cookbook (The Silver Palate), this illustration by Sheila Lukins has the flair and flavor of a personally published book. As a self-publisher you can use any kind of illustration you want—even if it seems a bit off-the-wall—if you're inventive and surprising, you'll get away with it.

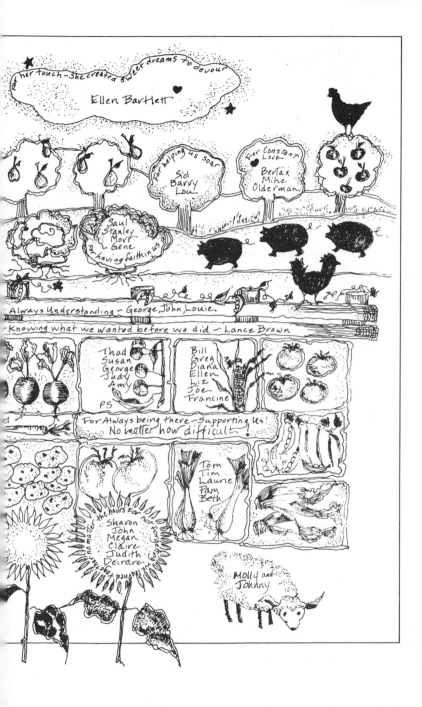

1844 wrote a book for her daughter-in-law to pass on recipes she had collected from relatives, from classes in a Philadelphia cooking school, and from her years of personal experience.

In her introduction to the facsimile reproduction of *Martha Washington's Booke* (sic) *of Cookery,* Karen Hess tells of family manuscripts filled with recipes written down "mostly as a reminder to oneself and to one's daughter . . . with no thought of impressing publishers or dazzling readers."

Nearly every Southern cookbook I have ever read includes comments about the treasured handwritten cookbook manuscripts that were passed from generation to generation. Often each generation added new recipes and additional notes in their own hands, showing the influence of each new black cook in the family's kitchen.

The strong emotional link we seem to feel between handwriting and recipes has encouraged more than one commercial publisher to try to duplicate that personal feeling. In Mollie Katzen's *Enchanted Broccoli Forest* and *Moosewood Cookbook,* her hand lettering and drawings and doodles are part of the design. In 1972 Nitty Gritty Productions published *To My Daughter with Love . . . A Collection of Family Recipes,* by Wanda Groceman, all written in such a graceful but imperfect penmanship that even now I have trouble believing that Mike Nelson, not Wanda, did the drawings and that it was a mass-market book, not a sweet little diary passed on to a few special people. Some gourmet and gift shops carry an entire line of little cookbooks about cookies, hors d'oeuvres, salads, and so on, all lettered in elegant calligraphy by P. Dutrey, who also publishes the books. I know they're commercial because they're sold in spinner display racks, but they *feel* personal.

Considering how well such stylistic devices can help sell cookbooks, I conclude that for many of us the personal element, the sense of being bound up in someone else's life, is what cookbooks are all about.

Writing What You Know—And Love

I think that those of us who love cooking harbor a built-in need to share what we know; we like the giving and the receiving. Shortly after I was married and still in that stage when experimenting with cooking didn't go much beyond pouring a can of tomato sauce on top of the meat loaf, a neighbor began to give me recipes she had typed carefully onto file cards. She gave me several a week.

Why? I hadn't asked for the recipes, and she, who had small children, was busy enough without typing up recipe cards. But I tried every one, and over the years I incorporated many of them into my permanent repertoire of good things to cook. In the ensuing years, I've passed some of them on to others through my cookbooks and cooking columns, and I've scribbled them on the backs of envelopes for my daughters and friends. When you try something and it works well, you want to share it with someone else; if you enjoyed it, you want them to enjoy it too. I think that's why my neighbor copied all those recipes for me, and I'm sure that's why I have continued to copy them for others. This is the first step in personal publishing.

The nice thing about personal publishing is that you can do what you like, since you are out neither to "dazzle publishers" nor to garner customers. You can even plagiarize if you want to. But you cannot be careless. The people who will try your recipes are those who matter most to you. In personal publishing you must adhere more strictly to the rules of recipe writing than in any other kind of cookbook publishing. Maybe it's not so bad to leave an unknown cook in Punxatawney wondering when and how to add the noodles to the Groundhog Paprikash, but you'd better not do it to your best friend if you want to have anybody to play tennis with next summer. Or, thinking ahead, suppose your great-granddaughter gets her hands on that recipe that directs the cook to set aside the half-cup of brown sugar and never mentions the ingredient again. There is *your* great-granddaughter, with a funny-tasting cake and an unused half-cup of brown sugar, and it's all your fault.

But in personal publishing, although you are constrained to put together the book as carefully, with as sound an organizational scheme, and with as much attention to detail as you would in publishing for a mass market, you are wonderfully free to write what pleases you, knowing that it will be meaningful to those who follow you in coming generations.

My Grandmother Pennington, the precise cook in the family, spent a lifetime mastering the traditional English recipes and some of the Pennsylvania Dutch recipes that my grandfather liked, and began to copy them down for me on lined notebook paper to fit into a little black binder. These were the foods I grew up eating at Christmas and Thanksgiving, for birthdays, and at family reunion picnics: English Plum Pudding, Ice Cream Cabbage, Pasties, Pepper Cabbage, Hot Slaw. She wrote these down for me a few at a time, along with advice to be sure to use kidney suet, not plain suet, for the Plum Pudding, because she hadn't known that when she was young and so her first pudding fell apart. As I read the recipe for Ice Cream Cabbage, I recall that my father gave it that name because it was so delicate, with just a hint

129

of sweetness. Reading the recipe for Pasties, a kind of meat pie, I remember that nobody but Grandma and Great-grandma Eyer had ever been able to fold those perfect half-circles on a cookie sheet. Everybody else had to use a pie pan. The Pepper Cabbage recipe reminds me how Grandma Pennington pushed the bowl under the food grinder to carefully catch every bit of juice from the ground celery to add to the dressing.

What other cookbook that I have could possibly be so special? Grandma was quite old when she began the book, and she lost the concentration to finish it long before she reached the end of her recipes. How much I have lost! Don't wait! If you have the urge to write a personal cookbook, do it *now*. If the idea of sitting down to do the actual writing puts you off, how about using a tape recorder in the kitchen to get started?

My sister, who is not enthusiastic about cooking herself but appreciates my interest, collected recipes for a year and put them into a ring binder to give me for Christmas. Her criterion was, "If it sounds weird, Sara will like it." I still use the recipes.

In Houston, Mona Gregg has spent time and energy to become an outstandingly good cook for an outstandingly discriminating husband. Since more and more people ask for her recipes, she has put the fruits of twelve years' experiments into her own cookbook, with the recipes in a heavy-duty binder on laminated pages. When she wants to share them, she has everything photocopied.

Write Now!

Perhaps because I write cookbooks, people tell me about their aspirations to do the same. Nearly every day the owner of a gourmet shop or a volunteer in the library or the manager of a natural-foods store or a neighbor with lots of kids or someone else actively involved with preparing food confides that she wants to write a cookbook of her own. Over and over I say, "*Do* it." What you create will ultimately have more value than the slickest book on any bookstore shelf. Consider that serious cookbook collectors and researchers value their inherited, handwritten manuscripts above all other cookbooks.

To give you some idea how valuable your recipes will be to those who come after you, think of those recipes in your file (if you use something as neat as a file; mine are all stuffed into an old corset box). Think of how many of those recipes are written in the hand of the person who gave them to you and how many of them have names like "Grandmother's Molasses Cookies" and "Mom's Favorite Bread." In my boxful, some of the old family recipes are written on the white papers that used to line boxes of nylon stockings. The ink has faded into the paper and has had to be retraced, but I treasure them because each one includes not only the directions for making a dish, but all the human touches that recall the people and the times when those foods were cooked and served. I have also my Grandma Dietrick's old diaries, in which recipes she made up are scattered among accounts of what the preacher said in his sermon on Sunday ("Paul, Paul, why must he always preach on Paul?"), how much she got for eggs that week (20 cents a dozen), and the progress of Daisey's pneumonia ("hanging on"). I find a recipe for Applesauce Cookies with a note that she created it from her recipe for Applesauce Cake. I read that Father went fishing the night before and brought back "a real nice eel," and then I come to a recipe for cooking it. Grandmother Dietrick has been dead for many years; Grandmother Pennington has also passed on, but their lives leap from the pages and invigorate my life.

Your personal cookbook can do the same, and the sooner you start it, the more lively it will be; the less your descendants will miss. As you set down the recipes, free yourself from the constraints you would feel if you were trying to write something suitable for a market of thousands. This is for the people who matter to you, for the people to whom you matter. Keep in all the comments about what happened the first time you tried to cook a new dish, what your best friend said the first time he tried your cake, how you discovered one particular recipe, why another has become your favorite. Use it all. That's what will make it special. And if you draw or doodle or take photographs, consider adding illustrations to your book or, if someone else in the family has more artistic ability than you, draft him or her to do some illustrations.

Physical Possibilities

How you proceed depends partly on how many copies you want to make. Blank books are one option. Nitty Gritty stopped printing theirs because they didn't do so well as the other books, but some stores still carry them. Crown publishes a blank book called *The Cook's Own Book*, which includes with its empty pages an index page and printed information about weights and measures. From Stonesong Press you can buy a ring binder with a cookbook-looking cover, entitled *I'm Writing My Own Cookbook*. This too includes illustrations; dividers for sections such as appetizers, entrees, and desserts; a glossary of cooking terms; and substitution and conversion charts. Somehow all these books appear too "commercial" to me, but that's my taste, and, as the saying goes, "There's no accounting for taste."

The main practical drawbacks to such books are that they are fairly

131

expensive and that you have to write them out one at a time. If you have decided to give up television forever to sit by the fire like Abraham Lincoln and transcribe recipes, blank books may be just right. But if you're busy and have a bunch of people waiting for their cookbooks, you may need to consider other possibilities. To me, the perfect way to proceed with this kind of publishing would be to do each one by hand on plain paper, illustrating and doodling as you went along, somewhat like the ancient monks illuminating manuscripts, but few of us have the skill or the patience for this option.

You need to consider two main factors: the medium in which you perform most comfortably and the number of copies of the book that you will need. This may help you decide whether it would be better to type, to write by hand, or to use a word processor. The legibility of your handwriting might be a factor too. Since the book is an extension of you, I think you should stick with what seems most natural to you. I know people with beautiful handwriting from whom I can't imagine receiving anything typed; I even know people with lousy handwriting from whom I can't imagine receiving anything typed. For me, on the other hand, the typewriter has become an extension of my brain. I think through my fingers. The last time I wrote anything by hand was when I flunked penmanship in Mr. Schucker's one-room school in Fleetwood, Pennsylvania. And then there's calligraphy. That art was mercifully unknown when I was studying under Mr. Schucker, or I suppose I'd have flunked it too. But if you can master the skill, calligraphy is a beautiful way to write a cookbook.

At the same time you're deciding how to create your original manuscript, consider how you want to reproduce it, because the means of reproduction could influence the size and format of your original. If you want to reproduce your pages on a photocopy machine, for example, you must use a size of paper that the machine can handle. For photocopy and for offset printing you will need to use either a good pen and indelible black ink or a new ribbon and clean typewriter keys to make your master as bright and sharp as possible. If you are planning illustrations and want to reproduce by offset printing, you should probably do your drawing in black and white for the sharpest reproduction.

The small print shops that are numerous everywhere can help you with these decisions. Most of these shops have high-quality photocopy machines and will reproduce your pages for a few cents per page. Some even have color photocopiers. These cost considerably more, usually at least a dollar per page, but the quality is surprisingly good. If you are planning books to be kept over the years, however, rather than to be enjoyed briefly and forgotten, consider offset printing instead of

TARRAGON

A small budget is no excuse for not illustrating your book. This assortment of clip art gives you an idea of how effective and appealing these drawings can be.

133

photocopying, even for a small number of books and even though it costs more. Here's why: the toner that a photocopy machine "burns" into the pages as part of the copying process is not stable. Long after you have made the copies, heat or pressure can cause type from one page to adhere to the page on top of it—hardly the stuff heirlooms are made of.

Once you've worked out the reproduction, your binding possibilities include ordinary ring notebook binders, pages folded and stapled into a cover, and craft covers bound with plastic spirals or tied with yarn. Again, a small print shop can help you with the more complicated options, while you, yourself, are perfectly capable of going to the five-and-dime to pick out nice ring binders.

Three very different effects that can be achieved with line drawings: the apple, **left,** *is a line drawing done in a stippled style; this technique works well with food and "gentle decorative settings." The apple,* **below,** *shows a screen (or transfer shading) applied to the line art. There are many kinds of screens available at art supply stores and they are an easy way to add many interesting effects to drawings. The apple,* **lower right,** *is a line drawing in a cross-hatched style. (Drawing by Barbara McFadyen, from* Bring Out Your Own Book)

The most important advice about personally published cookbooks, I think, is the same that professional growers give to people who are building hobby greenhouses: buy as much as you can afford; you're bound to need more than you think. Suppose, for instance, you decide to do ten books, one for each of your nieces and nephews. I guarantee that on the day you give away the last one, you will discover a niece you didn't know you had or you will meet someone so special you know you must give them a cookbook. But by then you'll be out of books, and there's no way any of those other nieces and nephews will give theirs back. So plan for extra books, even if you can't imagine right now who would want them. And whatever else you do, keep an original master copy against the day when you need to reproduce extras. Everybody who sees your book will want one.

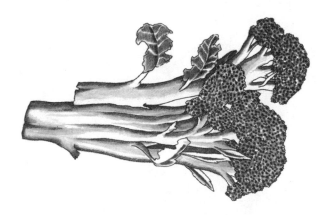

CHAPTER *6*

Looking at Trade Publishing

When we talk about getting a book published, most of us think first of trade publishing. The big houses—Doubleday, Little, Brown and Company, and random House—spring to mind. But in addition to such major publishing houses, most of which are based in New York City, the commercial world includes numerous smaller publishers, many on the West Coast. Their names are not household words, but nonetheless they are active publishers. Many of them specialize in cookbooks. If you collect cookbooks, you probably have some of their books on your shelves.

The Sunset Line, published in Menlo Park, California, includes ethnic cookbooks, appliance cookbooks, and a variety of single-subject cookbooks in addition to gardening, building, and craft books. Often you see these books on display in spinner racks in hardware stores and garden centers, as well as in bookstores. HP Books, published in Tucson, Arizona, are a similar, though somewhat smaller, line; so are Ortho Books. Owlswood Productions in San Francisco publishes a line of gourmet cookbooks especially to accompany the new applicances and tools designed for gourmet cooks. Another house, 101 Productions, in San Francisco, specializes in cookbooks that emphasize natural ingredients rather than processed convenience foods. Nitty Gritty Productions in Concord, California produces a line of specialty cookbooks geared to current cooking trends and leaning toward simple processes for busy cooks.

A surprising number of smaller publishers with smaller lists don't specialize but do offer cookbooks, some of them highly unusual. Ideal, in Milwaukee, publishes children's books, gift books, home-improvement books, and seasonal books, in addition to cookbooks. The cookbooks resemble those of HP and Sunset in format and display, and, to some extent, in subject matter. Like those companies, Ideal has a seafood cookbook, a Chinese cookbook, a food-processor cookbook, and others. The unusual aspect of this line is that it features an entire group of brand-name cookbooks: *Hershey's Chocolate and Cocoa Cookbook, Durkee Spice and Herb Cookbook,* and *The Official Budweiser Cookbook,* to name a few. A representative of the company says they are more receptive to freelance submissions than Sunset.

Barron's, of Woodbury, New York, takes cookbooks so seriously that the publisher, Manuel Barron, tries many of the recipes himself. The company also publishes books on every subject from computers and software to foreign-language arts and mathematics.

Brick House Publishing, in Andover, Massachusetts, concentrates on self-sufficiency, the environment, current affairs, and home and energy books. Brick House dipped into the cookbook waters, appropriately enough, with *The Airtight Woodstove Cookbook,* by Dale Darling and Julia Van Dyck, which shows that you can place the *right* cookbook with the appropriate publisher even when cookbooks are not usually part of their publishing picture.

Running Press, the Philadelphia-based publishers of those tough puzzle books, *Crosswords 1* and *2,* an assortment of children's books, and books about beer, unicorns, birth, and solar projects, also publishes *The Salad and Soup Book* and *The Ultimate Sandwich Book.*

Peanut Butter Publishing in Seattle, known for restaurant guides to major cities, also publishes appliance cookbooks, ethnic cookbooks, and some single-subject cookbooks. In Pownal, Vermont, Garden Way specializes in books related to self-sufficiency, gardening, do-it-yourself, and cookbooks that use natural ingredients. Stephen Greene Press of Brattleboro, Vermont, takes a similar slant. So does Rodale, in Emmaus, Pennsylvania.

Triad Publishing Company, a small Gainesville, Florida, house, features books for and about women and children, and has created a small, dynamic line of cookbooks about Jewish cooking. They also publish *Cross Creek Kitchens,* a seasonal cookbook based on the kitchen of Marjorie Rawlings, author of *The Yearling.* And the East Woods Press, housed in Charlotte, North Carolina, includes among its books on travel, sports, child care, and journalism, a series of cookbooks ranging from *The Catfish Cookbook* to *Sweets Without Guilt.*

From Chester, Connecticut, the Globe Pequot Press proves you don't have to be able to say it to sell it. Their books are mainly about New England: a series on short bike rides in various New England states, profiles of historic places in New England, and photographs and articles from the *Boston Globe.* As famous as the area is for its food, you won't be surprised to learn that the list includes several regional cookbooks as well: *The Modern Cook's Early American Recipe Book* (recipes

Triad Publishing Company of Gainesville, Florida, publishes a variety of cookbooks, all of which show a strong streak of genuine creativity. Each book is unique. In Cross Creek Kitchens *both the art and the text are especially effective in evoking feelings of nostalgia for a simpler, back-to-basics life. This illustration is "Kate's Kitchen," introducing a chapter by the same name. In it the author writes that Kate's kitchen, "with its rich hued wood counters, the hand-made pottery in all shapes and textures, the ferns, the baskets, and Kate's paintings on the walls, encourages guests to linger long after a meal is finished."*

140

from Old Sturbridge Village adapted for today's kitchens), *The Boston Globe Cookbook, The Martha's Vineyard Cookbook, Truly Unusual Soups, The Bluefish Cookbook,* and *What Cooks in Connecticut* are among the titles. These titles should help you see the potential cookbook ideas in your region.

Jack Williamson, in Charlotte, Vermont, includes cookbooks on the list for his young company, Williamson Publishing, but so far he has avoided the already competitive New England slant in favor of cookbooks such as *The Brown Bag Cookbook,* which deal with the difficulties inherent in the way we live.

No two of these publishers are alike. Some, like Sunset, publish many cookbooks a year; others, like 101, publish only three or four new titles a year. The only thing they all have in common is that they are businesses that are trying to make money publishing books, including cookbooks.

More Potential Publishers

University presses are another group of publishers you should not overlook. Although university presses have traditionally specialized in scholarly books that would not have a large enough market to justify their publication by the larger commercial houses, most of these presses have had to publish books in other areas to help support their non-profit scholarly books. The presses tend to rely on books that will appeal to nonscholarly taxpayers for this added income, especially if they are part of state universities. As a result many university presses publish a variety of regional books, including cookbooks, and some kinds of popular history, including cookbooks dealing with food history. Some of them are downright esoteric, like *Pleyn Delit: Medieval Cookery for Modern Cooks,* from the University of Toronto Press. Others are straightforward regional books such as the *South Carolina Cookbook,* a book full of recipes for grits, greens, corn bread, and other traditional dishes of the South, from the University of South Carolina Press.

The University of Pennsylvania Press has entered the cookbook world with *Savoring the Past,* a book about the French kitchen and table from 1300 to 1789. Their book *Sauerkraut Yankees,* which explores the eating habits of the Pennsylvania Germans, is based on a translation of an old Pennsylvania Dutch cookbook called *The Handy Housewife.* From the University of New Mexico Press, the *Mexican Cookbook* and *More of the Best from New Mexico Kitchens* are excellent examples of an ethnic and a regional cookbook with broad appeal.

The University of Virginia Press publishes a number of uncommon cookbooks, including some facsimile reproductions. Their series on ex-

CARNE ADOBADA
Chile-Marinated Pork   10 to 12 servings

For a traditional menu, serve sopaipillas or corn bread, a crisp green salad laced with a tart dressing, and cheese-topped refritos. Natillas or flan will nicely complete the meal.

1 cup chile caribe (p. 20)
4 cups water
2 teaspoons salt
3 garlic cloves, chopped
2 tablespoons ground Mexican orégano
2 tablespoons ground comino
5 pounds fresh pork, thinly sliced (loin chops are excellent)

1 Combine chile caribe and water in a blender container and whirl until mixed into a sauce. Add salt, garlic, orégano and comino to the sauce; mix well.

2 Trim excess fat from the pork and lay slices in a flat baking dish. Cover with the sauce; turn the meat once to coat evenly on both sides. If possible, allow to marinate in the refrigerator overnight.

3 To cook, cover the baking dish with a lid or sheet of aluminum foil and bake at 325°F. for 30 minutes. Uncover and bake for 30 minutes more, basting periodically.

Note: *Any remaining pork will keep in the refrigerator for up to 1 week. If desired, the pork will freeze well in the marinade. Any unused marinade also will freeze well.*
Variation: *This chile makes very good filling for spicy tacos or burritos.*
Maximum Recommended Freezer Storage: *3 months*

MEXICAN SPARERIBS   4 servings

3 pounds lean pork spareribs
4 garlic cloves, minced
2 teaspoons salt
6 tablespoons olive oil, or half olive oil, half salad oil
dash of freshly ground pepper
4 tablespoons vinegar
2 teaspoons ground Mexican oregano
2 cups Red Chile Sauce (p. 44)
2 tablespoons minced onion

128 PORK MAIN DISHES

You don't necessarily need to use pictures to illustrate your cookbook. Jane Butel's Tex-Mex Cookbok *relies on decorative borders for visual appeal, with each chapter featuring a different Mexican motif. You can find a variety of border designs in collections of clip art, have an artist create some for you, or if artistically inclined, you can even draw your own.*

otic cookery includes *Traditional Recipes of Laos, Cook and Entertain the Burmese Way,* and *Indonesian Food and Cooking.* Perhaps the most unusual of all is Calvin W. Schwabe's, *Unmentionable Cuisine,* a book of recipes for the foods Americans rarely eat, but which are standard fare for millions of others.

Many other university-press cookbooks are mentioned throughout this book; you will find details about them in the appendix of suggestions for further reading.

Clearly, university presses do not publish cookbooks along the lines of *Fifty Nifty Desserts to Make in Your Wok.* Usually these presses are looking for books with historical or regional implications or with some relation to scholarship. If a university press seems like a possibility for your cookbook idea, proceed just as you would with any other trade publisher: get a catalog to see what else the press has produced. Even if a press has not published a cookbook, don't assume that it wouldn't be interested. It never hurts to ask.

Now think of all those more familiar New York-based publishers who don't specialize in cookbooks, but do publish some of them each year, and you can see that the number of possible publishers for your book is mind-boggling.

Perhaps one of the most notable publishers in this category is the Alfred A. Knopf Company. Their list includes books in many categories, but they have developed a distinguished line that includes some of the best cookbooks published, written by some of the best-known authors. Alfred A. Knopf is the home of Julia Child's six cookbooks, the redoubtable *Fanny Farmer Cookbook,* five James Beard books, and more than thirty others that deal with everything from wine to cooking on the trail. Knopf has gone so far as to offer a complete consumer brochure of cookbooks, and will put you on a mailing list to receive advance information about their new cookbooks and wine books.

This is the end of my list, but it isn't the end of the possibilities. Every time you turn around in the bookstore, you come across another nice book published by someone you never heard of before, or you discover that a publisher who produces books on another subject also offers some cookbooks.

Some publishers, however, won't touch cookbooks. Chilton of Philadelphia, for example, has given up cookbooks to concentrate on how-to books, including their famous automotive repair series. And Chronicle Books in San Francisco has avoided the competitiveness of the cookbook market, although they have published related books about where to buy fresh produce and how to cut up meat.

To complicate matters more, Chilton *used to* publish cookbooks and

Having a picture of the author among a cookbook's illustrations certainly is not new, but this drawing of James Beard, from Beard on Pasta, *is remarkable because it seems to capture not only Beard's physical likeness, but also his exuberant approach to cooking.*

Chronicle's editor says that they *might* publish some in the future.

As you can see, if you decide that you want to publish your book commercially, you will have to become familiar with many publishers and their idiosyncracies in your search for the right place for your project. In trying to evaluate what publishers are doing about cookbooks, you should consult both *Writer's Market* and *Literary Market Place,* two resources devoted specifically to information about publishing. *Writer's Market* lists book publishers with a description of their requirements and includes a subject index of those who handle food and nutrition. *Literary Market Place* lists more publishers and gives more names of people in staff positions—and has a list of book publishers classified by the subjects they handle—but does not tell much about the requirements of each publisher. Also, more scholarly presses are listed in *Literary Market Place* than in *Writer's Market.*

The best way to proceed is to check both these publications in your library (if you do not have them at home) for publishers whose names you have seen on cookbooks or in advertisements. Get addresses and as much information as you can from the listings and then write to those publishers who seem appropriate, requesting copies of recent catalogs and authors' guidelines.

At this point you may wonder why anybody would bother to fight through this maze, which leads us to consider the advantages and disadvantages of trade publishing.

Is It Right for You?

Perhaps the greatest advantage of trade publishing is that once your book is done, so are you. You turn the manuscript over to the editors, who smooth out your sentences and fix your spelling and eventually turn it over to the design and production people. They plan the format and layout, and guide it through all the steps of printing and binding that turn it into a book. Then people in sales and marketing see to the advertising and distribution. The entire publishing process includes plenty of worry and many places where problems can sprout; when you publish commercially, someone else worries through the problems, not you.

Other advantages include the possibility that your book will get wide exposure and may earn some money for you. Realistically, however, you can expect big money only from a big publisher. Craig Claiborne and James Beard can expect to land big publishers; as a beginner, you will be better off looking for a specialty publisher who concentrates on just the kind of book you want to write. Not only do smaller and specialty publishers produce more new cookbooks, but they usually pay more attention to each new book and author they accept. The money you make may be modest, but the experience will please you.

In working with specialty publishers I have found that editors become not only friends, but business partners as well. They make suggestions that will help make your book more salable, and sometimes even suggest other publishers to approach if your next idea doesn't fit their own plans. In this situation, you enjoy the best of trade publishing: once you've finished your book, you know it will be edited, designed, printed, and bound with careful attention, even if the staff is tiny, because when a company publishes only a few books, the success of each one is important.

As for your success in terms of money—it all depends. Sometimes specialty publishers use what they call the "work-for-hire" option. They buy your manuscript for a flat fee, and that's all the money you'll get, no matter how well your cookbook does, unless a clause is written into your contract that assures you extra payment if sales go beyond a set number.

Generally, a flat-fee arrangement is not considered as desirable as a royalty agreement because it limits what you can make on the book. In reality, if you are dealing with a small publisher whose print run is apt to be small and whose marketing efforts are limited, you may make as much money on a flat fee as you would if you were collecting royalties. Moreover, if you want your work to be published, sometimes you have to settle for a flat fee or not be published at all. The fee may be negotiable; I have seen them range from $500 to $5,000.

More commonly you work on a royalty arrangement, in which you receive a modest advance, anywhere from a few hundred to a few thousand dollars, plus a percentage of sales when enough books have been sold to cover the initial advance. If your book sells well, you may make some money. Cookbook writers, even unknown ones, have made anywhere from a few hundred to many thousands of dollars on their work. Realistically, a profit of a *few* thousand dollars is most likely.

Trade-publishing a cookbook works to your advantage mainly in relieving you of the burdens of editing, production, and sales, but these advantages are also disadvantages. The people who produce your book will have more to say than you about how it turns out, and authors are sometimes disappointed by the look of the finished book. The authors of a book on cooking for one or two, for instance, disliked the finished version in which all their recipes were printed twice: once to give ingredients and quantities for one person, and then again to give quantities for two. The authors thought that most people could divide or multiply by two and that the double printing was unnecessary, but the editor and the art director felt that it added novelty and visual appeal to the book. The authors felt they should have been consulted; the publisher felt it was his decision. Nobody was really wrong in this situation, and many people who write cookbooks would not care one way or another about such details, but if you are the kind of person who would care, you might have trouble with a trade publisher.

Another disadvantage of trade publishing is that you have little to say about promoting and advertising the book. If the publisher does a bad job, you can't do much about it.

Still, all the discussion of the advantages and disadvantages of trade publishing are immaterial if you can't find a publisher who wants your cookbook. At this point, the subject of agents inevitably comes up. Do you need one? Can you get one if you do? Authors, would-be authors, editors, and agents debate these questions regularly without ever settling them. I have talked to many agents about it. They all have strong opinions and they all refuse to be quoted. Although they say an author stands a better chance of finding a publisher and getting a good contract through an agent, they agree, as I have mentioned before, that they would be reluctant to handle cookbooks unless written by celebrities or written around a strong gimmick. In other words, they would be delighted to handle Richard Simmons' *Never Say Diet* book, but not the offerings of us common folk.

On the other hand, one editor I talked to said that she enjoyed working with agents, but she was often surprised at how little they actually did for their clients.

All the authors I questioned said that an agent would have been helpful in negotiating a contract once the author had found a publisher, especially for early books. Most *unpublished* authors seem to believe they could be published if they had a good agent, but getting a good agent is at least as difficult for the beginner as finding a publisher. Many frequently-published cookbook writers say they are perfectly happy without an agent. I have never used an agent for any book, and although I might want an agent someday for a book of deathless prose, I probably never will for a cookbook. It seems to me that the best way to have a cookbook published commercially is to do good work and to submit the right idea to the right publisher at the right time.

To do all this, you must learn who is publishing what and get to know the editorial bias of many publishing houses. And as you study the world of cookbook publishing, you'll probably have a good time as you use (and expand) the awareness I mentioned in Chapter One. You can devise all kinds of ways to play detective and track down the motives of publishers.

Study the Markets

The most obvious place to begin is the cookbook section of a bookstore. As you browse, make notes not only of titles and publishers, but also of publication dates. To find the publication date, look at the copyright date on the title page. If a book has been reprinted or revised, you should also find those dates there. The point isn't so much to find out how old a book is as to find out whether or not that publisher is producing any new books, and if so, what kind. As you check the cookbook inventory of the bookstore, make a note of any publishers who seem to have concentrated on books *similar* to the one you want to write.

For example, if your idea for a book has to do with using a famous name-brand product, you might approach Ideal, whose list includes the Hershey cookbook and the Budweiser cookbook. If you are interested in compiling a new book of traditional Pennsylvania Dutch recipes typical of the Philadelphia area, you might contact the University of Pennsylvania Press, which has published *A Quaker Woman's Cookbook* and a book about the food customs of the Pennsylvania Germans.

Obviously, if a publisher has already published a book just like the one you're planning, you need either a different publisher or a different book idea. In deciding whom to approach, you need to understand the difference between new ideas and new topics. I heard it explained sharply by Rebecca Greer, the articles editor for *Woman's Day*, when she spoke about the voracious appetite all publishers have for new ideas. A woman in the audience challenged her, asking why, then, the magazine continued to publish articles on the same subjects—sex, beauty, money, and food—month after month. Ms. Greer said, "You are confusing topics and ideas. Sex, beauty, money, and food are *topics* people care about. What we want are *new ideas* for dealing with those topics." I think the same is true with cookbook publishers. If a publisher has specialized in cookbooks that emphasize gourmet equipment and ingredients, for example, he or she will look for books dealing with those topics in new ways. They will almost certainly not be looking for completely new topics, such as backpacking food or macrobiotic diets.

The Globe Pequot Press books give us an example of a fresh idea on a familiar topic. Whoever thought up *The Bluefish Cookbook* must be a genius. Seafood cookbooks are a dime a dozen, and a good many cookbooks concentrate on the New England area. But to publish a cookbook about bluefish is an inspired variation on the basic subject of bluefish.

Look at everything the book has going for it. First, bluefish is readily available. Everybody who goes deep-sea fishing catches bluefish. It's also sold in grocery stores and fish markets, relatively inexpensively. Moreover, the fish tend to be large. When you cook a bluefish, or a couple of them, you're cooking a lot of fish. Also, it's a fish people tend to like, even though they don't know many different ways to prepare it. And as a final touch, one of the authors, Jane Alexander, is a stage and film actress. She may not be well enough known for her name to sell many books, but being a public figure can't hurt.

Except that it lacks a star as one of its authors, the *Catfish Cookbook* has the same advantages in North Carolina, where it is published by East Woods Press. Since catfish is very cheap and available all over the South, the potential market for the book is huge.

Caroline House, in Illinois, has a number of titles that look routine and uninspired at first glance: *Breakfast and Brunch Cookbook, Bread and Cake Cookbook, The Fish Cookbook,* and so on, with at least fourteen titles in the series. They all seem like books that have already been done too often, until you learn that the title of the entire series is "Preparing Food the Healthy Way" and that it appears over the name of Frederick E. Kahn, M.D. With the growing interest in fitness and health, this was an ingenious idea for a cookbook series.

Here's one more example, which seems to me the ultimate new idea. Bobbs-Merrill advertises *Cooking Without Recipes* by Helen Worth. Since Bobbs-Merrill has many cookbooks *with* recipes, I imagine that this one is for people who have bought all the books, mastered all the recipes, and are looking for the next challenge.

When you have exhausted the possibilities in bookstores, visit libraries. Public and college libraries usually have good selections of cookbooks, although you may find more classics and old favorites than new books. This will show you what books have been around for a while and how they have influenced newer books. In some university libraries the cookbook collection is housed in the college of human development or home economics. At Berkeley, unlikely as it may seem, the cookbooks are in the agriculture library. If you don't find many cookbooks in what seems to be the obvious place, ask.

And while you're in the library, ask to see the current *Books in Print* subject listings. (*Books in Print* is an annual reference series that lists all the books currently available by subject, author, and title.) Here, under "cooking and cookery," you will find page after page listing the titles, authors, publishers, and publication dates of virtually all the cookbooks in print. The size of the list could overwhelm you and tempt you to abandon the idea because the world doesn't seem to need another cookbook, but don't despair. If your idea is fresh you'll find a place for your book. Industry research shows that people who buy cookbooks are those who already have cookbooks. Cookbook buyers are almost always collectors, and only sometimes cooks. On the other hand, don't ignore clear messages. If your idea was to write a cookbook for Sunday morning golfers and you find fifteen cookbooks for Sunday morning golfers already listed, you might at the very least decide to write a cookbook for Sunday afternoon golfers. Your objective is to identify a need and fill it.

Less intimidating than studying *Books in Print* are advertisements for cookbooks in food magazines, promotional material for cookbooks in book-club mailings, and cookbook catalogs. All will instruct you further in cookbook publishing. Keep a few notes as you work, because when so much information hits you from so many different sources, your mind is bound to rebel at some point and punish you by forgetting something pertinent.

Approaching Publishers

As you zero in on a few companies that seem appropriate for your work, make sure you have a complete mailing address where you can write for more information. Try to get the name of the appropriate editor to query. If you can't find it in *Writer's Market* or *Literary Market Place,* try a call to the company switchboard. Directing your query to the right person will get you the fastest answer. This is important because some publishers that look like surefire markets won't use freelance material at all; others may either have published something similar to your idea that you missed or may have it in the works. The only way to know is to ask. Sunset, for example, keeps the recipe creating and testing "in-house." As an editor who used to work there put it, "Everything has to be run through that great universal Sunset Typewriter in the Sky for standardization." This makes Sunset a poor bet for beginning freelancers, but until you get inside information on such policies, the best way to find out is to write and ask.

Jacqueline Killeen of 101 Productions, which *does* use freelance work, suggests asking publishers for a current catalog while you're inquiring whether or not they accept freelance proposals. "We get a lot of proposals for books we have already published," she said.

Once you know that a publisher accepts freelance submissions and has not already published something too much like your cookbook, you are ready to send a proposal. Never send the entire manuscript, even if you have it all ready. Every editor with whom I talked said that each publisher has ideas about style and format, and prefers to guide the author's writing so that no one has to rewrite after the book is accepted. Moreover, publishers are often looking for a particular book with definite characteristics. Your proposal may be close to what a publisher wants; in that case you might be asked if you would consider changing and developing your book to fit the publisher's requirements.

Inevitably, as soon as I offer an emphatic publishing rule like "never send an entire manuscript," somebody who doesn't know any better breaks the rule—and succeeds. Once, I remember, I told a writing class that they should write letters to magazines to describe their proposed articles because editors are too frantically busy to consider article ideas on the telephone. One student said sadly that he would hate switching to letters because he was already doing so well on the phone. I am telling you all this because someone reading this book is bound to think of a good reason for sending his or her entire manuscript to some publisher, and it's going to be accepted. But send an entire manuscript only if you already have it done, have a good history of being the exception to rules, and have strong vibrations about going ahead in spite of what Sara advises.

Ordinarily, publishers prefer to receive a letter that gives your background and qualifications, along with a proposal outlining the book you have in mind and a few sample recipes or sample chapters. What you submit should make very clear to the editors what kind of book you have in mind and what your work is like. If you have special credentials for writing a cookbook, such as teaching cooking classes, list them. The proposal package should be professional not only in content, but also in appearance. Every editor I asked said that the physical appearance of a proposal affected the consideration they gave its content. One editor, who used to work at Nitty Gritty Productions, said, "The single greatest flaw in submissions is messiness. Too often they're either poorly typed, handwritten, or sloppy. I was much more likely to take a submission seriously if it was presented well, even if we'd already done a cookbook on that subject. If the author seemed really good I might ask to see another outline on a different topic."

An editor at Garden Way grumbles about would-be authors who "send me bundles of recipes and wonder why I send them back."

And the editor at Owlswood Productions said, "The first thing I look for is professional approach."

My experience both as a writer and as an acquisitions editor substantiates this, not just for cookbook proposals but for all writing. The rate of positive responses to my proposals rose noticeably after I started to use an IBM self-correcting typewriter with a film ribbon, which made it possible for me to turn out perfectly typed pages.

Dress (Your Manuscript) for Success

When I look at submissions in my office at the University of South Carolina Press, I tend to keep shuffling messy manuscripts and proposals to the bottom of the pile, waiting, I suppose, until I feel strong enough to face working through the typos, smeared ball-point pen corrections, and strikeovers to get to what *may* be superior content. My mental bias expects a sloppy presentation to reflect sloppy thinking, and often it does. Especially in cooking, where accuracy and consistency are obligatory, sloppiness is a red flag that signals inaccurate recipes and inadequate instructions.

This does not mean that a perfectly typed submission automatically guarantees acceptance. As an editor at Writer's Digest Books observed, the growing use of word processors by authors makes even bad work look good, but ultimately, it doesn't disguise the fact that the work is bad. It brings us to a reality that sounds old-fashioned enough to embarrass you, but here it is anyway: your proposal should contain your best work, dressed up to reflect that excellence.

Even so, a proposal need follow no particular form. I personally prefer a short letter that introduces the author and describes his or her qualifications, along with an outline of the book and up to a dozen sample recipes. But my first cookbook assignment resulted from a letter, a proposal, and two sample chapters. My next assignment came from a letter, a skimpy outline, and three sample recipes.

As for the "dressing," let me repeat from Chapter Three that the pages you submit should be typed, double-spaced, on one side of good-quality white (*not* erasable) paper, with generous margins. The accompanying letter may be single-spaced, but should not be more than two pages long. The pages of your outline or proposal should be numbered. This sounds so obvious that you must wonder why I say it, but a lot of "word people," including me, have such an aversion to numbers that they resist using them even to number manuscript pages. I see a surprising number of outlines without page numbers in my office. (A crotchety fiction teacher broke me of going numberless during my college years by returning what I'd thought was a pretty good manuscript with no critical comment at all. Instead he covered the entire front page with vivid descriptions, written in four different colors, of what should happen to any writer who didn't number her pages. The commentary, as I recall, started out in red, "Dammit, Sara . . ." and got stronger with each successive color. By the time he got to blue, his comments were too blue to repeat here.)

Here is an example of a query letter and proposal I submitted. The editor did not use the proposed idea, but gave me another assignment because the proposal I submitted made her feel that I knew what I was doing.

Susan Herbert, Editor
Owlswood Productions
287 Harbor Way
South San Francisco, CA 94080

Dear Ms. Herbert:

I have noticed that each year you add one or two new books on cooking with special utensils to your gourmet cookbook line. Sales representatives who call on gourmet shop retailers tell me that clay pots are an increasingly popular item, and that both retailers and their customers have been asking for clay-pot cookbooks. *Books in Print* lists no books on the subject. I know that one has been written by Grover Sales, but it was commissioned by Romertopf, a company that manufactures clay pots, and sellers of other brands of clay pot would be reluctant to stock it.

I am sending you a proposal for a clay-pot cookbook. My qualifications for writing it include writing regular cooking columns for the *Local Tribune* and two years' experimentation devoted to developing unique new recipes for the clay pot. You won't find recipes like mine anywhere else. Several of my recipes have won cooking contests in this area. If you find the proposal and the accompanying recipes interesting, I would be delighted to start at once to develop a clay-pot cookbook with you.

Cordially,

Sara Pitzer
4405 Weeping Spruce Court
Concord CA 94521
(415)682-7725

A PROPOSAL FOR

A

CLAY-POT COOKBOOK

The clay-pot cookbook would include four major sections:

1. INTRODUCTION

    Advantages of clay-pot cooking, how to use and care for the pot.

2. RECIPES.

3. CREATING new recipes and ADAPTING old favorites

4. ENTERTAINING TIPS

    How to use the clay pot for serving, how to manage timing, how to prepare a meal using several different clay pots, clay-pot menus.

On the following pages I have outlined briefly the contents of each proposed section.

Three sample recipes follow.

1. INTRODUCTION

    ADVANTAGES

    Cooking in clay is fantastic. It's nearly foolproof. Even a novice in the kitchen would find it hard to spoil a recipe in the clay pot.

    When you're in a hurry, roasting in the clay pot is faster than conventional roasting. When you want to cook slowly, the clay pot can be used as a slow cooker.

Once the pot is in the oven or the microwave, it requires little further attention until the food is done.

It is so easy to prepare entire meals in the clay pot that you can use it to save energy.

Since you don't have to add extra fat for clay-pot cooking, the recipes tend to be good for dieters.

And food cooked in the clay pot tastes

DELICIOUS.

USE AND CARE

How to use clay pots for fast and slow cooking; how to clean pots; storing pots; choosing the right pot for the right job.

2. RECIPES

Fowl

Cornish Hen with Wild Rice and Petits Pois

Coq au Vin

Chicken in Mushroom and Ginger Sauce

Chicken Breasts with Zucchini

Chicken-Bean Pot   etc.

Fish

Steamed Salmon with Capers

Flounder-Shrimp Rolls

Parsley-Flavored Swordfish

Halibut Italienne   etc.

Basic Roasts

    Perfect Roast Chicken

    Turkey

    Pot Roast of Beef à la Mode

    Leg of Lamb

    Pork Loin and Variations

    Almost Traditional Ham   etc.

One-Pot Meals

    Cassoulet

    Beef in Beer

    Vegetable and Chicken Stew

    Vegetarian Stew   etc.

Side-Dish Specialties

    Ratatouille

    Stuffed Tomatoes

    Green Peppers Stuffed with Beans and Corn

    Turkish Eggplant (served at room temperature)

    Clay-Pot Potatoes

3. CREATING new recipes and ADAPTING old favorites

Rules for adjusting temperature

Rules for adjusting liquid

What NOT to try in a clay pot

4. ENTERTAINING

Timing is easy

Serving in clay requires some care

Menu suggestions

I think it is better to mail your letter and proposal flat, rather than folded, even if it consists of only a few pages that would fold neatly into a standard number-ten envelope, because once papers have been folded they never lie flat again. Trying to read a pile of papers that curl is one of those minor irritations that can make an editor frown even before she's begun to read.

Editors disagree whether a proposal has more appeal loose or in some sort of cover, but all agree that staples and paper clips hinder page turning and are a nuisance. I prefer to look at proposals that are not bound in any kind of folder because a stack of various-sized and different-colored folders on my desk always seems like clutter.

Finally, always include a self-addressed envelope with enough postage to return everything to you, if you ever want to see it again.

All this attention to details should reinforce your awareness that your beautifully prepared letter and proposal are going *somewhere* to be considered by *somebody*. The "somewhere" is probably a little office overflowing with papers; the "somebody" may have a headache and be worried about paying off the orthodonist's bills of two teenaged daughters before it's time to buy them wedding dresses. As with any other communicative art, the more you know about the audience and situation into which your missive will move, the more appropriate you can make it. You can't know much about the individuals who will handle your work, except that they are human beings with human concerns beyond your proposal, but you can learn something about the typical "consideration" process in publishing and at least keep your submission appropriate to that.

Survival of the Fittest

First, we must acknowledge that the details of the process vary from one publisher to another; in general, however, certain things happen to all submissions. Some large publishing houses have staff to serve as first readers, who go through proposals as they arrive, return those that are clearly unsuitable, and pass those that show promise on to higher editors. Smaller publishers have no such staff; a single editor may read proposals, answer or return them, work on books in progress, and deal with authors, among other things. Either way, sooner or later (usually later) the proposal reaches an editorial person with some decision-making power. One of the biggest disillusionments of my life was to learn that in trade publishing, editors seldom have the final say about what gets published. An idea that the editor likes must also survive discussions with marketing and sales people. In the end, even the best proposals live or die by the answer to the question, "Will it sell?"

This seems sad and cynical until you realize that even publishers have to make enough money to pay salaries and operating costs. In recent years many have gone out of business because they ignored too many business realities and made inaccurate guesses about what they could sell. Clearly, then, to help your proposal along, you should offer as much intelligence as you can about who will buy your cookbook as proposed; then you should demonstrate convincingly your ability to develop the proposed idea and help deliver the projected audience. I once almost sold a cookbook idea to a publisher with the suggestion that it could be marketed through the local newspapers, for which I was writing cooking columns. How about your book? Who will buy it beyond your friends and family? If you think it could be used in home economics classes because several home-ec teachers have tested it successfully in classes, say so. If it could be used by the members of every running club in the country or by every new bride or by every teenaged pizza lover, explain how. Help the publisher see the potential market for your book. If you can provide an impressive statistic that's pertinent, toss it in. "According to the USDA, 6 million Americans made berry jam last year, and 10 million more planted berry bushes in their home gardens."

Sell your idea as persuasively as possible. Describe how your book is different from all others and superior to any similar books. Communicate your own excitement about the project. If any of your other activities, such as teaching cooking classes or appearing on television, give you added exposure that might help sell your book, emphasize them. If you've won cooking contests or other related awards, mention them too. Be sure to mention that you recipes have all been tested.

It can be tricky to sell an idea without sounding hokey about it. If you have trouble striking the right tone between a sideshow barker and an ad on the *Wall Street Journal* financial page, try this. In the most enthusiastic tone you can muster, write out everything you want to say about yourself and your book idea. Then go through and edit yourself, taking out adjectives, hyperbole, and exclamation points as necessary until you have reached what feels like a nicely controlled but very positive pitch. If you have trouble hyping yourself, ask someone to brainstorm with you; if you have trouble subduing an overboisterous presentation, ask someone more conservative to suggest editorial changes.

Assuming you've delivered the right idea to the right publisher and convinced the marketing people that there's a market worth pursuing, you must subject your proposal to another test. You must persuade the publisher that yours is the best available treatment of the idea in question. I've never quite gotten used to the fact that no matter what unique, previously unconceived idea any of us develops, someone else, a stranger in a distant place, has had the same idea, developed it in remarkably similar fashion, and sent it to the same publisher where I sent mine. It happens—often.

What do editors look for, then, in deciding whose treatment of a particular idea wins the prize of publishing? What makes a proposal so conspicuously superior to others of its kind that editors choose it over other contenders?

Editors agree surprisingly well on the answer to these questions. First, they like flair. Your proposal should absolutely crackle with your excitement about the project; it must convince the editor that you can write a cookbook that will delight readers. Unfortunately, you can't fake excitement convincingly. Occasionally I see an article or a little book suggesting that if you want to make some money, all you have to do is gather up some recipes (not necessarily your own) and hook them together with a few cute lines of prose, and you're on your way to riches, whether you can cook or not. I think I've seen a book or two written that way—on the remainder and sale tables of book stores, reduced to 99 cents. Lots of exclamation points and underlined words may fool the writer into thinking that he or she sounds excited, but it won't fool the editors. If most of your enthusiasm is for money rather than cooking, write a book on investments. (I went against my own advice a while ago at the request of a publisher. I tried to write a book on say beans. It didn't work and eventually I gave up. I had to relearn what I already knew.)

Editors look not only for flair, but also for professional-quality workmanship. The editors I talked with agreed that your proposal must not only avoid sloppiness, but also sound as though you know what you're talking about. It must be impeccably typed and neatly packaged. And the recipes must be given in a format consistent with other good cookbooks. I made this point in Chapter Two, but it's worth repeating here.

Finally, the recipes you include in your proposal should be original (or perhaps historical) and good. Experienced cookbook editors can tell by reading a recipe whether it's really new and whether it's likely to be successful. This is just another way of saying, "You can't fake it." If you have unique old family recipes or previously unpublished historical gems or brand-new combinations of ingredients, that will show. If you don't, that will show, too.

Patience Is a Necessity

If you have submitted a proposal that meets all these exacting standards, you can't be blamed for expecting an enthusiastic letter of acceptance in a week or so. It's unlikely. Sometimes it takes longer than that for anybody to open the envelope. You will probably have to wait at least six weeks, maybe several months. Sometimes you will get a quick answer, but more often you will have to live through waiting while your proposal rests on the corner of a desk in a "to-be-considered" pile until an editor gets to it.

All kinds of things can slow down that consideration. Here are some things that have kept me from looking at manuscripts as quickly as I should have: I've been on the road attending professional book exhibits; I lost a contact lens and stepped on my glasses all in the same day; submissions doubled in the past year and I need help; the air conditioner broke in the office during a heat wave; the office converted to computerized order fulfillment and everybody's helping straighten out the mess; my boss put me on a priority rush project; I did look at all the manuscripts and wrote responses, but the postal workers went on strike; I wrote the responses on a word processor and the new computer ate them.

The point is, many things can happen in publishing houses to slow down the consideration process. It shouldn't work that way. It's unprofessional. But it happens. When you consider that editors, like other people, go on vacations, get sick, procrastinate, attend conventions, and do other things besides read and respond to proposals, it's easier to understand why it sometimes takes a while to get an answer. Think of any letter you've been meaning to answer for—how long? Weeks? Months? You've lost track? Sometimes it's like that for editors, too. But generally they try to be systematic and responsible in handling the proposals they get.

If you feel that you have waited an unreasonable length of time, say, three months, and want to know what's going on, write a short follow-up letter to the publisher and send it along with a photocopy of your original letter and a photocopy of an acknowledgement of your proposal, if you received one. Some publishers acknowledge receipt of all submissions; many do not. Mention the date on which you mailed the original proposal, summarize it in a phrase or so ("my proposal for a cookbook on cooking with Gloriosa daisies"), and ask when you might expect an answer.

If you still have no answer in another month, you can simply forget about it and go on with other business, waiting to see what will happen eventually; or you can write another letter to say that you are withdrawing the proposal from consideration to submit it elsewhere.

Waiting is an occupational hazard. Even now I'm working on a project that languished more than six months before I got a go-ahead. Another of my proposals is growing moldy somewhere in the vaults of a major publishing house. It's been there three years, and I have never been able to get any acknowledgement at all, except for a secretary's assurance on the telephone that my proposal was "still under consideration," and would I just "wait a little longer." I've lost interest in it and am simply letting it go to see if anything ever happens.

Telling you how the consideration process works and how to submit your proposal by mail forces me—again—to tell you a story that contradicts everything I have just said. When Jeanne Jones learned that she had diabetes and decided to write *The Calculating Cook* to demonstrate that it was possible to eat well on the exchange diet, she did not follow the procedure I have described. She said, "I found my publisher by going to all the bookstores and picking out the publisher that had the nicest artwork because I was an art major, and 101 Productions was the winner. Then I called and announced that they had won my 'contest'!" Jeanne made arrangements to meet with the 101 people at an American Booksellers Convention, where they worked out some more details, and she has been publishing health-oriented cookbooks ever since.

Do I recommend that you proceed similarly? No. Her success with that approach was a fluke. I recommend it only if you have strong reasons for believing that you, too, can pull off an unorthodox approach.

Inevitably, the traditional approach seems weighted in favor of the trade publisher and leads authors to ask about submitting proposals to more than one publisher at a time. Doing this used to be absolutely verboten, but now it is called "simultaneous submission" and is supposed to be all right because photocopy machines make copies as easy to read as the original. Some authors are doing it, but the old objection that reading smeary carbon copies was too hard was only part of the publishers' opposition to simultaneous submissions. A lot of time and discussion go into deciding to publish a book. Nobody wants to go to that much trouble only to be told that another publisher has just bought the manuscript. Some well-known writers' agents do contact more than one publisher about a new work, and sometimes the publishers bid against each other to get it. Unless you've found a way to make recipes read like chapters from *Scruples*, this is unlikely to happen with a cook-book.

If you decide to go ahead and try a simultaneous submission, be sure that each publisher knows you have submitted the idea elsewhere. You don't have to say where or even to how many other places, but it's only fair for the editorial committee who may consider your proposal to know that another group may be doing the same thing. Simply include a line in your letter saying something like, "I am also communicating with another publisher about this idea but have made no commitments and am very eager to learn your response."

The Big "Yes—Maybe"

But let's suppose you sent a proposal to just one publisher, waited your allotted three months or so, and, just about when you thought of giving up, got a letter from the publisher. They want to publish your cookbook. Sort of. That is, they like the idea but have some thoughts of their own about what should go into the book and how it should be developed.

Unless you are totally inflexible, this is the fun part, in which you discuss back and forth (one editor I know calls it "editorial back and forthing") the projected audience for the book, what that audience will expect, and how that audience might be expanded in the interest of selling more books. You should already have thought about these things in detail and be able to discuss them knowledgeably.

I encountered a good example of this when I wrote a book on jams, jellies, pickles, and preserves for Owlswood Productions. I like natural foods, cooking for big crowds, and eating in rustic settings. When I think about preserving food, I envision huge country kitchens, wood stoves, and iron kettles. In my mind, a cookbook about pickles and jellies implies that the cook ends up with row upon row of quart mason jars, glittering in all the colors of the harvest, stored in the pantry against the outdoor appetites of a huge family who must be fed during the long winter ahead. But Owlswood cookbooks are sold in gourmet shops, where they are bought especially by people who cook for a hobby and live in city apartments or suburban split-levels. These people choose shiny Cuisinart pans over old iron kettles every time. The storage space in their kitchens may not be much more than a shelf in the dish cupboard, and the family is probably small enough to fit around a tiny table in the breakfast nook. Even if they ate jelly three times a day, they wouldn't be able to finish a quart jar for months.

This means that an Owlswood cookbook must somehow marry the romance of country-kitchen fantasies with the realities of cooking small quantities in limited space and spare time, with modern gourmet gadgets. Since I am basically a country-kitchen cook myself, I had to experiment with the recipes to reduce their yield to a pint or so, and develop and describe preparation methods that use modern equipment and grocery-store ingredients. I suffered as I gave up my image of Amish women stirring cauldrons of apple butter over wood fires in favor of the image of a cook in designer jeans, neatly pouring three pints of strawberry preserves from her copper-bottomed saucepan, but in doing it, I wrote a cookbook that far more people are likely to buy and use.

If this kind of adjustment seems to you like giving up too much control over *your* idea, you must remember that the publisher is in the business of selling books—a particular kind of book to a particular audience—and if you can't or won't accommodate that audience, the publisher can't use your book.

In addition to negotiating content, you will also work out details about illustrations, indexing, and possible promotion. Some publishers provide their own illustrations for a cookbook, leaving you with little or nothing to say in the matter; others request rough sketches or photographs to guide their artists; still others expect you to provide all illustrations and captions.

If your heart is set on doing the illustrations yourself, or if you have strong feelings about not being involved with them, you may be able to negotiate, but not always. Mollie Katzen's *Moosewood Cookbook* ended up with Ten Speed Press rather than the big New York City publisher with whom she had been talking because the big publisher did not want to use her drawings and hand-lettered text, which she considered an integral part of her book. Ten Speed, on the other hand, was willing to take her book just as it was.

The question of who pays for the illustrations depends on the publisher and on your agreement with that publisher. Some publishers simply bear the cost outright. Others expect you to pay the artist directly. And in yet another arrangement, some publishers charge the cost of illustration against the author's royalties, and that cost must be worked off along with the amount of the advance before you begin to receive additional royalties. Another arrangement is for the author and publisher to split the illustration costs. In those latter two cases, protect yourself by making sure the contract specifies an upper limit on the costs for which you are responsible.

As for indexing, most publishers expect the author either to pro-

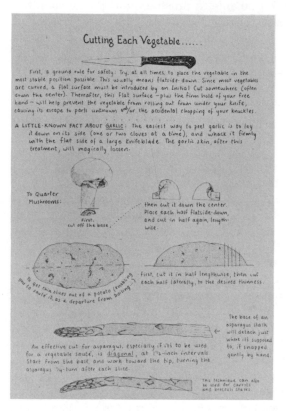

Less is more in cookbook drawings illustrating basic how-to information. Mollie Katzen was an art student before she became engrossed in cooking and restaurants. She said that the hard part of completing this page in the Moosewood Cookbook *was simplifying the drawings. She went back over each one several times, removing excessive detail each time. Doing this single page took her many hours.*

vide the index or to have the cost of a professional indexer deducted from royalties. If you decide to do the index yourself, be sure to get a copy of the little booklet, *Indexes*, reprinted from *A Manual of Style*, twelfth edition, published by the University of Chicago Press. It tells you exactly how to go about creating an index and what to include in it.

Although promotion plans are not usually spelled out in detail, the publishers like to have some indication that you will be willing to cooperate if they arrange public appearances or request suggestions from you for places to send review copies.

These details should be spelled out in your contract, along with deadlines, approximate number of pages or words, the royalties or flat fees you are to receive, when the money is to be paid to you, and who will hold the copyright—the author, the publisher, or the two jointly.

Although in the past it was considered preferable for an author to hold the copyright in his or her own name, the laws have changed recently, and many people feel that it no longer matters much whether the publisher or the author has the copyright. I thought that agents should be especially sensitive to the authors' side of the issue, and asked several about it. They all said that they *try* to have a work copyrighted in the author's name, but added that under the new laws nobody seems quite sure what's going on. With a cookbook you should probably ask to have the work in your name, but not to be too distressed if it is a point you cannot win. Some publishers insist on publishing everything with the copyright in *their* name. I would never give up a chance to be published by a house I liked because we couldn't come to terms on the copyright.

The contract will specify what is to happen to subsidiary rights for your book. This would include such things as the book being condensed or excerpted in magazines. Arrangements usually call for a split between author and publisher; 50 percent-50 percent or 60 percent-40 percent, for instance.

Also, the entire contract will hinge on your delivering what is termed "an acceptable manuscript." This sounds vague. In fact, it is usually not. It is common practice for a letter accompanying the contract to spell out in more detail what will be considered acceptable. If the publisher has gone so far as to negotiate a contract, it means that there are plans for your book, so if you have worked reasonably toward delivering what you promised, it is unlikely that the publisher would declare your manuscript unacceptable without trying first to work with you to get it the way they wanted it. Occasionally, however, an author does not deliver what a publisher expects, and in that case is asked to return all or some of the advance.

Some authors want an agent to help negotiate the best contract. Every agent I questioned said that she thought she could probably negotiate a better contract than an author could do for herself. Publishers, however, doubted that the difference would be enough to cover the agent's percentage. One editor said, "Our house has limits, especially for first books. No matter how persuasive an agent is, we can't go beyond those limits. We try to be fair."

What is fair? The only good answer comes from a real estate agent I know who is fond of saying, "The selling price is whatever price a buyer and a seller agree upon." A fair contract is any contract an author and a publisher agree is fair. Here are some realities to help shape your notions of what is fair in your contract.

Great Expectations

First, except for occasional blockbusters, neither authors nor publishers get rich on a cookbook, especially an unknown author's first cookbook. A few special cookbooks capture public imagination and sell beyond the wildest expectations of everyone, but the *Publisher's Weekly* report on mass-market titles published in 1982 includes no cookbooks at all in the two-million-plus category, where such authors as Sidney Sheldon, Stephen King, and Harold Robbins live. In fact, cookbooks aren't even seen in the 500,000-plus paperback category with Richard Simmons' *Never Say Diet* reprint and the Garfield books. At about 100,000 paperback copies published for the year, cookbooks begin to show up: Sunset's *Easy Basics for Good Cooking*, for example, H.P.'s *Appetizers*, and the unusual book by Mollie Katzen, *The Enchanted Broccoli Forest*, from Ten Speed Press. Many more cookbook sales number in the thousands than in the hundreds of thousands. You shouldn't expect to make as much money as the author of a book like *Real Men Don't Eat Quiche*; it's more realistic to expect that you will make anywhere from a few hundred to a few thousand dollars, either in a flat fee or through royalties.

Unless you made a work-for-hire arrangement for a flat fee, the common arrangement for payment written into a contract is that you receive royalties on sales. Royalties can be figured in a mind-boggling number of ways. You could receive a percentage of list price, but more likely you would receive a percentage of net sales (what's left after the discounts given to wholesalers and retailers are deducted). Royalties based on list price are more common for very high-volume books than for first cookbooks, but in negotiating your contract, at least you can *try* for royalties based on list rather than net. It will make you sound professional and it might work. Some publishers simply pay a set amount, as little as 8 or 9 cents, on each book sold. Usually, some part of the royalties is paid to you before the book is published, with a guarantee that you can keep the money advanced to you even if the publisher never sells enough copies of your book to cover that advance. Those big quarter-of-a-million-dollar advances you sometimes read about in slick magazines are for authors who have produced huge best-sellers, not cookbooks. For us mere mortals, advances on cookbooks usually range from $500 to $5,000. Regardless of its size, the idea of an advance is to give the author walking-around cash while she's finishing the book.

Unless you're a truly remarkable creature, you will spend that advance money while you are walking around with it, before you finish the book. What, then, if something happens and you can't finish it by the deadline? Or, worse yet, can't finish it at all? If you don't finish the book, you have to give back the money. If you are simply having trouble meeting the deadline, you can usually arrange for an extension. People miss deadlines more often than you might suppose; most of us have unrealistic ideas about how much we can accomplish in a given time. Most editors, all too familiar with authors' procrastination and crises, build a little fat into their schedules to allow for such problems. But if you find yourself falling behind, let your editor know right away. Don't wait until the day your manuscript is due in the publisher's office and then call up to say it will be late because you've just broken both arms and can't put stamps on the envelope. Editors are the only people in the world who hear more trumped-up excuses than college professors who teach Saturday classes. In fact, editors come to recognize whole categories of excuses and to discount all stories in those categories.

Excuses, Excuses

The editor of a hobby magazine I sometimes work with got the ultimate excuse. A man who was supposed to build a project he had designed and then send her the drawings, the built project, and a how-to manuscript called her the day everything was due. He said it wouldn't be coming because he had fallen into a big hole outside his shop and broken both arms and both legs. "Do you suppose it's true?" she asked me. I didn't suppose it was true, but I had been to his shop, and there *was* a hole out back big enough to break your arms and legs if you fell into it. To this day we haven't decided whether it was true.

The significant thing here is that deadlines do matter and excuses, especially if delivered at the last minute, tend to sound phony. On an even more callous level, it doesn't matter much whether or not the excuse is true. If a publisher has contracted for a book by a certain time, people are counting on it; editorial people need time to edit it; production people need time to turn it into a book; marketing people need to know when it is coming so they can promote it. In this formula, you are only the author. Your problems back there in the kitchen, with the measuring cups and the typewriter pages, matter very little to anyone at the publishing house. All that matters is your book.

Once you have mailed your manuscript to the publisher and an editor has acknowledged its arrival, you may think it is done. Wrong! The next stage is editing. Editing changes a manuscript and usually improves it. The number of people who work on your manuscript at this point will vary from one publisher to another, but whether handled by one editor or several, the manuscript will be edited in two ways. The first is what I call "shaping" your manuscript. In this stage an editor will look at the overall organization of your cookbook, including the arrangement of chapters within the book and of recipes within the chapters, and may decide that the book would be stronger with the chapters in a different order. When I wrote my book on whole grains, for example, I wanted to organize the chapters alphabetically by type of grain, like an encyclopedia. I wanted to begin each chapter with information about the grain, with instructions for growing, harvesting, and storing it and advice on buying it. I wanted to devote the second half of each chapter to recipes for using the respective grains.

The editor was the kind of man who can tell you that your idea is wonderful but that the work will be better arranged his way, and leave you believing both statements. We discussed organization and ended up arranging the chapters not alphabetically but in order of familiarity, with corn first and triticale near the end. But he agreed with me that recipes for each grain should go into the second half of the appropriate chapter. As editing goes, this was a pretty minor change. He could have decided to put all the recipes in one section and all the information about growing corn in another. I'm glad he didn't.

At this point, an editor might also suggest adding more recipes of a particular kind, taking out others, shortening or lengthening the instructions in a recipe, writing a stronger introduction, or adding a glossary of terms. You may be asked to do these things yourself, or the editor may just go ahead and make the changes.

In the second phase of editing, copyediting, someone will go over every word in your manuscript, correcting and improving your syntax and grammar, catching typographical errors and misspelled words, and checking the accuracy of measurements, instructions, cooking times, and temperatures. The editor will check routinely to make sure your instructions account for every ingredient in the recipe and that every ingredient mentioned in your instructions is specified in your list of ingredients.

This is detailed, precise work. For me, it is hard, but some people find it easy and natural. They make good editors. I am always grateful when an editor says to me, "You list salt right after stock in the ingredients, but you never say when to add it." Or, "In the recipe for Chicken Bordeaux you call for powdered thyme. Do you really mean *powdered* thyme or do you mean whole dried thyme?" Or, "Why do you say to crimp the edges of the aluminum foil in some recipes and to use a butcher's fold in others? Aren't they the same thing? Which do you want to use?"

This part of editing obviously improves my work and is easy to accept.

You will probably find that it's harder to accept the editing that tampers with your carefully chosen words and your painfully created phrases. In this book, I made a reference to Aristotle's saying that there is no accounting for taste. I've loved and used this line for years, and have always attributed it to Aristotle. The copyeditor changed it to "an old saying," and sent along a little note that it wasn't Aristotle who said it. She said she knew it had originally been written in Latin, but couldn't trace the saying to any one author. I was so upset I called the professor from whom I had first heard the phrase. His wife answered the phone, and when I told her what I wanted, she said, "He probably made that up. He does that to me all the time because I make up biology facts for him." He couldn't possibly have done such a thing to me. I called back to ask him to confirm Aristotle as the originator of my beloved line. The professor said, "Oh, I think that's just an old saying. I've seen it in the Latin. I haven't any idea who said it."

Well, here's a new saying. You can't trust your old *perfessers*, but you can count on your copyeditor to find mistakes almost every time.

Sometimes, though, you have expert information that your editor does not; you have the right to insist on your version when meaning is at stake. In this book, when I wrote about the importance of accuracy in recipes, I told the story of a friend who ate a whole loaf of pasty nut bread because I'd forgotten to write in sugar and his wife had accepted my version of the recipe. The editor asked me if that bread would really have been pasty. It would. In quick breads, sugar changes the structure of the baked product, and if you leave it out, the resulting "bread" is heavy, dense, too floury—pasty. We kept the word.

I think the best way to read editorial changes is to try to read the revised text the first time without noting what was changed, and stop to examine the change only when you come across something you know you would not have said. This is hard to do if the marked-up manuscript is all you have to look at, but if you have copies of page proofs or galleys of the set type, it's easy. Once you have gone through the text this way and become comfortable with it, you should find that you can go back and look at each change to be sure it is correct without taking it all personally.

Occasionally I have disagreed with the way my writing was edited, but only rarely. In my experience, professional editors are very good at improving my copy. (Many of them kindly tell me they are not good at writing their own copy, though I know some are.) I appreciate what they do because in the end, the result is a better book.

The remaining steps for turning your manuscript into a book include designing, typesetting, pasteup, printing, folding and gathering the pages, and binding. The designer, usually in cooperation with the marketing and editorial departments, decides what size and shape the book will be, the kind and size of type in which it will be set, the arrangement of pages, and how to display charts, diagrams, and art. The type is then set according to the designer's specifications, and the pages of the book are pasted up either manually or by computer. Sometimes the book is printed by the same people who set the type; more often it is sent to another place for printing. Similarly, the printer may also bind the books, or the pages may go to a separate bindery. And at some point in all this activity, the marketing and art people are designing a jacket for your book, if it is a hardback, or the cover if it's a paperback.

A writer with sixteen books to his credit once said, "I have learned never to argue about jackets or titles." It's just as well, because in trade publishing the author has little to say about either. I don't have any statistics on this, but I doubt that one book in a hundred is published under the author's original title, and for a good reason. The jacket and the title must do far more than merely identify the book; they have to sell it. And authors rarely sense what will work in the bookstore, in the publisher's catalog, and in advertisements. Of course marketing professionals can goof too. Miriam Ungerer, whom I mentioned earlier, thinks an earlier book of hers, *The Too Hot To Cook Book,* would have sold better with a less cutsey title. Her publisher, she said, was too heavily influenced by the success of Peg Bracken's *I Hate to Cook Book.*

Titles usually come from brainstorming sessions. In a really good session, everybody knows the book and its working title, and has spent some time thinking about it. They get together to dream up possible titles. If the group gets a little silly and really starts to play with the thing, so much the better. A good title is apt to come of it. (I've always wished I could have been in on the Junior League meeting that created the title *Applehood and Mother Pie.*)

The publisher will ask for your title suggestions. If you want to have some control over the title, it wouldn't be a bad idea to brainstorm with your friends to see if you can come up with something sharp and salable, pleasing to the ear and eyecatching in the bookstore. There's always the chance that you can out-brainstorm the publisher's marketing people and enjoy your own title on the book.

It feels like forever, but sometime after the day you sent your beautifully typed manuscript to an editor, you will receive your copies of the finished book. This usually takes nine months to a year; sometimes the time is less and sometimes much longer.

After that, your publisher will advertise the book and get it into the hands of sales representatives, wholesalers, and (eventually) book-stores. Of course none of this will happen as fast or as extensively as you would like, but yours won't be the only new book the publisher is pushing, so try to be reasonable in your expectations. Also, ask what you can do to help promote the book. Send in any suggestions you have for reviewers and places to advertise. And if it appears that the publisher really isn't doing anything at all with your book, try to pro-mote it yourself, using as much as you can the approaches I've suggest-ed for marketing in the chapter on self-publishing.

Regardless of how book sales go, unless you started the project on-ly for money, you should get a hoot out of your first trade cookbook. A commercial publisher thought it was worth bothering with. They published it, but *you* wrote it. There's no other feeling in the world quite like it.

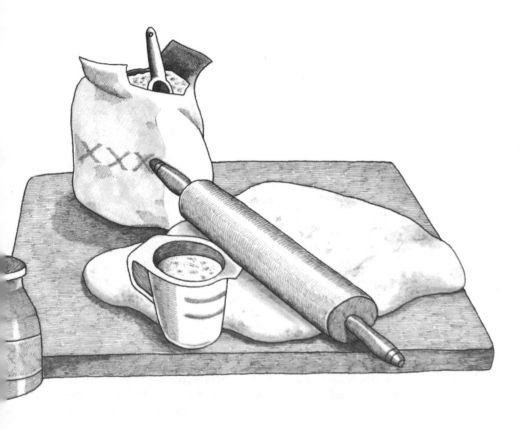

CHAPTER 7

Illustrating Your Cookbook

*T*he earliest cookbooks were not illustrated. Even today, a surprising number of cookbooks have little or no illustration, but concentrate instead on squeezing as many recipes into the pages as possible. But sometime in the past, I suspect, words failed a cook who was trying to write down just how to fold flour into beaten egg whites or how to disjoint a bird, and she drew a little sketch of the process to show her absent reader what words alone couldn't communicate.

If you doubt for a second that words do sometimes let us down in describing processes and intricate devices, think of the game you played as a child in which you went around asking people to describe a spiral staircase or to tell you what a goatee was, and then made fun of them because they had to use their hands to do it.

Of course, technology has also had a part in creating our modern-day expectations that cookbooks be full of pictures. Now that it's possible to make full-color photographs and reproduce them in the printing process, it's inevitable that books and magazines on a subject as colorful and visual as food often rely heavily on pictures.

Certainly the luscious photographs in the gourmet magazines play an important part in our enjoyment of those magazines, and such illustrations tend to make us expect something similar in other publications dealing with food. A little later in this chapter I will discuss the many important, practical functions that illustrations serve in cookbooks, but let's pause for a moment and reflect on the sheer pleasure we get from good color photographs of food. I can't begin to guess how often I have been lured into trying to prepare a particular recipe because I have seen it beautifully illustrated somewhere—in a magazine or cookbook, in an advertisement, or even in a grocery-store brochure. I have seen photographs that make lobster, prickly, bright red, full of claws, and monster-shaped as it is, look mouth-watering. Photographs of a hot cherry pie, with the crimson syrup just bubbling to the top of the latticework crust, or of a three-tier chocolate cake, iced with white seafoam frosting and covered in a blizzard of grated coconut, have made me forget I shouldn't eat sugar. The other day I saw a photograph of assorted stuffed eggs that was enough to make me buy my own laying hens. The stuffings were pink with salmon, green with avocado, and bright yellow with curry powder, and the eggs were arranged in alternating colors on a bed of fine alfalfa sprouts garnished around the edges with brilliant green watercress. Each egg was garnished further with a bit of red pepper, a green pea, or a square of carrot. The detail in the photograph was splendid—so fine you could make out the tiny husk on each alfalfa seed. And I thought that if I couldn't have a salmon- or avocado-stuffed egg, within an hour, I would die. No question—the color illustrations in cookbooks, especially photographs, can have a powerful influence on us.

Yet, in deciding whether or not your book should be illustrated, you may be surprised to discover that some of your favorites are not. Looking at the books on my own shelves, for instance, I find that Julia Child books are illustrated, but not lavishly. Craig Claiborne books are sparsely illustrated. The self-published books run about half and half, but the illustrations tend to be simple.

Until I started to plan this chapter, I never thought about illustration much one way or the other. I provided roughs for illustrating my own books if a publisher asked for them, and once I cooked and photographed thirty-five different dishes in one day for a book, but it was just part of the job. I responded with pleasure, as we all do, to those expensive cookbooks that are crammed with color photographs of perfect-looking foods, the kind you suspect spirits whisk onto the dining tables of those perfect dining rooms you see in decorating magazines. Although I looked at those books, I never particularly wanted to do one like them.

If you are planning to publish your book with a trade publisher, decisions about the illustrations will probably rest largely with the publisher. Some publishers expect you to provide illustrations; others handle the art themselves. Often the cost comes out of your royalties, but not always. But if you turn to self-publishing or publish a personal book, it will be up to you to decide what to do about pictures.

You should find it easier to make this decision after you consider what we expect from cookbook illustrations. If you, like me, had never given it much thought before, you may be surprised at all the different reasons we have for illustrating cookbooks. (Every picture you include should have a definite purpose for being in the book that you can explain in a single sentence.)

When I styled the food for the black-and-white photographs in Whole Grains: Grow, Harvest and Cook Your Own, *published by Garden Way, my main goal was to show what unfamiliar recipes look like after they have been prepared, and to make the food look appetizing. This photograph of a barley salad relies on a variety of textures and shapes to add visual appeal in the absence of color.*

Worth a Thousand Words

The first use, as I have already suggested, is functional. Illustrations can show what words alone are inadequate to describe. Often illustrations can reduce the number of words you have to use in describing a complicated process or device. Imagine trying to tell someone in words alone how to bone a duck and reassemble the meat to serve as the Chinese do. Or imagine how many words it would take to explain what an expresso coffee maker looks like. And how would you have described spaghetti squash in words alone, back when it first began to appear on the market as an exotic vegetable unfamiliar to most shoppers? Even simple line drawings can help in these cases.

Another purpose of an illustration is to show a finished dish that looks so good you want to try it. The pictures in cooking magazines and women's magazines are especially adept at this. Some cookbooks, such as the Life International Series, are famous for striking "try-this" illustrations. The food growers and the manufacturers of all kinds of food products hire advertising agencies to style these foods in dishes that look so tempting that people will want to buy and use the products. Come to think of it, making something like prunes or raisins look good must be the ultimate challenge. This kind of illustrating is usually very expensive. It's done with full-color photographs or occasionally with oil or watercolor paintings, which are then photographed for reproduction.

Sometimes illustrations are used to emphasize a feeling, a tone, or a theme in a book. In this kind of illustrating, pictures of actual dishes may not be shown. You're more likely to see drawings than photographs for this kind of illustrating: drawings of some of the ingredients, of an appropriate serving piece, or of some related objects. *Beard on Bread* and *Beard on Pasta* are two beautiful examples of books in which drawings are used to emphasize on the theme of the book. Holiday books, too, lend themselves to such illustrating; so do any books with a theme beyond the food itself.

Another use of illustration is "spot art," which fills up what would otherwise be an empty spot on a page or breaks up the gray of a large block of type. In these cases, good illustrating can also work to develop the theme and establish the tone of the book. All too often, however, the pictures are little more than bits of vaguely related art stuck in here and there. I feel strongly that good design demands a clear relationship between the art and the subject matter of a book.

For one type of cookbook, however, some people argue persuasively against this idea; I refer to the regional or organizational cookbook, in which pictures of local landmarks are interspersed among the reci-

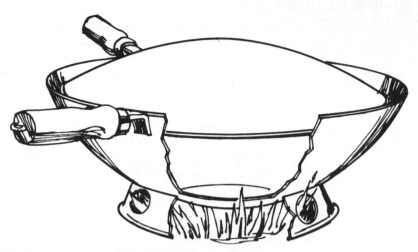

This line drawing by Mike Nelson seems to be explaining a device, but if you look closely you see that it doesn't really say much that anybody who has a wok hasn't already figured out. The real function of this drawing is to fill out the page. (From Wok: A Chinese Cookbook *by Gary Lee)*

pes. Some museum-sponsored cookbooks are illustrated with pictures of paintings and objects from the museum, and I have seen a Mexican cookbook filled with pictures of people from the countryside going about their daily chores. As I said, one can make an argument for such illustrating. It's especially tempting if you are producing a regional cookbook and have access to plenty of good photographs or drawings of the area, but I would always vote against it.

Probably you have also seen cookbooks in which illustrations were used to fatten the book. There's nothing wrong with using illustrations to increase the number of pages in your book, provided they relate to the text, but if you decide at the last minute that you are running short and try to find a few extra pictures to fill in the gaps, the book will look padded.

I haven't yet mentioned a major reason for including pictures in cookbooks: people like them. They help sell books. I have watched people flip through a few pages of a cookbook, see that it contains nothing but type, and then lay it aside to look for one with pictures.

If you are self-publishing a book and wondering whether or not to use illustrations, your best guide will be the nature of your expected readers. Are they picture people, or would they prefer all the available space to be used for recipes? And how can you know whether or not they are picture people? At best this is only a rough guide, but I think you can safely assume that if you are publishing for people whose interest is historical, practical, or related to fitness and health, they will be more concerned with the amount of information you can pack into your pages than in elaborate illustrations. I do *not* mean to imply that a book of recipes from the days your ancestors drove the wagons West will please its audience less if you put pictures in it. Nor am I suggesting that illustrations would offend the readers of a cookbook for workaday meals, or that the potential readers of a cookbook for maintaining sports-level nutrition would reject a book if it had pictures. But if the information in such books is sound and useful, I think the readers will be more or less indifferent to whether or not the book has illustrations.

On the other hand, I can see that people who are looking in a book for party ideas would expect to see illustrations of table arrangements, serving ideas, and attractive garnishes. If you hope to sell a self-published book for a profit, you must consider the expectations of your audience. If they are buying a book on entertaining, is it because they want to see pictures of how to do it? And if they are buying a book of practical tips, do they prefer more tips than pictures? These are serious considerations in self-publishing for profit.

On the other hand, if you are working on a personal book to give to important people in your life rather than to sell, I think your decision can be guided by your own skills. If you have a knack for drawing or know someone who would like to help, or if you have photographs, it seems a shame not to illustrate. But if the attempt to include illustrations will stymie you to the point where you never finish the book, forget them.

. . . But Are They Worth $2,500?

As anyone who buys books knows, illustrations add to the cost of a cookbook. Simple line drawings add the least; black-and-white photographs add more; full-color photographs increase the cost of a book substantially. If you wonder, then, how heavily illustrated books from HP, Sunset, and Ideal manage to offer so many color photographs at comparatively low prices, remember that they are printed in huge quantities, which lowers their unit cost. Many a publisher mutters that full-color illustrations do not begin to be cost-effective unless you print at least 20,000 copies of a book. That would eliminate full color from most self-published books. For the amount of charm they can contribute, line drawings add very little to the cost of the book, especially if made in the exact size in which they are to be used so that they don't have to be blown up or reduced. It may even be feasible to print the drawings in a different color from the text, thus making a two-color book.

When deciding whether to add illustrations or color, another thing to consider is what else you could do with those same dollars. If you want a book for people to take to the kitchen and use, rather than just to collect and read, you might prefer to put the extra money into a spiral or other stay-flat binding or a washable cover. The people at Time-Life showed their awareness of our reluctance to take a heavily illustrated book into the kitchen when they published each book of their "Foods of the World" series in two volumes—one gloriously illustrated with color photographs, the other a little spiral-bound book to use stoveside, which contained the recipes that went with that elaborate photography.

Your publisher or printer is your best source of information about the technicalities of illustrating a book, but you will be surprised at how little you have to know to deal successfully with the matter. Here are a few basics that will help you sound reasonably knowledgeable when you talk with a printer or publisher, and will help you understand more easily what they are telling you.

Printing ABC's

Line drawings are reproduced in the same way as type, by printing the actual lines (or letters) as they appear in the original. These days the reproduction is almost always done by offset printing.

Black-and-white photographs are usually reproduced in halftones. By a process called "screening," halftones reproduce the full range from black to white, including the grays, in the photograph. The screen is placed between the illustration and the film negative, and it breaks the continuous gradations in the tones of the illustration into dots that vary in size. The size of the dots determines the blackness or grayness of the image. The variation in the sizes of the dots makes the printed halftones look as if they had been printed with varying densities of ink. Halftone screens are measured by the number of lines per inch in the screen, which ranges from 55 to 300 lines. The more lines, the finer the screen; the finer the screen, the sharper the reproduction. A newspaper photograph is reproduced with a fairly coarse screen; the black-and-white photographs in an art book are reproduced with fine screens.

A more expensive process for reproducing pictures is duotone, in which the same illustration is photographed twice, with the screen at different angles. Then the picture is printed with dots in two colors, one from each of the two angles. The first image, which is black, is usually a regular halftone. The second, which may be gray to give a black-and-white effect or another color to give the effect of a colored picture, is added in dots between the first set of dots. The two sets of dots to-

This photo of Salad Nicoise is from **Glorious Food**, *which features hundreds of entertaining ideas, menus, and recipes from one of New York's leading caterers. The book is a feast for the eye and the imagination, extravagantly illustrated with more than 150 color photographs of gourmet food set in sumptuous surroundings. Oversized at 12x9,* **Glorious Food** *costs $40 and is probably more at home on a coffee table than in the kitchen—who would want to risk dribbling zabaglione cream across its lovely pages? Such lavish productions are probably most safely executed by trade publishers experienced with elaborately illustrated books; even at that, a very expensive book must be well targeted at its market to be successful. (Photo by Richard Jeffrey)*

To make use of color, you don't have to include all the shades of the rainbow. Although this photograph features relatively few and subtle colors, it would be totally uninteresting and unappetizing in black and white. (Photo by Bobby Greenlaw, food stylist, and Glen Millward, photographer)

Two-color printing can give the effect of color without all the expense. Casseroles and Salads, *from which this illustration by Craig Torlucci was taken, is printed half in blue and green ink (for the salad recipes), and half in gold and brown ink (for the casserole recipes). You can add additional color interest by printing on colored stock; just be careful not to sacrifice readability in the process.*

The importance of the art of presentation might be hard to appreciate from a simple text instruction: "Spread each slice of toast with layer of guacamole and arrange alternate rows of shrimp and avocado." (From Small Feasts)

Unless you had seen Eight Treasure Rice before, it would be almost impossible to understand how to make it from the written instructions alone. The photograph makes clear how to arrange the jujubes, apricots, and other fruit and nuts in a pattern. The photograph doesn't tell the whole story, however, because this dessert contains a half cup of red bean paste in the center, where you can't see it. (From The Cuisine of Cathay)

This is a photo they didn't use in Creative Soups and Salads. *The bright multicolored stripes and colorful ceramic crockery used here as a setting for a stew (in itself an interesting combination of shapes and colors) make this shot cluttered and busy and almost totally upstage the alleged focus of the picture, the stew itself. The photo they* did *use cropped out most of the place mat and eliminated the pile of bowls in front, then angled in from one side.*

Nostalgia Pepper Anchovies ("crunchy salted anchovies") must be seen to be believed. The Chinese eat this as a snack or a side dish. From an artistic point of view, the fine greenery against the dark-green cloth makes an effective background and contrasts nicely with the shiny masses of the anchovies. A recipe with such visually striking ingredients almost had to be displayed against a solid white plate. If you are not overly fond of anchovies, you may decide this picture demonstrates that some foods are better unphotographed. (From The Cuisine of Cathay)

A photographic backdrop gives you more control than you'd have if you set up your table in the woods, at the county fair, or in a field of daffodils. The sun can't go behind a cloud, it won't start raining, and the wind can't blow your accessories away! (From Farm Journal's Complete Decorating Book)

Small Feasts *features beautiful color photography—more than 65 pictures in 288 pages. But the 400 recipes in* Small Feasts *are relatively down-to-earth—soups, salads, sandwiches—and the backgrounds are very stark and simple for the most part. Only a few of the photographs feature accessories, so all our attention is focused on the food, which stands out beautifully.*

Sugar
Snap
pea

golden
beet

Royal
Chantenay carrot

roquette

Lo
Po
be

Short
'n Sweet

Burpless
cucumber

Buttercrunch
lettuce

Roma
tomato

Royal
Burgundy bean

Color is more psychologically important in the vending of food than of most subjects. Top left, by Laura Cornell, for an article in Cuisine *magazine on vegetable hybrids that are especially good for cooking; this watercolor style is a soft, pleasing, and evocative "frame" for the subject matter. Bottom left, done by Joan Blume for* The Early American Cookbook, *features antique utensils that reinforce the authenticity of the recipes. The simple yet vibrant style and the exquisite coloring do an amazing job of rendering life in a line drawing. The drawing* above, *done by Lauren Rosen for the* Toll House Heritage Cookbook, *reflects a homespun scene where fresh-baked cookies are a delightful fact of life—you can almost smell them.*

How the four-color printing process works: **Above:** *are the "separations" (printed in the four so-called process colors of black, yellow, blue, and red) that will ultimately be combined to make the final image or "composite"* **below.** *This photo was used as a general "motivational" illustration for sheer visual appeal in a salad cookbook. The variety of colors in this photograph seems to contradict my contention that the number of colors in a photo should be limited. But because the colors are the natural ones of the vegetables, the results do not seem garish or excessive. Though the arrangement here may seem random, it was carefully designed by the food stylist. (Photo by Bobby Greenlaw, food stylist, and Glen Millward, photographer)*

gether can create the effect of a third color in the shadow areas.

To reproduce full-color illustrations your printer should work from a transparency, or what we commonly think of as a color slide. If you start with a color painting, for example, it must be photographed to make the transparency. If you have a photographer take pictures for color illustrations, ask for transparencies, not for color prints.

A color separation is made from the transparency by making four copies of the transparency into screened halftones, each in one of the colors used for color printing: magenta, yellow, cyan (a shade of blue), and black. These separated images are "reunited" by printing them one on top of another in transparent inks, so that all together they look like the original, full-color subject. Because each color has to be printed on the paper separately, and because each colored image has to be lined up to fit perfectly on top of the others (it's known as being "in register"), color printing is much more expensive than black and white.

Another consideration in the cost of color illustrations is the total number of color separations that must be made, not just the total number of color pages you will have printed. Suppose, for example, that you have four color transparencies, each measuring four inches by five inches, that you want to reproduce on a single page in your book. A color separation of one four-by-five transparency costs about $100. Thus, the cost of separations for that one page would be $400. And that cost is separate from the actual printing. It costs roughly three times as much to print an illustrated page in full color as in black and white.

If you want the effect of color in your book without going to the trouble or expense of reproducing full color, you can have the book printed in colored ink or even in two colors of ink, which will give the illusion of more color. A single colored ink costs only a little more than black ink. Two colors will cost more, but still far less than full-color reproduction. Another inexpensive trick to give the illusion of color is to use colored ink (but only one color) on colored stock. Since our eyes are accustomed mostly to black and white in printing, we will have the impression of more color.

Regardless of the method of reproduction, the results can never be any better than the original. During my days at the newspaper I was mystified when people brought in photographs that were out of focus, badly composed, or lacking contrast, and assured me that the pictures would look better when they were printed. On the contrary: each step beyond the original takes a little more away from a picture. The first copy is less good than the original; a copy of the copy is still less good. Each "time removed" reduces sharpness and color intensity. For this reason it's a poor idea to try to reproduce a picture that has already been reproduced in a book or magazine. So, whether you decide to use photographs or drawings, in black and white or in color, the quality of the original is most important.

If the illustrations are black and white photographs, look for sharp contrast and good detail in the grays. The blacks should be truly black; the whites should be bright white, not muddy; the shades in between, the grays, should be so well defined that you see many gradations. The focus should be sharp, not blurred or fuzzy.

Focus is important in color transparencies too. And the colors in the picture should be faithful to the colors of the food. Red apples should be red, not orangish; green lettuce should be clear green, not faintly blue.

With original art, especially line drawings, be sure that the pictures are not smudged and that the lines clearly define what is to be shown. Although I would not rule out pencil drawings, pen and ink reproduces more sharply.

Remember that too much detail in line drawings, too many objects in black and white photos, and too many patterns in color photographs and paintings all reproduce poorly in cookbook size. Instead of reproducing as interesting pictures they shrink to confusing clutter.

In addition to the technical points of printing and reproduction, you must consider the style and the tone of the illustrations. Let me offer you some suggestions, which were given to me by illustrators, art directors, and book designers.

● Choose art that is not too fussy or cute. Just as you decorate a dress with small amounts of lace rather than smothering it in billows, be sparing with very elaborate or intricate drawings.

● The line drawings used to illustrate processes or devices should be simple and avoid extraneous lines.

● The art should fit the tone of the book. A book that treats old family recipes as serious history, for instance, would look silly if illustrated with cartoon drawings.

● The pictures in a cookbook should not overpower the subject matter. Unless you are producing an art book, remember that the recipes are the main reason for the book's existence. Don't let the book become top-heavy with illustrations.

● Try to find ways to inject a sense of life and motion into all cookbook art. The illustrations should reflect the feeling that this is real food, to be prepared and eaten by real people. One reason line drawings work so well in cookbook illustration is that the artist has the means to convey action. And one reason elaborate photography is so difficult is that it often looks as if it belongs with the plastic mannequins in the department-store windows—too perfect to be real.

Never underestimate the power of editors. They have a voice not only in your text, but also in how your book is illustrated. This is a drawing that didn't make it into a Weight Watchers cookbook because the checkered background was too busy and because the shoes beside the tablecloth were "too suggestive." A later drawing turned the tablecloth white and eliminated the shoes. I agree with the first judgment but feel sad about the shoes. Somehow I think the suggestion that if one sticks to her diet she'll end up frolicking barefoot on the picnic green would be a great incentive to a Weight Watcher. (Illustration by Janet Nelson)

Haute Cuisine

The business of arranging food so that it looks appetizing in photographs is called "food styling." In a publishing house where food photography is taken very seriously, the team responsible for the pictures may include an art director, a food stylist, and a food photographer. Often the prices that food stylists and food photographers command for their work seem high. The reason, in the words of an advertising-agency director who often uses such people, is that food stylists and photographers "have only one product to sell." These advertising agencies whose clients include food producers and processors create some of the most magnificent food photography available.

If you want photographs to be part of your book and if it's your responsibility to have them made, the most desirable option is to hire a food stylist and a photographer with experience in photographing food. In a major city you can probably find all the help you need by consulting the Yellow Pages or contacting an advertising agency that specializes in graphics for leads. In smaller communities you may not be able to find such specialists, but you may be surprised at how much talent you can track down in unlikely places. The local newspaper offices may be a good place to inquire, as well as home economics extension offices and high school and college home economics departments.

If you have to style the food for photography yourself, prepare to be patient and devious. Making photographed food look perfect includes all kinds of tricks.

The first thing you must accept is that you won't be able to eat some of the food you prepare for photography. Some food is not cooked to doneness because it gets too soft and loses its shape. Instead, the food is cooked just enough to brown it. Sometimes it is not cooked at all, but is colored or otherwise treated to make it look cooked. The old pros had all kinds of tricks: substituting shaving cream for whipped cream; using a blowtorch to brown the skin of a turkey perfectly; pouring lighter fluid instead of brandy over a plum pudding to make the flame brighter; and filling crepes with raw rice before saucing them so that they would hold their shape.

Today, government regulations require food to be prepared for advertising photographs exactly as it would be prepared for eating, and since we all learn and borrow from each other, this regulation will inevitably affect cookbook photography too. We will learn new ways to make food edible as well as photogenic.

Here are some suggestions from food photographers and stylists for getting the best possible pictures for your cookbook:

- For color photography, plan settings that contrast colors or harmonize a range of colors.
- For black-and-white photography, contrast interesting textures and shapes.
- Avoid attempts at perfect symmetry.
- Use patterned dishes sparingly.
- When using patterned dishes or linens, limit yourself to one pattern per picture.
- Make sure you and the photographer agree on what is to be the center of interest in a picture.
- When working with fragile foods such as cakes, ice cream pies, meringues, and gelatin molds, make at least two so that you will have a perfect one to use in the final shot. The first one is apt to wear out as you arrange and rearrange the setting and the lights.
- In photographing soups and stews, save a few barely cooked ingredients to float on the top at the last minute.
- Don't line up such small foods as egg rolls, stuffed mushrooms, deviled eggs, and cupcakes like soldiers on the plate. Instead, try to arrange them in pleasing patterns; rely on garnishes, napkins, and doilies to soften the "naked plate" look.
- Don't try to crowd too many objects into a picture; keep it simple.
- Make some test shots with a Polaroid camera to see how the picture will look before you take the final photograph. This will give you an idea of the differences between how the food looks to a camera and how it appears to your eye.

If you must have photographs, the important thing is to begin the adventure with a willingness to handle food in what seem like unorthodox ways; remember that a camera and a diner make wildly different demands on food. I remember vividly that I had to overcome my concepts of how food should be served when I wanted to set up a picture of a complicated bean soup in a six-quart tureen. The tureen was perfect for the picture, but I really didn't want to make six quarts of bean soup, so I devised a jerry-rig of upside-down custard cups to support a flat cake pan just inside the top of the tureen. Filled with just four cups of soup, the tureen looked full. But because the cake pan didn't fit snugly against the sides of the tureen, the soup leaked below the level of the top and revealed the edges of the pan if we dallied too long. I kept stirring in extra water dyed with soy sauce, floating more half-raw beans on top of the soup, and urging the photographer to get his head out from under that silly rag and take the picture. When I told this story to a food stylist, I got a lecture about the importance of being patient and allowing a photographer to work at his own pace.

Black-and-white photographs don't always do a good job of making a dish look so good you want to try it. This photograph of Eggs Benedict was used for publicity for the book Brunch *by Christie Williams. The original, in the book, is in full color. In black and white, the sauce looks cold and gummy; in color it appeared warm and tasty.*

Taking black-and-white photographs of food is even more of a challenge than making good color photographs. It may be because we have become so accustomed to seeing pictures of food in color that it often looks unappetizing in black and white. To give you an idea of this, I have been studying a full-color advertisement from the California Raisin Advisory Board, intended to suggest new and presumably appetizing uses for raisins. The photograph in the ad shows a large black kettle of pork and beans with raisins sprinkled on top. A few wisps of steam are wafting from the open pot. Next to the pot, a pork chop glazed in a shiny orange sauce, dotted with raisins, rests on a wide spatula with a blue handle. And on an orange and white polka-dot napkin, next to the pork chop, is a cheeseburger on an open toasted sesame bun, garnished with lettuce and raisins. The advertisement is bordered in blue and decorated with a regular pattern of raisins around the edge.

Now try to imagine the entire picture in black and white. The kettle is black. The beans are gray. The raisins are black and the steam is gray.

The spatula handle is black or dark gray; so is the orange background of the polka-dot napkin. The pork chop is dark gray and the raisins on the chop are black. The meat in the cheeseburger and the raisins are both black. So is the lettuce garnish. The bun is gray. The border around the ad is gray, with a pattern of black raisins. Yum, yum.

I have worked (patiently) with photographers to overcome other challenges such as photographing a bowl of cottage cheese in black and white so that it didn't look like a bowl of oatmeal; photographing a bowl of oatmeal so that it didn't look like a dead volcano; and finding a way to keep flat biscuits from looking like drops in a cow pasture. The answers lie in garnishes, accessories, and the artful tilting and arranging of the ingredients.

Let me warn you at once that if you are working in black and white you should avoid that most ubiquitous of garnishes—parsley. Like the lettuce on the cheeseburger, it will look black. In black and white the most successful garnishes are those with contrasts of color and distinctive markings, but not so elaborate that they cast strange-looking shadows. For salads and vegetable dishes, thin whole scallions photograph well because they range in color from near white to dark green and photograph as gradations from white to black. For desserts, cottage cheese, yogurt, and some entrees that use orange sections and partly peeled oranges can be effective because of the varied textures of the peel and segments and the added interest supplied by the fine white threads that adhere to the skin of the orange segments. As you look at foods, imagine them in black and white. More ideas will come to you.

What you can do in black and white with dried peaches, tomato soup, and grilled-cheese sandwiches is beyond me. Still, I imagine that nobody would see a need to illustrate those things in cookbooks anyway, except those people I told you about who wanted to warn novice cooks to pit the avocados.

When you work in color, the important thing is not to go overboard with too many colors just because it is possible. My best (or worst) example of this error comes not from the field of food but from newspapers, back when color printing was just becoming popular on the front pages of daily papers. It was the first issue of a new paper in the community, and it was supposed to be a very big deal that the paper was going to have color on the front page. So was the fact that the town would finally have a morning paper.

In that first edition, the entire top half of the front page was festooned with a headline in huge colored letters: GOOD MORNING! Every letter was a different color.

For subsequent issues, the editor sent the photographer out with

Getting flat cookies to look like they belong on a table and not in a cow pasture is especially difficult in black and white. Here the result was not fully successful. Baking a pecan half in the center of each cookie would have helped—I think. (From Whole Grains: Grow, Harvest and Cook Your Own *by Sara Pitzer)*

balloons of many colors to blow up and work into his pictures some-how so that the readers could appreciate the paper's fine color repro-duction. It wasn't too bad for the county fair or stories about local schools, but the National Organization for Women didn't care much for the added touch of color in the coverage of their march for the ERA.

With food, the counterparts are all the obvious temptations: too many red radishes around the yogurt, serving dishes decorated with six-color designs, sandwiches decorated with little American flags (ex-cept for the Fourth of July), and multicolored bouquets of flowers next to the chocolate marble cake. You will stay out of trouble if you remem-ber that nothing should detract from the food, not even its garnishes. Props and background pieces are helpful, but only if you use them sparingly.

An excellent way to test the effectiveness of the photograph you have set up, whether for color or for black and white, is to take a Polar-oid shot of the scene. This will show you at once approximately how the finished photograph will look.

Cuisine Art

Working with an artist seems somewhat easier to me, but it can also present a few challenges. The main thing an artist needs is a sense of how *everything* is supposed to look. That includes the crumbs from the cake on the plate, the way steam rises when you drain pasta, the shape of a drumstick after it's cut off the bird, and the way your fanny sticks out when you lean over to put something into the oven.

In addition to examples of actual prepared foods, cookbook artists rely on what they call "scrap art." The more and better scrap you can provide them, the better their illustrations. Scrap is simply pictures from everywhere—photo albums, magazines, newspapers—showing all these angles and shapes and motions. I have personally provided the scrap for the fannies in oven pictures for three different cookbooks.

It happened because I gave a cookbook illustrator a handful of snapshots left over from the photographs taken to illustrate my cook-book on whole grains. One of them showed me in work shoes and blue jeans, leaning over to put a cookie sheet full of homemade pretzels into the oven. In the photograph that went into my book, the art director mercifully cropped off most of the sticking-out fanny, but that other il-lustrator took the original and went wild. In one illustration the cook is leaning over to pull a pizza from the oven. She's wearing high heels, peg-leg pants, and a ruffled blouse, but that's unmistakably my fanny filling the rest of the picture. In another illustration the cook is bending over to put bread pans into the oven. She's wearing sneakers and trim pants—and *my* fanny. After I have mentioned so many cookbooks by name, giving all kinds of specific details about them, you're bound to notice that I have been uncharacteristically vague about the two that contain the illustrations drawn from scrap. But I'm sure you'll understand.

To give you some less blatant examples of the way artists use scrap, I have seen them use a Polaroid to take photographs of people's hands folding a won ton. I have seen them pose a model over a table with a glass and a pitcher to get the right angles and attitudes for pouring. Any pictures you provide to show these kinds of activities will serve as foundation material for an illustrator. You can also help an illustrator tremendously by talking to her or him about what is important in a particular recipe, what is difficult in a process, and what is to be emphasized in the look of a given food. The more the illustrator understands about the whole cooking process, the better she or he can communicate the essence without words. In line drawings it is important for the artist to know exactly what you want to show, because in that kind of illustration many nonessential details are left out of the picture.

Line drawings are used in cookbook illustrations in three distinctly different ways. The first and most practical use is to show in realistic and easily understood fashion how to do something, such as cutting vegetables or cleaning squid. A second use is to give a general impression of the ingredients of cooked foods. Often such drawings suggest not a single recipe, but an entire class of recipes. A nice example of this kind of drawing is found in the chapter headings of *The New 365 Ways to Cook Hamburger and Other Ground Meat*. Artistically you can't do much with a lump of ground beef, but the artist, Lauren Rosen, manages to show uses for it without subjecting us to the fine details of each tiny ground bit. The illustration in the heading for "Sandwiches" includes a hamburger garnished with sauce, sliced onion, and bacon. A loaf of French bread is shown beside the hamburger to suggest other possibilities that might be developed in the recipes of that chapter. The drawing for "Casseroles and Oven Dishes" centers around some indeterminate concoction in a casserole, which contains mushrooms and possibly noodles. Around the casserole are arranged a box of noodles, a can of tomatoes, and a couple of potatoes, to imply that ground-meat casseroles need not be limited to noodle mixtures.

A third, more subtle use of line drawings in cookbooks is to create a feeling in the reader about the entire process of preparing the recipes. In the James Beard books *Beard on Pasta* and *Beard on Bread*, Karl Stuecklen's drawings illustrate such processes as kneading; beyond that, they create a sense of action, enjoyment, and pleasure. The bread book contains mostly drawings that show how to shape and handle the various breads; the pasta book shows basic processes too, but has more drawings that communicate the feeling that making pasta is as much fun as eating it. Stuecklen's jacket illustrations are in color and more detailed, but still reflect an almost abstract sense of how much fun James Beard has cooking. I think the potential buyer begins to feel that if she buys this book, she's going to have as much fun as James Beard does.

Somehow, original art works better than photographs when you want to get across more than just the notion of a gorgeous meal. Of all the cookbook art I have ever seen, I have been most affected by the paintings of Kate Barnes, which illustrate *Cross Creek Kitchens* by Sally Morrison. As I mentioned earlier, the book is a thoroughly nostalgic collection of recipes with narrative about the pleasures of living close to nature, growing your own vegetables and fruits, and working in old-fashioned country kitchens. Most of the illustrations show not food, but the kitchens, gardens, and out-of-doors surroundings of the author and the illustrator. I've tried several of the recipes in the book and found them outstandingly good—unusual and delicious. (In particular I liked the Tangerine Chiffon Pie, which turned out billowy and light and full of a better-than-orange flavor.) But more than that, I've turned back to look at the illustrations again and again and I've developed an itch to move back to the country, grow my own vegetables, and cook in an old-fashioned kitchen. The overall effect came from the near-perfect unity of the art and the narrative and from the skill with which the paintings were executed. And as if to prove that no rule is ever hard and fast, the paintings were all done originally in color, but only the cover of the book is reproduced in color. The paintings inside are reproduced in black and white. Ordinarily, color photographs and color paintings make disappointing black-and-white reproductions.

This observation about color pictures leads me to comment further on what generally does *not* work in cookbook art. Avoid photographs of people, especially women, demonstrating cooking procedures. They will make your book look dated within a year or two because hair styles and fashions change so rapidly. As a child of the fifties myself, nothing embarrasses me more than to flip through the pages of a cookbook and find a picture of somebody who looks like Sandra Dee, wearing a circle skirt with a cinch belt, made up with dark lipstick and perfectly penciled eyebrows, and coiffed in a bubble hairdo. Worse yet, she's holding an old, old electric mixer, and I can tell that at the time it was brand new. So don't show appliances in cookbook photographs either (unless it's an appliance book), because they, too, date the book.

Another caveat: some food doesn't lend itself to being photographed. This feeling may stem from our preconceived notions about what is nice to eat and what's unmentionable, but pictures of tongues, kidneys, sweetbreads, and brains, showing every biological detail, don't appeal to most of us, however much we may enjoy these foods once they are prepared. I know someone who claims she saw appetizing pictures of these organ meats, but since I haven't seen them, I remain unconvinced.

This discussion of cookbook art will not turn you into an illustrator, but along with the pictures and captions in this chapter, it will help you decide what you want to do about illustrating your own cookbook and let you talk knowledgeably with the people you approach for help.

As I said in my discussion of food styling, how you find an artist or photographer for your cookbook depends on where you live. In cities where people specialize in such work, the telephone book or a referral service is the most direct route. But in smaller areas, and sometimes in cities, too, you will find that the old-buddy system is still the best way to get what you want. Ask people who should know where you can find an artist or photographer who has worked with food. Ah, but who should know? Home economists; newspaper and magazine editors; art directors, other photographers and artists; college teachers in departments of advertising, art, food science, and photography. And don't forget cookbook publishers. The country seems to be dotted with small trade publishers and self-publishers. The people in your bookstore or library can help you contact one nearby.

When you find an artist or photographer you think might be suitable, ask to see samples of her or his work. If your candidate has not worked previously with food, ask her to prepare you a sample picture on speculation. Most people are glad to do this if they believe the effort stands a reasonable chance of leading to a job. In this way you also have a chance to be sure you're dealing with someone who will be responsive to your wishes.

How much do you pay for illustrations? The closest I can come to an answer is that you should expect to pay the going rate in your area for other kinds of photography and art. That sounds terribly vague, but I have seen prices for a good food photograph range from $15 to $500. Quality was not the determining factor—the situation of the photographer was. Similarly, artists may charge anywhere from a few dollars to a few hundred or thousand dollars for their work, depending on their experience and inclinations. Generally, if you hire a person who does this kind of work for a living, it will cost you more than if you find an amateur or hobbyist. On the other hand, while the work from either may be equally good, you will usually get what you need from a professional with much less grief.

Here I must state strongly that unless you are a professional or a very talented amateur photographer or artist, it is not a good idea to do your own illustrations. You should use your own only if you know that you can produce top-quality photographs or drawings. Inferior pictures are worse than no pictures at all. They will ruin your book. And since most of us have trouble being objective about the quality of our own work, especially in hobbies, I recommend getting some advice about the quality of your pictures from an art teacher or director or from a professional photographer, should you decide you want to use your own. Producing cookbook art requires skill that usually has to be developed through practice.

Two other sources of art deserve mentioning here: one a source of photographs, the other of line drawings. The publicity departments of advertising agencies and product-promotion organizations often have test kitchens and studios in which they not only create and test recipes, but also photograph the finished products. Often they will let you have color transparencies or black-and-white photos. Such organizations vary in what they will do for freelance writers, but in general their job is to promote their clients' products as widely as possible, and they tend to be cooperative.

The best way to figure out whom to approach is to consult the *Standard Directory of Advertisers* in your public library. This amazing book lists an incredible number of food companies, along with information about what agencies each company uses (some use more than one), the addresses of those agencies, and the name of a contact who handles the account. Since some food-promotion organizations do not use advertising agencies but do their own publicity, you should also consult the *Encyclopedia of Associations* and the directory for the *National Trade and Professional Associations of the United States,* which I mentioned in my discussion of food and product promotion organizations in Chapter One.

Advertising is also the source, indirectly, for inexpensive or free line drawings known as "clip art." Clip art drawings are assembled by category in books and magazines to be cut out, or clipped, and pasted onto a page for illustration. The most common use of clip art is by newspapers in creating advertisements for local clients who do not use advertising agencies. Small agencies also may use clip art in making up camera-ready ads for their clients. The drawings are usually repeated in a variety of sizes for various-sized spaces. These simple drawings can sometimes be effective in breaking up a page of type in a cookbook.

One rich but seldom-used source of free art for cookbooks can be found in the public library. Most larger ones have some very old cookbooks in the public domain illustrated with wonderful, detailed pictures from before the days of photography. These examples are from Tales of the Table: A History of Western Cuisine *by Barbara Norman.*

You can find books of clip art at well-stocked art-supply stores, especially those that cater to students in advertising, or your local newspaper may be willing to give you the clips you need. And Dover Books (31 E. Second St., Mineola, NY 11501) publishes quite a few reasonably priced books of clip art.

If you decide your cookbook doesn't need to be illustrated, remember that many other cookbook authors have decided the same thing. Maybe you can work up your own version of the comment with which Christie Williams introduced her "What's Cookin'?" series on cooking with a food processor. She said that there were no pictures of the recipes in her books so that the cook at home wouldn't feel bad if her attempts turned out looking less than picture perfect.

I'll mention one other interesting source of free art. Most of the larger public libraries have some very old cookbooks, long since out of copyright and in the public domain, that are illustrated with wonderful old pictures from before the days of photography—ornate etchings of food scenes, elaborate drawings of pastries, and a wealth of other food pictures that would add grace and a hint of antiquity to some present-day cookbooks. If you find such books, they may be in the rare-book room, which means you cannot take them from the library. In that case, ask the library to make a photostat of the pictures you like. You can reproduce beautifully from that.

CHAPTER *8*

Beyond Cookbooks

*P*eople get around to writing cookbooks in funny ways. Look what happened to Marion Brown. She'd never thought of writing a cookbook until she became a women's page editor for a local newspaper. Like most newspapers, hers carried a regular column of recipes, contributed by readers, which she edited. Because of her involvement with that column, the auxiliary of her church asked her to edit and design a cookbook for the benefit of the church, the Episcopal Church of the Holy Comforter in Burlington, North Carolina.

Sometime after that, she took a creative writing class at the University of North Carolina, where her instructor became interested in her church cookbook. He sent her to meet the director of the University of North Carolina Press to talk about publishing a cookbook that would be *the* authority on the classic cooking of the South. Then she really got involved: the secretary of the local chamber of commerce wrote to chambers of commerce in every Southern state, which brought her the names of regional cookbooks and the help of all kinds of people, from librarians to broadcasters. She went to hotels and restaurants for recipes and—most difficult of all in the South—she convinced many families to share their old, treasured secret recipes.

After more than five years of research, which Ms. Brown says "involved thousands of miles of travel and many thousands of letters," she had collected more than 25,000 recipes. "Needless to say," she added, "the manuscript was culled." Her *Southern Cookbook*, a whopper containing nearly 1,000 recipes, was first published in 1951. She revised and updated it in 1968, and since then it's been reprinted five times. And it all started with a recipe column in the local newspaper.

Pretty much the same thing happened to Miriam Ungerer. She worked as editor for a fashion magazine where the staff was so small that, as she puts it, "I also art directed and changed all the typewriter ribbons." And that's where she published her first food piece. "Since the staff was mostly me," she said, "I wrote the food things under the name Phoebe Lancaster, my daughter's first name and my maiden name."

As she became increasingly interested in food, she wrote about it more and more. After living (and cooking) all over the United States and abroad, she settled into writing a regular food column called "Long Island Larder" for the East Hampton *Star*. In her column she concentrated on ways to cook what was in season in her area.

A roving editor for a small publishing house saw her column and asked her to write a book. She said, "I wrote it mostly for the people I saw in the summer in and around East Hampton, but it had a decent success nationally. Perhaps focusing on a specific audience is a good idea." Her most recent book, *Country Food*, comprises work first published in somewhat different form in her newspaper columns.

One Thing Leads to Another

My first book, too, was the indirect result of writing for newspapers. I was feature editor of the *Pennsylvania Mirror*, responsible for filling several pages a day—sometimes a burden, especially on Friday nights, when I had to fill up not only Saturday's paper but also Monday morning's, if I didn't want to work Sunday night. Although other reporters wrote for me, I wrote many of the features myself.

One Friday, when I really wanted to get out early to go to the Grange Fair, a story I had been counting on to fill a lot of column space fell through. The only thing I knew enough about to write fast at the last minute, without doing research or interviews, was cooking. My special interest at the time was natural foods, so I gave myself a headline, *Straight from Nature*, and wrote about eighteen column inches to go with it.

I still remember that one of the reporters walked by as I was writing, and, seeing that I was working without notes, said, "Are you just making that up as you go along?" I nodded and kept typing. I wrote about how to use natural foods, made some wisecracks about how hard it was to keep the kids from sneaking out at night for Twinkies and Dr Peppers, and filled the rest of the space with recipes I liked and knew by heart.

People liked it. They called the office and wrote me letters and sent me recipes. The next thing I knew, I was a food columnist. Later, I went freelance and sold the columns to a couple of other newspapers in the state; then I was a *syndicated* food columnist.

The columns were humorous, mainly because nobody but my

mother has ever let me do anything with a straight face, but also because I thought people were turned off when a subject like natural foods was treated too solemnly. Food should be fun. My friends have always insisted that I have a weird sense of humor, so I started to send my columns to a friend on the West Coast who was the president of a national radio syndicating company, because he has a weird sense of humor too. And one day, when my mind was on something else altogether, he called up and asked me to write a radio program for Christmas, plus a little premium cookbook to go with it, for participating radio stations to give to their listeners. The show and the cookbook would be called *Christmas at Our House*.

I met with him and a New York advertising agent at one of those resorts in the Poconos where the main athletic activity is napping in the row of rockers on the porch. The advertising man who was supposed to promote the show and the book to radio stations said to me, "No offense and nothing against your talent, but nobody knows who you are. How can I make it sound like a big deal to have a cookbook written by you?"

Well, if *he* didn't know, I certainly didn't. None of this had been my idea in the first place. But then he perked up. "I know," he said, "We'll call you a culinary expert. 'Culinary expert Sara Pitzer.' "

He did it. Before long, publicity material for the cookbook *Christmas at Our House*, written by culinary expert Sara Pitzer, was circulating all over the country. That little book opened up all kinds of other doors for me in the years that followed.

Create Your Own Opportunities

As you may begin to see, food writing doesn't have to begin or end with cookbooks. Writing for newspapers and magazines, publishing little premium cookbooks, and producing specialty food brochures can all make it much easier to break into the world of commercial cookbook publishing. As an editor who spent years at Prentice-Hall said, "I always am inclined to look at a cookbook proposal more seriously if it came from a writer who has worked in other media and can show me samples."

Nor are the possibilities limited to print. Other outlets that can provide the same kind of credentials, fun, and sometimes even a little money include television demonstration shows; giving cooking demonstrations for gourmet shops and health-food stores; teaching cooking classes; and appearing on radio shows.

The great thing about all these possibilities is that getting into them is mainly a matter of ingenuity, persistence, and luck. There is no one right way. In food writing, more than in any other area in which I've worked, one thing leads to another; you get the chance to do things because you've done things. It's a weird world. You have to be ready to grab the opportunities when they come along. I've been lucky that way. I once landed a cooking demonstration series on public television because the director always ate Thanksgiving and Christmas dinners at my house, and she observed that my hands "looked like they knew what they were doing." I fell into the opportunity to do a radio show because the person who had done it before moved away; except for me, no one was left in the office who knew anything at all about cooking.

But this is more than a string of stories about serendipity. I have two points to make here. First, serendipity takes you only so far. When the opportunities come, you have to seize them immediately and with almost brazen confidence. You can't stop to agonize about what might go wrong, and you have to work your tail off to make it right. The *Christmas at Our House* cookbook had to be finished in three days. Looking back, I don't know quite how I managed it, but the only mistake that slipped in was that my seven-layer cookies had only six layers. It's hard to overestimate the importance of that little book to me; it introduced me to a whole series of magazine and book editors from whom I subsequently received assignments. I couldn't have used the book that way if it had been a bad job. In food writing one thing leads to another, but only if you do a good job. Do it poorly and one thing leads to nothing.

Second, the great danger of a serendipitous life is that you will begin to count on the neat opportunities coming to you rather than going out and pursuing them. Sometimes I wonder where I would be now if I had learned that years sooner. For a long time I waited for these lucky breaks to come my way, and moped around during those idle periods when none did. For me it took a move from the East Coast to California to learn to pursue opportunities aggressively. The mortgage payment was my greatest motivator. I taught cooking classes in California because I went to the store and asked to be one of their instructors. I was hired by a cookbook company there because I called them up and said I could sell their books. I received cookbook contracts because I sent proposals to publishers. I had a column in a regional magazine because I went to their office, recipes in hand.

If I, after years of counting on getting good breaks, could learn how to go out and create my own opportunities to publish my food writing, anybody can do it. *You* certainly can. Here's the story of a woman whose ingenuity in pursuit of opportunity serves as a paradigm.

Barbara Christensen knew that the *Benecia Herald* had no regular food column. She knew also that editors are always being approached by somebody who wants to write some kind of a column for a newspaper, and tend to become hardened against these suggestions. So she invited W.A. Silva, the editor of the *Herald,* to lunch—not lunch on the credit card, but lunch at her house, a lunch she cooked and served herself. She served him a series of delectable dishes, each beautifully garnished and perfectly prepared. At the end of the meal she showed him her recipes and made her pitch for a food column in his newspaper. He went for it. I know the story because Mr. Silva wrote it himself and used it to introduce her and her cooking column to the *Herald's* readers.

In St. Petersburg, Florida, Jo Anne Parke went to the *St. Petersburg Times* to look for a reporter's job and found that what they needed was a food editor. "I can write and I can edit and I'm a good cook," she said. She showed them how she would handle it, and thus became the food editor of the *St. Petersburg Times.*

What these women did was spot a need, demonstrate the ability to fill it, and then present a plan for doing it. All successful proposals work on some variation of this strategy.

Newspapers Are Hungry Markets

One reason so many of these stories involve newspapers is that newspapers are such an outstandingly good outlet for food writing. We have a lot of newspapers and they gobble material voraciously. Editors are always looking for bright writing that will interest their readers. It's true that the big-city dailies have been dwindling in number and that those remaining are hard to break into. But in their place a proliferation of suburban newspapers, community newspapers, weekly papers, feature papers, and "shoppers" (handouts consisting mostly of advertising), are vying for readers and writers. Many of these publications are put out by small staffs and don't pay a lot. Their focus usually is local rather than national, and they're hungry for good material that people will want to read. They're receptive to food writing because people like to read about food.

In communities outside the major metropolitan areas, those newspapers that publish their own weekend supplements often use freelance writing. And the special tabloids devoted to holidays and special events, such as weddings, are usually loaded onto editors who arc already carrying full schedules; often they are delighted to be able to buy some appropriate articles about food. Some don't pay, but are still glad to have the material if you will contribute it. They are worth your time, especially if you haven't published much food writing before, because with each piece you publish, paid or not, you accumulate valuable credits.

Magazine Markets

In addition to newspapers, consider approaching all kinds of magazines. Of course the big national magazines—*Woman's Day, Family Circle, Gourmet,* and *Good Housekeeping*—come to mind first. They carry many food articles and sometimes run recipe contests, such as the *Woman's Day* Silver Spoon Contest. But these are not the best place to start. Most of their food writing is done by their own staffs or by long-time professional food writers. Even when they consider your freelance work or when you enter major contests, you're in competition with thousands of other submissions. That need not discourage you from trying, but you should save some of your effort for all those other magazines that use food articles even though they are not food magazines. You'll encounter less competition there.

Start checking the magazines that come to your house, those that clutter the racks in waiting rooms of medical people and beauty shops, those that are tucked into the pocket of your airplane seat, those that are artfully arranged on coffee tables in the lounges of car dealerships, those in your friends' bathrooms, those on the magazine shelves in the supermarket, and even those published by the companies where your friends work. You will be astonished at how many publications carry food articles. Somebody's sending recipes to every publication from *Field and Stream* to *Friends—the Chevy Owners' Magazine*.

If you decide to look seriously for places to send your food writing, try to find magazines besides the slick national-circulation giants. Some magazines have national circulation but are devoted to a narrow field of interest; others are more general but are circulated only to certain people.

Look for magazines of general content circulated to specific audiences, such as the *Rotarian,* which goes to all members of Rotary, and *Organic Gardening* are examples of magazines on special subjects.

Look for magazines of general content circulated to particular audiences, such as the *Rotarian,* which goes to all members of Rotary, and *50 Plus,* for people in their middle and later years. Similarly, check into the general-interest magazines offered to customers of insurance companies, car manufacturers, military personnel, and so on. *Ford Times* is a classic example.

Look for trade journals that are written for the practitioners of specific professions and trades. In book publishing, the leading trade journal is *Publisher's Weekly*. Librarians read *Choice* and *Library Journal*. The journals for the textile industry include *Bobbin*. And to give a far-out example, people who sell miniatures and doll houses subscribe to *Miniatures Dealer*.

Don't forget the church and religious magazines. Baptist to Roman Catholic, all those readers eat.

As you systematically collect and study these publications, you will see that some use food writing all the time, while others apparently never do. Probably your best chances lie with those who already have a history of carrying recipes and food articles, but it never hurts to try out a "just right" idea on a publication in which you've never seen a word about food. For example, although I have never seen a word about food in *Miniatures Dealer*, I've noticed that many of the people who work in miniature tend to be overweight, maybe because such delicate, painstaking work doesn't give them a chance to burn off many calories. I've always thought that magazine might welcome an article dealing with the special diet problems of miniaturists, including some recipes, or an article suggesting how owners of miniatures shops could increase business by starting a miniaturists' recipe exchange.

Cook Up Some Publicity

When you approach any of these magazines, *Runner's World* or *Ford Times* or *Miniatures Dealer*, remember that each has special requirements toward which all their writing, including food writing, must be slanted. You can't take an article about cooking and just drop it into any available publication, any more than you can place an unslanted article about anything else in different magazines. *Runner's World*, for instance, is concerned about recipes that build health and provide energy. They would probably not run a diet recipe for cutting calories, but they would use recipes for runners who are "carbohydrate loading" before a marathon. And if you're not sure what carbohydrate loading is, you haven't studied the magazine well enough to write for it. In short, it's not enough to send off a letter or an article to a publication you've heard might use food pieces. You have to study the magazine to see what kind of food writing it might use and what its readers' attitudes toward food would be. There's no point in sending *Organic Gardening* an article on how to make great casserole combinations with canned soups!

To me, magazines are obvious places to sell recipes and food writing. They're a good place to start, but I think we should also explore the less tried possibilities of writing for food growers and manufacturers, writing premium cookbooks, and writing for the makers of small appli-

Even the lowly sweet potato has an organization to promote it. The South Carolina Sweet Potato Board published a recipe for Sweet Potato Pie in newspaper advertisements. (From Cross Creek Kitchens—Seasonal Recipes and Reflections, *by Sally Morrison, with illustrations by Kate Barnes.)*

205

ances and kitchen equipment. These are uncertain areas because no two operate alike. Big companies like Hunt-Wesson hire big agencies like Botsford-Ketchum, home of Maggie's Kitchen in San Francisco, to conduct elaborate recipe-development programs and to produce exquisite photographs that show the products to advantage. Not a good place to take your first set of recipes. But on a more modest scale, every region in this country produces some food product as a mainstay of its farming industry: chickens in Maryland, milk products in New Jersey, peaches in Georgia, beans in Michigan and Idaho, and apples in Washington. They are represented by the boards, councils, associations, and cooperatives I mentioned in Chapter One. Not all of them use expensive advertising agencies or teams of home economists; the resources of many are much more modest. As I paw through my box full of recipe clippings and booklets, I find brochures, little cards, multifold flyers, and single sheets, all with recipes for cooking a single product. At random I see material from the Gulf South Atlantic Fisheries and Development Foundation, Inc.; the Seafood Marketing Authority; the Idaho Bean Commission; the Western Growers Association; and the South Carolina Egg Board. All these handouts are quite modest. I have somewhat more elaborate ones from a prune producer, a manufacturer of Chinese sauces, a Cornish hen company, and turkey raisers.

I also have pamphlets for my slow cooker, my blender, my electric frying pan, my crepe maker, and my clay pot. Somebody writes all these things. Why not you? General Electric and Westinghouse probably don't need you, but the makers of many smaller items and the marketing people in many smaller companies might. A few years ago, Gourmet-Topf, a manufacturer of clay pots in competition with Romertopf, needed someone to edit recipes sent in by users to create a little cookbook that would encourage more people to cook in clay. And the company that makes Apollo strudel leaves (phyllo) has printed right on the box an invitation to send them your own recipes for using the product. If you use any products or pieces of equipment with especially good results, write to the company and see if you can interest them in your recipes. The worst they can do is say no.

Another kind of little cookbook you can write is the premium book, which businesses and organizations like banks, insurance companies, and department stores use as incentives in promotions. Watch to see who in your area engages in a lot of promotion; then think up a way they could use a cookbook in one of their promotions and offer to write it for them. If I wanted to write a premium cookbook right now, I think I would approach the local RV dealership that advertises the most heavily and is always running some kind of special gimmick, and offer them an idea for a seasonal or holiday cookbook to be given to everybody who comes to the showroom.

When you get these ideas, don't be shy about approaching people with them; they may not even know they want a cookbook until you tell them. Whenever you go to a businessperson with an idea for improving business and customer relations, you're doing that person a favor.

This discussion doesn't even scratch the surface of possible markets for food writing in your area. The best idea is to read everything in print to see whether it's a potential market for your recipes. Look at every food producer and equipment maker with the thought of sending them your recipes. Look at every organization as a possible buyer for a premium cookbook.

Your market potential isn't limited to print. Don't forget local television and radio stations. Some have trouble filling awkward times, like Sunday mornings, with good local programs. A cooking show might be the answer. Department stores with appliance centers need demonstrators, especially around holidays. Gourmet shops and natural-food stores can increase their business by offering cooking lessons. If they don't have a kitchen, offer to bring a hot plate! All kinds of women's clubs, church groups, and professional organizations look for new speakers to pep up their meetings. Get some engagements to demonstrate and discuss what you know about cooking, and become a local culinary expert almost overnight.

Cook to Write or Write to Cook?

These are all good ways to break into the cookbook world, good ways to enjoy food writing without taking on a whole book, and good projects to keep going along with a book. There's something about food writing: once you begin, you get hooked. As Marion Brown says, "A warning! Once you get into food writing, you are stuck—happily—forever!" Oh, you'll think you're giving it up; you will swear at the end of a project that you'll never write another recipe as long as you live. In fact, I've been known on occasion to swear that I will never even eat again, but inevitably, before the ink is dry on such declarations, the next idea pops up and I'm off on a new project.

Getting the first project going is the hardest. After that first idea gets under way, your challenge is to sustain the pace so that you always have something interesting in the works. I don't think there is any one way to get an idea and make it work, but over the years I have developed a set of guidelines based on what has worked for me. They might be useful for you too.

1. Look at everything and every place as a potential outlet for your work. Examine every publication, every store, every public occasion to see whether you could make an opportunity for yourself there.

2. Be willing to start small. That may mean writing for free at first. I used to know a woman who left me purple with frustration because she was forever getting good ideas, half starting them, and then dropping them without putting the time and energy into developing them because she couldn't get anybody to promise ahead of time to pay her generously. "What's the use of going to all that work if I'm not going to get anything out of it?" she'd say. She envied me because I got paid. I never could make her understand that I had put in an ample share of volunteer time, writing for free, just to get the clips and the credibility for the paying job that might come along next.

This frustrating woman also refused to try to understand the needs of the markets for which she wanted to write. "I shouldn't have to change what I do to suit somebody else," she would say. (I suppose she still says it, come to think of it, but not to me. I avoid her.) It just doesn't work that way. Let's listen again to Rebecca Greer, articles editor for *Woman's Day*. She talked about the editorial process, how decisions are made about what to publish, and the fact that the writer must her work to the requirements of the magazine and accept the magazine's going rate of pay. She said, "It's a buyers' market. It may not be fair, but that's the way it is. It's a buyers' market."

Okay, it is. The answer to that is simply to do whatever it takes to make yourself one of the more valued sellers. And to do that, you've got to start somewhere, probably small, probably for minimal payment.

3. Tackle only projects for which you feel genuine enthusiasm. I have said this several times already. By now I hope you believe me. You may say, "Of course I wouldn't work on a project I didn't like," but sometimes these things sneak up on you. You are asked to do something, and out of duty or habit or greed you agree.

About a year ago I was asked to write a cookbook on tofu, and in my usual offhand manner I said, "Oh sure." I bought some tofu and I made it into cream soup. I stuffed it into mushrooms. I spread it on toast. I tried all kinds of other creative, novel ideas with it. I hated it. But, as usual, the mortgage was motivating me. "A job's a job," I thought. "If they want a tofu cookbook I'll give them a tofu cookbook." And I kept on inventing recipes at the rate of three or four a day.

Then an internal integrity keeper I didn't know I had took over. The next thing I realized, I was trying to figure out ways to test my tofu recipes in servings for one, so I wouldn't have so much of it around. Then I slipped from testing four recipes a day to four a week; then weeks went by with no tofu testing at all.

About the time I should have been asking for a contract, I got a call from the editor, who wondered how I was doing with my tofu recipes. I wasn't home. My daughter took over. She said succinctly, "Mom hates tofu. She can't make it taste good." Well, the editor said later, she had about decided there would be a better market for a Japanese cookbook anyway, and she had an excellent Japanese cook and writer right in the neighborhood. Maybe we should just postpone tofu a while. I can't say which of us was more relieved at avoiding a project for which neither of us could sustain any enthusiasm.

4. When you do feel enthusiasm, protect it. Avoid people who tell you why your ideas won't work. People like that can ruin your forward momentum. I call them "yesbuts." You say, "Here's a great idea," and launch into it, and they say, "Yes, but aren't you afraid that. . . . " For a while I worked in an office surrounded by "yesbuts." No matter what I proposed one of them would always tell me why the idea was too difficult, another would say the plan was too complicated, and everybody would assure me it had never been done before, which meant it was tantamount to impossible. That environment kills creativity. I remember jumping up and down in the hall one day, screaming, "It's damned hard to be enthusiastic all by yourself."

As things worked out, reinforcements arrived and we went on to do all kinds of "impossible" things. I learned a valuable lesson: pitting yourself and your enthusiasm against negative people costs too much; it uses you up. You will never communicate your enthusiasm to them, and you may become so discouraged in trying that you ruin it even for yourself. If you can't avoid such people, at least don't tell them your good ideas. Give them something less valuable to shoot down.

5. In fact, don't risk talking away your ideas with anybody. Many a good storyteller has never seen a story in print because once it's been told, she or he loses the need to communicate it. When you get an idea, do something about it first—then talk.

6. Accept the fact that not all your ideas will work. When you try one that doesn't work, don't take it personally. Don't even take it as a reflection on the idea. Just try it again somewhere else, or try something else.

I think persistence may be the single most important characteristic you need for getting into publishing. I know it is more important than talent. A lot of talented people have never pushed themselves into print. A lot of untalented but terribly persistent people have. If you believe that what you are doing is good, keep trying. You will succeed.

7. Be professional. Even if cooking, collecting recipes, and writing about food are hobbies for you, the work you present for consideration should be thoroughly professional because publishing magazines, newspapers, and cookbooks and selling foods and equipment are not hobbies for the people you are approaching. Always address the person to whom you are making your presentation in terms of what the project will mean to him or her, to readers, to the audience, or to customers. Do not ask for the opportunity as a favor. People may do each other favors across the fence in the yard after work, but not when they're engaged in the business that earns the money to make the payments on that fence and yard.

No matter to whom you make a proposal—editor, businessperson, gourmet shop owner—your ideas should flesh out the following skeleton:
- What you are offering
- The advantages to the person to whom you're offering it
- When you would like to begin
- How you would proceed
- When you would finish
- What you want in return

Do not say how much it would mean to you to have the opportunity to do this job. Do not talk about needing the money or making your mother proud or needing something to do with your time. Do not even talk about how wonderful other people think your cooking and recipes are.

Instead, tell how your offering may be used to increase business, improve readership, or improve customer relations. Tell how similar enterprises have benefited from such work as you propose to do. Your goal should be to leave the person you've approached with the feeling that they've got hold of a wonderful opportunity in you and that they're lucky you showed up when you did.

8. Always try to have several possibilities in the works at a time. The more places you're trying to settle an idea, the less disappointed you will be when one doesn't come to fruition and the better your chances, statistically, that at least one will.

9. Never give up.

10. NEVER give up.

This is a glimpse of the world beyond cookbooks. For some people it's a starting place; for others it is sufficient unto itself. What this book, and especially this chapter, should make you realize is that if you love food, cooking, and recipes, your possibilities for living out that enthusiasm are limited only by your own energy.

A Round Tuit

The editors of this book asked me to write a few words about how to find or make time for writing a cookbook. I have never been able to think of an answer to the people who say they would write a book if they just had the time. I still can't. Instead, I offer this motivational device that I first saw taped to the mirror of Leslie Fleming when she was a high-school girl in State College, Pennsylvania.

This is *your* ROUND TUIT.
Now that you have it you can accomplish anything you want. Not having a round tuit often keeps people from doing the things they would like to do. You hear them say, "I am going to write a cookbook just as soon as I get a round tuit." These people must search passionately, because when you see them again they are very sad and say, "Oh, I still haven't gotten a round tuit." Fortunately, I have been able to locate an extra round tuit for you.

Now you won't have to spend time looking for one. You can collect recipes and create them; test recipes and write them in fine prose. You can publish your cookbook. Others may talk about how much they would like to do these things, but you now have a great advantage over them because you have gotten A ROUND TUIT.

Congratulations!

Bibliography of Cookbooks

I offer the following list of cookbooks for your perusal. Most of them are discussed elsewhere in the book, but I have included a few I like which didn't seem to fit into what I had to say in the rest of the text. My list is unquestionably idiosyncratic—it includes the books that seemed to *me* to have merit. The list is by no means exhaustive, and you will certainly think of others.

Baylis, Maggie and Castle, Coralie.
REAL BREAD.
San Francisco: 101 Productions, 1980. When I was looking for a bread book to send my daughter, who was recently married, living in England, and newly involved in the delights of baking bread, I checked at least ten different books. This was the one I chose. The book begins with a good discussion of the various ingredients in bread, moves on to a basic how-to that covers kneading, mixing, and so on, and then offers 200 recipes that make wonderful breads. A special section on sourdough is especially appealing.

Beard, James.
BEARD ON BREAD.
New York: Alfred A. Knopf, 1974. This is a detailed, opinionated book about breadmaking. The recipes are unusual and interesting, and have the great advantage of producing small quantities—wonderful if you are not feeding ten anymore. For my taste the recipes are a little heavy on salt, but that is easily corrected by using less. The book opens with some observations on how to bake bread and on basic ingredients. I have seen better treatments of ingredients in some of the more recent bread books, but this book is worth owning for the recipes and whimsical line drawings alone.

Beard, James.
BEARD ON FOOD.
New York: Alfred A. Knopf, 1974. Composed of a selection of Beard's weekly syndicated newspaper columns, *Beard on Food* is my favorite Beard cookbook because of the number of new and interesting ideas. In my edition, his commentary for the book is printed in brown, and the recipes from the newspaper column are printed in green. The colors are difficult for me to read, but I see the necessity for separating what came from columns and what was written just for the book. One nice thing about the book is that it was written before we all became so self-conscious about health and nutrition, and it contains such hard-to-find information as two full pages on how to make real French fries. Another recipe calls for a half-pound of butter plus heavy cream. Oh, ecstasy!

Beard, James.
BEARD ON PASTA.
New York: Alfred A. Knopf, 1983. Of all the pasta books around, I think this one is the best I've seen. The 100 recipes go well beyond the typical Italian treatment to which we're accustomed. There are also recipes for Chinese wontons, Jewish kreplach, Greek pastitsio, and a whole slew of hot and cold sauces to go with all kinds of pasta shapes. Somehow Beard seems to have more fun with his pasta than other cookbook writers.

Beck, Simone; and Louisette Bertholle and Julia Child.
MASTERING THE ART OF FRENCH COOKING. (Vol. I.)
New York: Alfred A. Knopf, 1964. This is *the* classic American cookbook of French cooking. It fascinates me that the title page of my copy, an early printing, lists the authors in the order given above, while promotional material recently published puts Julia at the head of the list. Volume II is by Julia Child and Simone Beck. Both are teaching volumes, which give step-by-step instructions for preparing many classic French recipes, along with detailed commentary on French techniques for basic cooking processes.

Brown, Marion.
MARION BROWN'S SOUTHERN COOK BOOK. (Second Edition)
Chapel Hill: University of North Carolina Press, 1968. Marion Brown said that her goal was to produce a book from which one could produce a complete meal "in the true Southern manner," and she collected everything from old plantation recipes to gourmet restaurant specialites. The resulting book of nearly 1,000 recipes is culled from files of more than 30,000. The recipes are not all as detailed as in our more contemporary cookbooks, but anyone with even a modicum of experience should be able to follow them. I can recommend the book to anyone who likes Southern cooking.

Boy Scouts of America.
HOW TO SURVIVE WHEN MOM'S AWAY.
California: self-published, 1981. A 68-page, 56-recipe paperback, written by three boys for other kids and their fathers, this little book earned enough to take its three authors from California to the Boy Scout Jamboree in Virginia. Finding a copy could be a challenge. Start by contacting:
> Boy Scouts of America
> Supply Division
> 1325 Walnut Hill Lane
> Irving TX 75062

Castle, Coralie.
SOUP
San Francisco: 101 Productions. This nice little book, direct and to the point, contains recipes for about 300 soups, along with chapters on homemade stocks, accompaniments for soups, ways to improve canned soups, and ideas

for using leftovers. Coralie says that in testing recipes for this book she ate soup "morning, noon, and night." That doesn't seem like such a bad thing if all the soups were as good as these.

Castle, Coralie and Killeen, Jacqueline.
COUNTRY INNS COOKERY.
San Francisco: 101 Productions. Castle and Killeen present recipes from North America's famous country inns, emphasizing regional cooking. The book ties in logically with the 101 Productions series on country inns.

Castle, Coralie and Lawrence, Barbara.
HORS D'OEUVRE ETC.
San Francisco: 101 Productions. Done with the usual tasteful competence of 101 Productions, *Hors D'Oeuvre Etc.* consists of about 600 recipes and ideas, including a section on Chinese dim sum.

Castle, Coralie and Newton, Astrid.
THE ART OF COOKING FOR TWO.
San Francisco: 101 Productions, 1976. The 380 recipes in this book emphasize natural ingredients. The directions are brief and clear, and the recipes produce good food. This is one of my favorite cookbooks because it shows some genuine originality.

Child, Julia.
FROM JULIA CHILD'S KITCHEN.
New York: Alfred A. Knopf, 1975. A cookbook bibliography without a book by Julia Child would be unthinkable. I like this the best of her books because she has moved away from the restraints of classic French cooking to try all kinds of unorthodox combinations. The recipes are good and her writing is fun.

Claiborne, Craig.
THE NEW YORK TIMES COOK BOOK.
New York: Harper & Row, 1961. I've had this book for about twenty years. It was the book my friends and I used during the years we discovered that there was more to cooking than pouring a can of tomato sauce over meatloaf, and gave elegant little dinner parties for each other. These days I hardly ever use it, but I still think it's a good book, especially for younger cooks. It contains nearly 1500 recipes from Claiborne's columns in *The New York Times.*

Claiborne, Craig.
THE NEW YORK TIMES MENU COOK BOOK.
New York: Harper & Row, 1966. The recipes in this book always seemed more interesting to me than those in Claiborne's *New York Times Cookbook.* I never actually prepared an entire menu from the book, but I ate at the homes of people who did and enjoyed the food very much. The front of the book con-

sists of a variety of menus: An Elegant Spring Luncheon, A Party Picnic, A Fall Dinner, and more. The rest of the book comprises recipes for the foods in the menus. Like Claiborne's other *New York Times* cookbook, this one contains recipes from his newspaper columns—more than 1200 recipes, if his introduction is to be believed. I never counted.

Claiborne, Craig and Virginia Lee.
THE CHINESE COOKBOOK.

New York: J.B. Lippincott Company, 1972. One of the most interesting parts of this book is Claiborne's introduction, which describes his feeling that while he could master French cooking because it seemed "so logical," Chinese cooking seemed to him too vast and complex to tackle—until he met Virginia Lee. An outstanding feature of this book is the number of recipes for foods that are *not* stir-fried, a real boon if you are trying to serve a multidish Chinese meal and have the only pair of hands available for the last minute stir-frying.

Colquitt, Harriet Ross Ed.
THE SAVANNAH COOK BOOK.

New York: Farrar & Rinehart, 1933. A collection of old fashioned "receipts" from colonial kitchens, this out-of-print book can probably be found in secondhand book shops or tracked down for you by book locators. Its charm lies in what it tells us about attitudes toward food and cooking in the South in an earlier time. It also reflects an earlier attitude toward blacks in daily life, acknowledging the skill of black cooks and perhaps overemphasizing their casualness about it.

The Congressional Club.
THE CONGRESSIONAL CLUB COOK BOOK (tenth edition).

Washington, D.C.; self-published, 1982. For about 60 years Congressional Club cookbooks have been best sellers among self-published cookbooks. The current edition includes recipes from congressmen, ambassadors, governors, and President and Mrs. Reagan. The book contains 1300 recipes.

The Congressional Club
2001 New Hampshire Avenue, NW
Washington DC 20009

Crown.
THE COOK'S OWN BOOK.

New York; Crown Publishers, Inc., 1982. This is one of several available blank books for you to write recipes in, and it features several pages of information about weights, measures, and conversions, as well as a specially marked index page. It is a ring binder with punched pages, which gives you the options of adding pages or taking some out to replace them with others.

The editors of Consumer Guide.
FOOD PROCESSOR COOKBOOK.
New York: Simon and Schuster, 1976. This is an outstandingly good book. The recipes are clear and easy to follow and the results are excellent. Basic processes are illustrated with step-by-step color photographs, as are many of the finished dishes, but illustrations do not dominate the book. The final chapter on the test reports for ten food processors may be outdated, because more processors have come on the market and the old ones have been changed, but the basic observations are still sound. Knowing what the reporters looked for serves as a good guide for a purchaser in any year. I especially like this single-subject cookbook because it does not give recipes unsuitable for the appliance simply to prove that they're possible.

Daughters of the American Revolution.
A DAR SAMPLER: DINING WITH THE DECORATIVE ARTS.
Washington, D.C.: self-published, 1982. Compiled by Paul Wright, the book features recipes related to the items on display in the DAR Museum in Washington, D.C. The recipe for "Molly Stark's Recipe for Dolly Madison's Whim Cake," for instance, is illustrated by a picture of a wool bed rug made by Molly Stark, which is on display in the museum. The museum is filled with Americana, and the cookbook features related American recipes from each of the fifty states.
> Daughters of the American Revolution
> NSDAR, 1776 "D" Street, NW
> Washington DC 20006

Davis, Adelle.
LET'S COOK IT RIGHT.
New York: New American Library, 1970. One of the very first "health-food" cookbooks, this one still holds its own in the marketplace. Compared to the newer books and recipes available, the recipes seem a little "hair shirt" with their considerable emphasis on wheat germ, brewer's yeast, and blackstrap molasses. But if you don't already own the book, it's worth buying just to see how the earlier approach differs from today's. The recipes are not entirely reliable but can be used anyway. A recipe for wheat-germ dinner rolls, for instance, seems to be short about five cups of flour, but once you add the flour, the rolls turn out to be delicious.

Day, Avanelle, and Lillie M. Stuckey.
THE SPICE COOKBOOK.
New York: David White Company, 1964. It may not seem like such a big deal today, but when this cookbook first came out, it was remarkable because relatively few people were cooking with spices and herbs beyond such basics as cinnamon and parsley. I think this is one of the those books that contribute to our current eclecticism with seasonings. I object to such ingredients as instant minced garlic and instant minced onion in the recipes, but it's simple

enough to substitute the fresh ingredients and the results of the recipes are good. I also like the history of the spice trade, the description and history of individual spices, and charts for using spices and herbs.

Eckhardt, Linda West.
THE ONLY TEXAS COOKBOOK.
Austin: Texas Monthly Press, Inc., 1981. This book abounds with enthusiasm for Texas and its food. Eckhardt collected Texas recipes from every conceivable source in the state and has accompanied them with many stories about the origins of the recipes.

Ewald, Ellen Buchman.
RECIPES FOR A SMALL PLANET.
New York: Ballantine, 1973. Written as a companion to *Diet for a Small Planet*, this book is a collection of meatless recipes that use the "balanced protein" concepts.

Firnstahl, Timothy.
JAKE O'SHAUGHNESSEY'S SOURDOUGH BOOK.
San Francisco: San Francisco Book Co. Inc., 1976. This is one of my favorite cookbooks. I used it to learn about handling sourdough, and although I do not agree with everything Firnstahl says, his dictates are a sound base from which to deviate. Jake O'Shaughnessey's was a famous saloon in Seattle in 1897. It has been revived, and the recipes in Firnstahl's book represent the kind of food the saloon served.

Goldbeck, Nikki and David.
THE GOOD BREAKFAST BOOK.
New York: Quick Fox, 1976. A cookbook of alternatives, almost 400 of them, for breakfast foods. The recipes emphasize high nutrition and low calories. Meat is played down as a protein source. Although the commentary on the importance of a good breakfast sounds overfamiliar, the recipes are novel and appealing.

Goldbeck, Nikki and David.
NIKKI & DAVID GOLDBECK'S AMERICAN WHOLEFOODS CUISINE.
New York: New American Library, 1983. What this encyclopedic volume doesn't tell you about cooking with "wholefoods" (unprocessed foods), you probably don't need to know. The book includes more than 1300 meatless recipes, as the jacket says, "from short order to gourmet." It is an almost overwhelming piece of work. I suspect it is the yardstick against which forthcoming natural-food *and* vegetarian cookbooks will be measured.

Greene, Bert.
HONEST AMERCIAN FARE.
Chicago: Contemporary Books, Inc., 1981. A nostalgic collection of those

recipes considered basic a few generations ago: meatloaf, macaroni and cheese, beef stew. Greene is a regular contributor to many magazines, and writes a syndicated column called "Bert Greene's Kitchen." His emphasis is on down-home, regional cooking.

Groceman, Wanda.
TO MY DAUGHTER WITH LOVE.
Concord, Ca.: Nitty Gritty Productions, 1972. A collection of family recipes for family days and celebrations, this book is handwritten to produce the effect of a personal cookbook. Although it is available in some stores, Nitty Gritty is no longer publishing this book.

Grossinger, Jennie.
THE ART OF JEWISH COOKING.
New York: Random House, 1958. This is a modest but thorough book of traditional Jewish recipes, an ideal book for cooks just beginning to experiment with kugels, knishes, and knaidlach. My copy sports multicolored smudges on nearly every page from much use.

Harwell, Richard.
THE MINT JULEP.
Charlottesville, Va.: University Press of Virginia, 1975. A true Southerner and a true gentleman, Rick Harwell has gathered classic old recipes for mint juleps, along with history and anecdotes about the venerable libation, into a slender volume so charming it almost makes getting crocked seem respectable.

Hess, Karen (Ed.)
MARTHA WASHINGTON'S BOOKE OF COOKERY.
New York: Columbia Press, 1981. A facsimile reproduction of two books of recipes that date back to Elizabethan and Jacobean times, the book takes its title from the fact that Martha Washington had the recipes for fifty years. It has been edited and annotated by one of the country's foremost food historians. In this book Hess shows the relationship of the culture to American colonial cuisine. For those interested in the history of cookbooks, she traces the line of ownership of some of them and discusses the tradition of English household recipe manuscripts, or what we might now call "personal cookbooks."

Hieatt, Constance B. and Butler, Sharon.
PLEYN DELIT: MEDIEVAL COOKERY FOR MODERN COOKS.
Toronto: University of Toronto Press, 1979. The present-day English tradition of the title is "Plain Delight." This little book contains more than 100 recipes from the Middle Ages, adapted to twentieth-century cooking. It's a good source for new ideas when your imagination goes stale.

Himes, Genia Lee.
THE CUISINE OF CATHAY.
Gainesville, Fla., Chopping Board, Inc. (self-published), 1983. This is the

most elaborate self-published book I have ever seen. Even at $40.00, Genia Lee says she does not expect the book to make money. It contains 250 pages and 380 illustrations, most of them color photographs, which demonstrate step-by-step procedures and show how finished dishes should look. If you can bring yourself to take such a fancy book into the kitchen, you really can prepare unfamiliar Chinese recipes from the instructions.

Chopping Board, Inc.
Box 2549
Gainesville FL 32602

Hoffman, Mable.
CHOCOLATE COOKERY.
Tucson, Ariz.: HP Books, 1981. Here are recipes for more chocolate than anybody should ever eat. The book is illustrated with many color photographs in the usual HP style. Recipes include Black Forest Cake, Grasshopper Pie, and dipped chocolate candies.

Hsiung, Deh-Ta.
CHINESE REGIONAL COOKING.
New York: Quarto Publishing Limited, 1979. Although this is not the most comprehensive Chinese cookbook I own, it is one of the best. Beyond the fairly standard explanation of Chinese cooking ingredients, techniques, and utensils, the introduction classifies Chinese cuisine by region, describing the geography and food of each. Succeeding chapters contain recipes for the outstanding dishes of each region, many of them illustrated with color photographs of the dishes as prepared by the chefs of ten different restaurants. Other photographs, all in color, show the market scenes and the countryside where ingredients for the recipes are procured. I find that I cook very successfully with the recipes from this book, and every so often I browse through it just to enjoy its beauty.

Jones, Jeanne.
DIET FOR A HAPPY HEART.
San Francisco: 101 Productions, 1981. The author has earned the respect of good cooks and of the medical profession for her books devoted to low-cholesterol, low-fat, low-sodium, and low-sugar recipes that taste good. In 1981 she revised *Diet for a Happy Heart* to eliminate artificial sweeteners. She also adapted the exchange lists of the American Diabetes Association. The recipes in this book, as in all her books, make perfectly respectable eating for anyone, with or without health problems.

Jones, Jeanne.
THE CALCULATING COOK.
San Francisco: 101 Productions, 1972. A gourmet cookbook for diabetics and dieters, approved by the American Diabetes Association, this is one of Jeanne Jones' nine health-and-diet-oriented cookbooks. Worth having even if

diabetes is not your problem, because the recipes provide sound eating for anybody.

Jones, Judith and Evan.
THE BOOK OF BREAD.
New York: Harper and Row, 1982. If there is anything more to say about bread, I can't imagine what it would be. The Joneses are two of the most knowledgeable food and cookbook people in the country. Their book dispenses new information and offers new recipes for an old staple.

The Junior League of Baton Rouge, Inc.
RIVER ROAD RECIPES I.
Baton Rouge, La.: self-published, 1959. The Baton Rouge Junior League has sold more than 90,000 copies of *River Road Recipes I* since the first printing in 1959, and the book has outsold all other Junior League cookbooks in the United States. The 650 recipes come from all over Louisiana; many have been handed down from one generation to another. The Junior League says that each recipe has been tested.
> Baton Rouge Junior League
> 4950C Government St.
> Baton Rouge LA 70806

The Junior League of Baton Rouge, Inc.
RIVER ROAD RECIPES II—A SECOND HELPING.
Baton Rouge, La.: self-published, 1976. This sequel to *River Road Recipes I* reflects the same Creole heritage, but all the recipes are new. This volume was inspired by the tremendous success of the first book, and is clearly intended for those who already have volume I, as well as for a new market. *River Road Recipes II* contains 600 recipes.
> Baton Rouge Junior League
> 4950C Government St.
> Baton Rouge LA 70806

Junior League of Charleston.
CHARLESTON RECEIPTS.
Charleston, SC.: self-published, 1950. A classic among the Junior League cookbooks, this one features traditional low-country recipes for ribs, ham, seafood, and other dishes that have come to be associated with the Charleston area. Spiral bound, with no illustrations, the book is in its 24th printing.
> Junior League of Charleston
> Box 177
> Charleston SC 29402

Katzen, Mollie.
THE MOOSEWOOD COOKBOOK.
Berkeley, Ca.: Ten Speed Press, 1977. This book proves that sometimes

good books can defy existing commercial standards and succeed beyond anyone's wildest dreams. *The Moosewood Cookbook* was created by Mollie Katzen to offer in home-sized proportions the recipes used at the Moosewood Restaurant in Ithaca, New York. I bought the book for myself after I had eaten several wonderful dishes prepared from it at the Millheim Hotel in Millheim, Pennsylvania. The drawings and hand lettering, also by Ms. Katzen, add to the book's "noncommercial" feeling. Although the recipes are vegetarian, the real emphasis of the book is good food prepared from scratch.

Katzen, Mollie.
THE ENCHANTED BROCCOLI FOREST.
   Berkeley, Ca.: Ten Speed Press, 1982. This sequel to the *Moosewood Cookbook* has even more recipes than the first book. They are unique, delicious, and vegetarian. The book overflows with exuberance, love of good food, and enthusiasm for preparing it. Like the previous volume, it is hand lettered and illustrated by Ms. Katzen.

Keys, Margaret and Ancel.
THE BENEVOLENT BEAN.
   New York: Doubleday, 1967. When this book was published, the idea of a single-subject cookbook devoted to dried beans seemed almost bizarre. Each recipe includes information on calories, grams of protein, and fat. The Keyses were ahead of their time; their book is a fascinating example of the earliest nutrition-oriented cookbooks.

Kimball, Marie.
THOMAS JEFFERSON'S COOK BOOK.
   Charlottesville, Va.: University Press of Virginia, 1976. Thomas Jefferson spent a prodigious amount of money on food, drink, and entertaining, even compared to today's costs. As a result of his travels in Europe, his tastes went far beyond the Virginia tradition of fried chicken, ham, and greens. This book reflects those eclectic tastes, especially the French influence, in recipes for foods not commonly found on Southern tables at the time. The author has reduced the recipes from their original huge quantities (a dozen eggs, a pound of butter) to today's smaller proportions. Each recipe has been tested, and includes enough standarized measurements to be used by a reasonably knowledgeable cook.

LaFray, Joyce.
FAMOUS FLORIDA. (Series.)
   St. Petersburg, Fla.: La Fray Publishing Company (self-published), 1983. The *Famous Florida* series comprises four books, the most recent being *Cracker Cookin'*. The first book in the series, *Famous Florida! Restaurants & Recipes,* was published in 1981. Ms. LaFray actively promotes the series, which relies heavily for its success on its tie-in with dishes served in Florida restaurants. The

books include directions for finding the restaurants where the recipes are served.
>Joyce LaFray
>Box 7326
>St. Petersburg FL 33734

Lappé, Frances Moore.
DIET FOR A SMALL PLANET, Revised Ed.
New York: Ballantine Books, 1975. In this book, Frances Moore Lappé presentes a rationale for obtaining the proteins we need in our diet by combining the proteins in grains, legumes, dairy products, and other nonmeat foods to act as whole proteins. This method allows us to cut down or eliminate meat from our diets. Many of the pages are devoted to charts and information about nutrition, but about half the book is recipes, most of them very good even to the average meat-and-potato palate. This was the first book to introduce the concept of balanced proteins in popular style and to offer recipes that apply it. It has sold, and continues to sell, voluminously, and has influenced many more recent vegetarian recipes.

Lawrence, Barbara.
FISHERMAN'S WHARF COOKBOOK.
Concord, Ca.: Nitty Gritty Productions, 1971. The Fisherman's Wharf is to the Bay Area of San Francisco what Charleston is to the Southeastern shore—a place for tourists to find magic, legends, and good food. The cookbook contains seafood recipes from some of San Francisco's most popular restaurants, including The Mandarin at Ghirardelli Square; Fishermen's Grotto No. 9, on the wharf; and Tadich's Grill, a few blocks from the wharf. All the recipes are distinctly West Coast in their ingredients and seasonings.

Lee, Gary.
THE WOK.
Concord, Ca.: Nitty Gritty Productions, 1970. A best seller for Nitty Gritty for over a decade, this little Chinese cookbook is a curious combination of rambling Chinese philosophizing, kitchen instructions, and recipes—some traditional Chinese and others contemporary inventions of Mr. Lee. It's the kind of book that goes nicely with a wok as a gift, which probably accounts for many sales.

Lee, Gary.
WOK APPETIZERS AND LIGHT SNACKS.
Concord, Ca.: Nitty Gritty Productions, 1982. Illustrated with an unusual combination of full-color photographs, line drawings showing scenes of Chinese life, and how-to sketches of cooking processes, this follow-up to *The Wok* contains a variety of interesting recipes for both classic and novel Chinese appetizers and dim sum. Gary Lee's commentary tends to ramble; it often relates

only marginally to the recipes. To me it seems the book was put together by several people with differing (and equally strong) ideas about how it should be done. Nevertheless, the recipes are good and relatively simple to follow.

Miller, Gloria Bley.
THE THOUSAND RECIPE CHINESE COOKBOOK.
New York: Grosset & Dunlap, 1970. Gloria Bley Miller's book gives lie to the popularly held notion that Westerners cannot write about Chinese cooking. This book of more than 900 pages covers virtually every cooking process used by the Chinese, with variations on everything. Contrary to the usual pattern, Miller is a professional writer who became interested in cooking, rather than a cook who decided to write. If I could have only one Chinese cookbook, this is the one I would want.

Mock, Lonnie.
DIM SUM COOKBOOK.
Walnut Creek, Ca.: Alpha Gamma Arts, 1977. Dim Sum are snack foods served by the Chinese, and they differ considerably from the stir-fry dishes and egg rolls most of us associate with Chinese restaurants. This modest little paperback gives easy, clear directions for preparing most of the common dim sum dishes.

Morrison, Sally.
CROSS CREEK KITCHENS.
Gainesville, Fla.: Triad Publishing Co., 1983. The illustrations by watercolor artist Kate Barnes, although reproduced in black and white, contribute strongly to the gentle mood of this book, as do the musings of Sally Morrison about restoring an abandoned orange grove, picking food fresh from the garden, and sharing fresh-baked breads and desserts with friends. The subtitle of the book is "Seasonal Recipes and Reflections," but seasons are a major theme only in one section. The author lived for a time in Cross Creek at the old farmhouse of Kate Rawlings (author of *The Yearling*), and helped restore life to the old place, which is now a state historic site. Rawlings herself wrote a famous cookbook, *Cross Creek Cookery*, which combined lengthy prose descriptions of the area with some very rich company-fare recipes. Morrison's book is avowedly influenced by Rawlings', but the recipes are lighter, emphasizing natural foods and little cream. A blurb on the cover claims that the recipes are "so unique you won't find them anywere else." And they are. Those I have tried are delicious. I rate this cookbook far above average.

Olney, Judith and Klingel, Ruth.
THE JOY OF CHOCOLATE.
Woodbury, N.Y.: Barron's Educational Series, 1982. Here is a testament to the power of well-done illustrations in a cookbook. I looked over the beautiful glossy pages and their chocolate-laden recipes and decided I didn't really need an entire cookbook on chocolate in my collection. Then, for days, my mind was

filled with memories of the color photographs of tortes, mousses, fudge, and such exotic concotions as apricot cream in a chocolate sack. I went back and bought the book. I learned that to make the chocolate sack you spread a paper back with melted chocolate, let it harden, and then peel the bag. A similar method using cabbage leaves is used to create a chocolate cabbage cake. A delightful, unusual book.

Pepin, Jacques.
EVERYDAY COOKING WITH JACQUES PEPIN.
New York: Harper & Row, 1982. Some, though not all, of the recipes in this book are demonstrated in Jacques Pepin's television program of the same name. His emphasis is on French country cuisine as it is cooked in the home kitchen. As you might expect of a book based on a television show, the recipes are illustrated with many step-by-step color photographs. The results of the relatively simple recipes are tasty, and the book makes a nice addition to a cookbook collection.

Pitzer, Sara.
WHOLE GRAINS: GROW, HARVEST & COOK YOUR OWN.
Charlotte, Vt.; 1981. Of course this is a splendid, spectacular, sensational cookbook. One chapter is devoted to growing, harvesting, storing, and cooking each of the grains: corn, wheat, triticale, barley, buckwheat, millet, oats, rice, and rye. This book contains relatively few bread recipes on the theory that bread recipes using all kinds of flour are available in almost all complete cookbooks and bread books. Instead, the emphasis is on new ways to prepare grains as a part of daily meals.

Pitzer, Sara.
THE MORE THAN CHICKEN COOKBOOK.
Charlotte, Vt.; 1984. More than 100 recipes for chicken, turkey, duckling, cornish game hens, quail, game birds—and eggs. How to buy, butcher, dress, and store these birds. All recipes are coded to indicate where such appliances as food processors, clay pots, and slow cookers can be used. Some recipes are marked "1 to 100" to indicate that they can be multiplied to serve any number of people, a unique factor.

Randolph, Mary.
THE VIRGINIA HOUSE-WIFE.
Columbia, SC.: University of South Carolina Press, 1984. *The Virginia House-Wife* was first published in 1824. This is a facsimile of that edition, with excerpts from the editions of 1825 and 1828, and is edited with historical notes and commentaries by Karen Hess. This little book provides a fascinating look at how the women of the new republic went about putting meals on the table. The book includes a glossary of cooking terms and phrases of the time, which makes the reading easier.

Rhett, B.S.; Gay, L.; Woodward, H.; and Hamilton, E.
TWO HUNDRED YEARS OF CHARLESTON COOKING.
Columbia, SC.: University of South Carolina Press, 1976. A reprint of an old classic, the book contains more than 300 recipes from Charleston, emphasizing traditional dishes and spicing them with local history and gossip as it has been passed down through generations. Although Lettie Gay tried to translate the casual old "pinch-of-this, bit-of-that" approach of the recipes into standardized measurements, I think the book is better used for reading and as a source of ideas than for following recipes step-by-step.

Ridgway, Arlene Martin (Ed.)
CHICKEN FOOT SOUP AND OTHER RECIPES FROM THE PINE BARRENS.
New Brunswick, N.J.: Rutgers University Press, 1980. Ms. Ridgway's collection of recipes from local people demonstrates that the people of the Pine Barrens learn how to use everything their environment provides, from the nuts on the trees to the game birds and seafood available for the catching. Ms. Martin has left the recipes pretty much as they came to her, which means that there is little standardization in measurements and that some of the directions for proceeding are casual in the manner of long-time, seat-of-the-pants cooks. This is no problem for an experienced cook, but could frighten a beginner who needs to be told what to do down to the last quarter-teaspoon of spice.

Robertson, Laurel, and Carol Flinders and Browen Godredy.
LAUREL'S KITCHEN.
Petaluma, Ca.: Nilgiri Press, 1976. *Laurel's Kitchen*, billed as "A Handbook for Vegetarian Cookery and Nutrition," is more than a collection of recipes. It contains a wealth of information about whole foods, nutritional content, and cooking methods. The book has become a classic, and is available in paperback, hardcover, and spiral binding. Even if you never use any of the recipes, you will appreciate the positive view of one of the alternative lifestyle movements that have influenced the American culture. The *Laurel's Kitchen* people were working on fitness before it became a fad.

Robinson, Mary Ann, Stancil, Rosemary, and Wilkins, Lorela.
SIMPLY SCRUMPTIOUS MICROWAVING.
Athens, Ga.: self-published, 1982. Three home economists saw a need for more and better recipes using the microwave oven, and created this book of 550 tested recipes. It is unique in offering recipes for clay-pot cooking, jams and jellies, special recipes for children's amusement, and techniques for such unlikely activities as blanching fruits and vegetables and drying flowers and herbs. A valuable book if you are interested in getting more use from your microwave oven.

Romagnoli, Margaret and G. Franco.
THE ROMAGNOLIS' TABLE.
Boston: Little, Brown and Company, 1974. This book grew out of the Ro-

magnolis' television cooking show on WGBH, Boston. The program was characterized by recipes that were so easy they could be executed from beginning to end in less than thirty minutes, but so delicious it seemed the cook should have slaved all day over that infamous hot stove. The book reflects the same characteristics. The recipes, which are billed as "Italian family recipes," go far beyond the triteness of lasagna and pizza. This is one of my favorite cookbooks. Everything I have ever prepared from it has been wonderful.

Romagnoli, Margaret and G. Franco.
THE ROMAGNOLIS' MEATLESS COOKBOOK.
    Boston: Little, Brown and Company, 1976. The distinction may seem subtle, but this is not a vegetarian cookbook; rather, it is one for meatless meals. Many of the traditional Italian recipes in it originated when the Roman Catholic Church demanded fasting and abstinence from meat during Lent and Advent and on Fridays. You will not find the vegetarian concern for protein and nutrition. The book is organized by course—appetizers, first courses (pasta or dumplings), second courses (fish, vegetables, and eggs), side dishes, and desserts. This book teaches you quickly that not all Italian food swims in tomatoes.

Rombauer, Irma S. and Becker, Marion R.
THE JOY OF COOKING.
    New York: The Bobbs-Merrill Company, Inc., 1964. A classic American cookbook, consulted daily by countless cooks everywhere, *Joy* started out as a self-published book for the benefit of a Unitarian group in St. Louis. *Joy* tells you how to do practically everything. It is a splendid source of general information and ideas about temperature, cooking time, and so on, when you are trying to create your own recipes and are not sure about such details.

Rutledge, Sarah.
THE CAROLINA HOUSEWIFE.
    Columbia, S.C.: University of South Carolina Press, 1979. Edited by Anna Wells Rutledge, this facsimile of the 1847 edition includes a checklist of South Carolina cookbooks published before 1935. The introduction, also by Anna Wells Rutledge, gives a colorful glimpse of daily life in South Carolina up to 1847, and is especially interesting in its comments on the role of women. The book was originally published anonymously, Miss Rutledge explains, and attributed only to "a Lady of Charleston," because at that time (and until about 1920) the name of a Charleston lady appeared in print only three times: "when born, when married and when buried—the legal necessities." In addition to getting history and ideas, an experienced cook could cook from this book.

St. Nicholas Roman Catholic Church Choir.
FAVORITE RECIPES FROM OUR BEST COOKS.
    Palisades Park, N.J.: self-published, 1979. You might have a hard time finding a copy of this little book; only 3,000 copies have been printed as of 1982. The recipes in the book were donated by parishioners in the church, many of

whom submitted old family recipes written on the backs of envelopes. The recipes were not tested, but the editors did check with the donor if something in a recipe did not look right.

Sales, Georgia MacLeod and Grover.
THE CLAY-POT COOKBOOK.
New York: Atheneum, 1980. This is not only the best, but just about the only available book of recipes for cooking in the clay pot. Some of the recipes are a little far out for my taste, but even they suggest possibilities and adaptations for more conservative cooks. The book is especially valuable for its information on basic handling and use of the clay pot.

Sahni, Julie.
CLASSIC INDIAN COOKING.
New York: William Morrow and Co., Inc., 1980. A collection of easily followed recipes for preparing some of the best-known traditional Indian dishes. The book contains extensive information about spices and herbs typical of Indian cooking, and, like so many good ethnic cookbooks, reflects the influence of the author's family as well as her ethnic background.

Samuel-Hool, Leonie.
TO ALL MY GRANDCHILDREN: LESSONS IN INDONESIAN COOKING.
Berkeley: Liplop Press, 1981. Although she is one of those cooks who believe that cooking is taught better in person, Leonie Samuel-Hool has gathered many classic, traditional Indonesian recipes and surrounded them with commentary about the circumstances under which she previously prepared them. Charming reading, even if you don't plan to cook Indonesian food. This book is a good example of what one can learn about another culture by studying the cooking of its people.

Seaver, Jeannette.
SOUPS.
New York: Bantam Books, 1978. I like the recipes in this little paperback better than those in any of my other soup books. After I had tried quite a few of the recipes and found them all successful, I even bought copies of the book for several other people. Seaver divides the book into clear soups, hearty soups, creamy soups, au gratin soups, and so on, and includes information by which (for example) hearty soups can be puréed to make creamy soups. Many of the recipes offer genuinely new, but not outlandish, flavors.

Shulman, Martha Rose.
FAST VEGETARIAN FEASTS.
New York: The Dial Press, 1981. According to this book, you can prepare any of these 200 recipes in less than 45 minutes. All the recipes are amply annotated with information about preparation time, supervised and unsupervised cooking time, suitability for low-sodium diets, and metric equivalencies. The

presence of the equivalencies in the recipes strikes me as typographically un-appealing, but would certainly be useful if you were trying to convert to the metric system. The recipes reflect ethnic diversity without flying off into what nonvegetarians would consider "weird."

Skinner, Kay.
WHAT'S FOR DINNER MRS. SKINNER?
New York: Key Books, Inc., revised ed. 1977. Written by the wife of the board chairman of the Skinner Macaroni Company, this little paperback is in-tended to explain the home cook's uses of commercial pasta. It includes recipes for pasta with meat, poultry, and meatless ingredients. Although the book has a good range of recipes, some readers may object to the frequent use of such in-gredients as canned soups and commercial lunch meats.

Stone, Marilyn, Ed.
THE CHOSEN: APPETIZERS AND DESSERTS.
Gainesville, Fla.: Triad, 1983. This collection of recipes comes from the best of 120 Jewish fund-raising cookbooks. All the recipes were tested, and range from such traditional Jewish dishes as knishes and kugel to regional special-ties, including blueberry buckle and key lime pie. The book is worth studying for its marketing genius.

Editors of Sunset Books and Sunset Magazine.
MEXICAN COOKBOOK.
Menlo Park, Ca.: Lane Publishing Co., 1977. This is a consumer-oriented book of recipes for the most popular traditional Mexican recipes, as well as some less commonly known to Americans. The illustrations reflect a "tourist view" of Mexico: the recipes use ingredients available in practically any super-market. If you are thoroughly familiar with real Mexican cooking, you might not be interested in this book, but as an introduction to Mexican food for the uninitiated, it is fine.

Tarr, Yvonne Young.
THE NEW YORK TIMES BREAD & SOUP COOKBOOK.
New York: Ballantine, 1976. The recipes in this book are arranged geo-graphically: New World, Mediterranean, Northern Europe, Eastern Europe, Near East and Far East. Recipes for breads appropriate to the soups are printed near the soup recipes. I like the author's use of *** to indicate recipes that have been particularly successful in her family.

Texaco Company Employees.
TASTE TREATS FROM TEXACO.
Self-published, 1981. *Taste Treats* is out of print, but finding it would be worth lurking around second-hand shops if you enjoy eclectic cookbooks. This 192-page book includes recipes from Texaco employees located in every Texaco facility in the United States.

Thomas, Anna.
THE VEGETARIAN EPICURE.
New York: Alfred A. Knopf, 1972. When this book first appeared, it presented the almost revolutionary idea that vegetarians could be gourmets. The book has definite undertones of what, at the time, we called "the counterculture." But the recipes are novel and good; the writing is charming; and the counterculture doesn't seem so "counter" these days. When I first found this book I was astonished and dismayed to learn that one of the reasons Anna Thomas wrote it was to make money to produce a film. Imagine writing a cookbook because she wanted to make films, when so many of us just wanted to write cookbooks!

Thomas, Anna.
THE VEGETARIAN EPICURE—BOOK TWO.
New York: Alfred A. Knopf, 1978. The recipes in this sequel are considerably more exotic than those in the first volume, reflecting the influence of foreign cuisines. The book contains 325 recipes; few of them are duplicated in any other book. Both volumes are worth owning if you are interested in meatless cookery. The section devoted to Indian foods is especially interesting.

Tolbert, Frank X.
A BOWL OF RED.
New York: Doubleday, 1972. Billed as a book for people who see chili "not as a food, but as a way of life," this is a revised and expanded edition of the classic "Natural History of Chili Con Carne." It includes other foods from the Southwest as well.

Truax, Carol (Ed.)
LADIES' HOME JOURNAL COOKBOOK.
New York: Doubleday. This is the first cookbook I ever owned. For at least a year it was the only one I owned. I still love it. Because it was put together before the craze for convenience foods took over, few of the recipes call for canned soups or anything powdered. Although the recipes are easy to follow, they call for some rather exotic combinations as well as for such basics as sautéed liver and baked potatoes. In other words, the book could take you from the beginning steps of cooking through the advanced stages. I never used a recipe I didn't like from the book. Today I imagine the only place you could find a copy would be in a used-book store or library. Either would be worth the trouble. The recipes have held up well over the years as times have changed.

Ungerer, Miriam.
COUNTRY FOOD: A SEASONAL JOURNAL.
New York: Random House, 1983. I knew I was going to like this book as soon as I read in the acknowledgments, "I wish I had a faithful typist to thank, but I don't . . . that would be me, and it would be right." The book is based on Ungerer's columns for the East Hampton *Star*, and emphasizes simple prepa-

ration of the fresh foods native to the Long Island area as they come into season. As much as anything, I enjoy the author's tart comments on the foibles of cooks and diners alike, making fun of people who refer to "pawhasta" rather than calling each shape by its own name, and saying elsewhere, "No one can convince me that foods cooked without salt or salads served naked are anything but a penance. . . ." Fun for reading, even if you don't have access to all the ingredients.

Wallace, George and Inger.
THE MEXICAN COOK BOOK.
   Concord, Ca.: Nitty Gritty Productions, 1971. Here is a book in which to study the problems you can have with a cookbook even though the recipes are outstanding. The book contains authentic recipes collected by the Wallaces during forty years of travel in Mexico. It is illustrated with photographs taken by the Wallaces of the Mexican people in their home settings. The photographs are reproduced in shades of brown and sepia rather than black and white.
   The text of the book explains a great deal about the history and foodways of the people. The photographs and text are fascinating. But somehow they never came together as a cookbook in the minds of consumers, who prefer the Mexican cookbooks of other publishers, illustrated with colorful photographs of meals containing green avocado, red tomato, and bright yellow cheese, all grandly displayed in the kind of pottery that is painted for export. The lesson here is that a cookbook may have all the elements of excellence in the minds of the purist, and yet not succeed in the cookbook market because it fails to conform to our expectations for a cookbook.

Weaver, William Ways. (Ed.)
A QUAKER WOMAN'S COOKBOOK: THE DOMESTIC COOKERY OF ELIZABETH ELLICOTT LEA
   Philadelphia: University of Pennsylvania Press, 1982. A facsimile reproduction of the book *Domestic Cookery,* published in 1845 by Mrs. Lea as a handbook for the inexperienced bride. In addition to recipes typically used by the Quakers of Pennsylvania, the book describes homemaking in a well-run nineteenth-century American home. Although the book is especially interesting for its exploration of the history of Quaker cooking, an experienced cook could also use it as a source of unfamiliar and interesting recipes.

Weiner, Marjorie, Ed.
JEWISH COOKING MADE SLIM.
   Gainesville, Fla.: Triad, 1983. Although the title sounds like a contradiction in terms, the editor of this book is a counselor at Weight Watchers of North Florida, and she knows about calories. The book contains more than 340 recipes. They go beyond strictly Jewish cooking, but include those traditional Jewish dishes that could be "decalorized." Recipes are preceded by the number of calories in a serving.

Wilford, Charles D.
ADVENTURES IN SOURDOUGH COOKING AND BAKING.
   San Rafael, Ca.: Gold Rush Sourdough Company, Inc., 1977. Published by a company that makes and sells sourdough starter, this book is clearly intended to tell you what to do with starter once you've got it. As you might expect, the book gives no directions for making a starter except with the company's product. I think Wilford gets a little excessive in his enthusiasm for the "adventure," but the recipes are basic and the procedures sound. They make an excellent base from which to begin developing your own recipes. You probably will find the book where the starter is sold, or you can write:
   Gold Rush Sourdough Company, Inc.
   65 Paul Drive
   San Rafael CA 94903

Wilkinson, Elviara; Claudia O'Brien, and Margaret Howard.
THE GREAT CALIFORNIA LIFESTYLE COOKBOOK.
   Los Angeles, Ca.: Lawry's Foods, Inc., 1981. Lawry's published this book to encourage people to use Lawry's seasonings. The book seems to be based on the assumption that people everywhere are impressed by anything Californian. I find the typeface of the book inappropriate to the subject matter, and I am also put off by a page at the end of the book entitled "Eating to Feel Great and Look Good," which makes a flat-out pitch for eating animal proteins, especially red meat. It is simply not ture that a nutritionally complete meal is difficult to provide from vegetable sources, and while I do not object to adovacy for any style of eating, I do object to the author's sneaking it in under a misleading label. But the book is worth studying for its clear, effective layout, outstanding color photography, and ingenious incorporation of brand-name ingredients into the recipes.

Williams, Christie.
WHAT'S COOKIN'? Vols. I, II, III.
   Seattle: SunKing Publishing Company, 1979, 1980, 1981. These three volumes of menus and recipes for the food processor were originally created for Cuisinart, but the rights have reverted to Ms. Williams. Although many of the recipes are at least slightly familiar, they reflect a wonderful variety of ethnic influences and show some real creativity in using a good processor (Christie calls hers "Jaws") to cut down on the amount of time and work required to make some delicious dishes. To locate copies:
   SunKing Publishing Company
   Box 68503
   Seattle WA 98168

Yankura, Lynn, ed.
COOKING ON EXTENDED BENEFITS: THE UNEMPLOYED COOKBOOK.
   McKeesport, Pa.: self-published, 1983. Unless you know somebody in McKeesport, it could be difficult to find a copy of this little book, published for

people who get their groceries from the Mon Valley Food Bank in St. Peter's Roman Catholic Church. The book, which includes recipes for cheese, dried milk, and such meat stretchers as macaroni, sold out its first 6,000 printing in a month. Some people in the area see it as a keepsake of the hard times. Anyone who can get a copy probably has a collector's item.

Williams, Jacqueline B. and Goldie Silverman.
NO SALT, NO SUGAR, NO FAT.
   Concord, Ca.: Nitty Gritty Productions, 1981. One of the Nitty Gritty cookbooks series, this book delivers what it promises: recipes using no salt, sugar, or fat. The recipes are varied; the tone is upbeat. Information about calories, grams of protein, milligrams of sodium, and so on is not provided. I don't see this as a lack; instead, it contributes to a sense that this is a perfectly reasonable way to eat, which can be accomplished without a lot of counting and measuring of nutrient values. But without such information, the book certainly could not be your only source for maintaining a diet low in salt, sugar, and fat.

COOKBOOK HALL OF FAME

1977   *The Settlement Cookbook* by Lillian Kander

1978   *The Joy of Cooking* by Irma Rombauer

1979   *The Fannie Farmer Cook Book* by Fannie Merrit Farmer

1980   *The Cordon Bleu Cook Book* by Dione Lucas

1981   *The New York Times Cook Book* by Craig Claiborne

1982   *Betty Crocker's Cookbook* Edited by Marjorie Child Hustad and created by the General Mills Home Services Department

1983   *The James Beard Cookbook* by James Beard

The R.T. French Company's Tastemaker Awards

1966	*Outstanding*	*The Thousand Recipe Chinese Cookbook* by Gloria Bley Miller.
1967	Outstanding	*America Cooks* by Anne Seranne. G.P. Putnam's Sons.
	Basic/General	*House & Garden's New Cook Book* by Jose Wilson. Condé Naste Publications Inc./Simon & Schuster.
	Foreign/Regional	*The Complete Book of Mexican Cooking* by Elizabeth Lambert Ortiz. M. Evans & Company, Inc.
	Specialty	*Nobody Ever Tells You These Things About Food & Drink* by Helen McCully. Holt, Rinehart & Winston.
	Soft Cover	*Clementine Paddleford's Cook Book* by Clementine Paddleford. Essandess Special Editions/ *This Week Magazine*.
1968	*Best*	*New York Times Large Type Cookbook* by Jean Hewitt. Golden Press.
	Basic	*New York Times Large Type Cookbook* by Jean Hewitt. Golden Press.
	Foreign/Regional	*American Cooking* by Dale Brown and Editors of Time-Life Books. Time-Life Books.
	Specialty (tie)	*Annemarie's Personal Cookbook* by Annemarie Huste. Batholomew House Ltd.
	and	*Better Homes & Gardens Cooking for Two* by Editors of *Better Homes & Gardens* and Meredith Press.
	Soft Cover	*Sunset Cook Book of Desserts* by Editors of Sunset Books and Sunset Magazines. Lane Book Co.

1969	No Best Cookbook This Year.	
	Basic	*Kitchen Primer* by Craig Claiborne. Alfred A. Knopf.
	Soft Cover	*Main Dishes* by Jean Hewitt. Golden Press.
	Foreign	*Italian Regional Cooking* by Ada Boni. E.P. Dutton & Company.
	Specialty	*Better Homes & Gardens Ground Meat Cook Book* by Editors of *Better Homes & Gardens*. Meredith Press.
1970	Best	*Splendid Fare* by Albert Stockli. Alfred A. Knopf.
	Basic/General	*Splendid Fare* by Albert Stockli. Alfred A. Knopf.
	Foreign/Regional	*California Cookbook* by Jeanne Voltz. Bobbs-Merrill Company.
	Soft Cover	*Sunset Oriental Cookbook* by Editors of Sunset Books and Sunset Magazines. Lane Magazine and Book Company.
	Specialty	*All Manner of Food* by Michael Field. Alfred A. Knopf.
1971	Best	*The New York Times International Cook Book* by Craig Claiborne. Harper and Row.
	Foreign/Regional	*The New York Times International Cook Book* by Craig Claiborne. Harper and Row.
	Specialty	*The New York Times Natural Foods Cookbook* by Jean Hewitt. Quadrangle Books.
	Basic	*The Four Seasons Cookbook* by Charlotte Adams. Holt, Rinehart & Winston.
	Entertaining	*Hostess Without Help* by Helen Worth. Westover Publishing Company.
	Softcover	*Herb Cookery* by Alan Hooker. 101 Productions.

1972	Best	*American Cookery* by James Beard. Little, Brown, & Company.
	General/Basic	*American Cookery* by James Beard. Little, Brown & Company.
	Foreign	*The Chinese Cookbook* by Graig Claiborne and Virginia Lee. J.B. Lippincott.
	Organic/Natural	*The Natural Foods Primer* by Beatrice Trum Hunter. Simon & Schuster.
	Special Diet	*Better Homes & Gardens Low-Calorie Desserts* by Editors of *Better Homes & Gardens.* Better Homes & Gardens Books.
	First	*The Cuisines of Mexico* by Diana Kennedy. Harper & Row Publishers, Inc.
	Specialty	*Pâtés and Other Marvelous Meat Loaves* by Dorothy Ivens. J.B. Lippincott Co.
	Entertaining	*Summertime Cookbook* by Marian Burros and Lois Levine. The Macmillan Co.
	Soft Cover	*Cooking with Wine* by Editors of Sunset Books & Magazines. Lane Magazine & Book Co.
1973	Best	*The Seasonal Kitchen* by Perla Meyers. Holt, Rinehart & Winston, Inc.
	Basic	*The Seasonal Kitchen* by Perla Meyers. Holt, Rinehart & Winston, Inc.
	First	*The Seasonal Kitchen* by Perla Meyers. Holt, Rinehart & Winston, Inc.
	Foreign	*The Classic Italian Cookbook* by Marcella Hazan. Harper & Row Publishers.
	Organic/Natural	*Bread: Making it the Natural Way* by Diana Collier and Joan Wiener. J.B. Lippincott Co.
	Specialty	*Dinner Against the Clock* by Madeleine Kamman. Altheneum.
	Special Diet	*Anne Seranne's Good Food Without Meat* by Anne Seranne. William Morrow & Co. Inc.
	Entertaining	*Feasts for Two* by Paul Rubenstein. Macmillan Pub. Co.

	Soft Cover	*Sunset Ideas for Cooking Vegetables* by Editors of Sunset Books and Sunset Magazines. Lane Magazine & Book Co.
1974	Best	*Simple French Food* by Richard Olney. Atheneum.
	Foreign	*Simple French Food* by Richard Olney. Atheneum.
	Specialty	*The Complete Book of Breads* by Bernard Clayton. Simon and Schuster.
	Basic	*I Cook as I Please* by Nika Hazelton. Grosset and Dunlap.
	Health and Diet	*Diet for One, Dinner for All* by Beryl Marton. Western Publishing Co.
	Entertainment	*Helen Corbitt Cooks for Company* by Helen Corbitt. Houghton Mifflin Co.
	Soft Cover	*Classic Greek Cooking* by Daphne Metaxas. Nitty Gritty.
1975	Best	*The Doubleday Cookbook* by Jean Anderson. Doubleday & Company.
	Basic	*The Doubleday Cookbook* by Jean Anderson. Doubleday & Company.
	Foreign/Regional	*The Better Homes & Gardens Heritage Cookbook* by Nancy Morton. Meredith Corp.
	Specialty	*Craig Claiborne's Favorites from The New York Times* by Craig Claiborne. Quadrangle/NYT Book Co.
	Entertainment	*The New York Times Weekend Cookbook* by Jean Hewitt. Quadrangle/NYT Book Co.
	Natural/Special Diet	*Salt Free Cooking with Herbs and Spices* by June Roth. Henry Regnery Co.
	Soft Cover	*Crockery Cookery* by Mable Hoffman. HP Books.
	First	*American Food, The Gastronomic Story* by Evan Jones. E.P. Dutton and Co.

1976	Best	*Michel Guerard's Cuisine Minceur* by Michel Guerard. William Morrow Co.
	Foreign/Regional	*Michel Guerard's Cuisine Minceur* by Michel Guerard. William Morrow Co.
	First	*Michel Guerard's Cuisine Minceur* by Michel Guerard. William Morrow Co.
	Basic	*The Six-Minute Souffle and Other Culinary Delights* by Carol Cutler. Clarkson N. Potter Inc.
	Specialty	*The Unabridged Vegetable Cookbook* by Nika Hazelton. M. Evans Co.
	Entertaining	*The Pleasure of Your Company* by Diana and Paul von Welanetz. Atheneum.
	Health and Nutrition	*The Slim Gourmet* by Barbara Gibbon. Harper and Row.
	Soft Cover	*Crepe Cookery* by Mable Hoffman. HP Books.
1977	Best	*James Beard's Theory and Practice of Good Cooking* by James Beard. Alfred Knopf.
	Basic and/or General	*James Beard's Theory and Practice of Good Cooking* by James Beard. Alfred Knopf.
	American/Regional	*The Flavor of the South* by Jeanne A. Voltz. Doubleday & Company.
	European Cooking	*Great Cooks and Their Recipes: From Traillevent to Escoffier* by Anne Willan. McGraw Hill.
	International Cuisine	*The Key to Chinese Cooking* by Irene Kuo. Alfred Knopf.
	Natural Foods/ Special Diets	*A Celebration of Vegetables* by Robert Ackart. Atheneum.
	Soft Cover	*The Book of Salads* by Sonia Uvezian. 101 Productions.
	Specialty	*Maida Heatter's Book of Great Cookies* by Maida Heatter. Alfred Knopf.
1978	Best	*Julia Child & Company* by Julia Child. Alfred Knopf.

	Basic and/or General	*Julia Child & Company* by Julia Child. Alfred Knopf.
	American/Regional	*American-Regional Cookbook* by Editors of Time-Life Books. Little, Brown & Co.
	Foreign	*More Classic Italian Cooking* by Marcella Hazan. Alfred Knopf.
	Specialty	*The Joy of Giving Homemade Food* by Anne Seranne. The David McKay Co., Inc.
	Single Subject	*Veal Cookery* by Craig Claiborne and Pierre Franey. Harper & Row Publishers.
	Natural Foods	*Pure and Simple: Delicious Recipes for Additive-Free Cooking* by Marian Burros. William Morrow & Co., Inc.
	Special Diet	*The International Slim Gourmet Cookbook* by Barbara Gibbon, Harper & Row.
	Soft Cover	*Cooking for Two . . . Or Just for You* by Editors of Sunset Books & Magazine. Lane Publishing Co.
1979	Best	*La Methode* by Jacques Pepin. Times Books.
	Europe and The Americas (tie)	*The Book of Latin American Cooking* by Elizabeth Lambert Ortiz. Knopf Publishers.
	and	*San Francisco a la Carte* by the Junior League of San Francisco. Doubleday & Company.
	International	*My Stomach Goes Traveling* by Walter Slezak. Doubleday & Company.
	Oriental	*The Great Tastes of Chinese Cooking* by Jean Yueh. Times Books Publishers.
	Natural Foods/ Special Diets	*The Vegetarian Feast* by Martha Rose Shulman. Harper & Row.
	Single Subject	*Lenotre's Ice Creams and Candies* by Gaston Lenotre. Barron's.
	Specialty	*Better than Store Bought* by Helen Witty and Elizabeth Schneider Colchie. Harper & Row.
	Soft Cover	*Fowl & Game Bird Cookery* by James Bear. Harcort Brace and Jovanovich.

1980	Best	*Craig Claiborne's Gourmet Diet* by Craig Claiborne and Pierre Franey. Times Books.
	Basic	*The Four Seasons* by Tom Margettai and Paul Kovi. Simon & Schuster.
	American Regional/ International	*American Home Cooking* by Nika Hazelton. Viking Press.
	Natural Foods and Special Diets	*Craig Claiborne's Gourmet Diet* by Craig Claiborne and Pierre Franey. Times Books.
	Specialty	*Half a Can of Tomato Paste and other Culinary Dilemmas* by Jean Anderson and Ruth Buchan. Haper & Row.
	Single Subject	*Maida Heatter's Book of Great Chocolate Desserts* by Maida Heatter. Alfred Knopf.
	Meat, Fish, & Dairy	*The Fish Lovers' Cookbook* by Sheryl and Mel London. Rodale Press.
	Original Soft Cover American Regional/ International	*La Verenne's Basic French Cookery* by Anne Willan. HP Books.
	Original Soft Cover Specialty	*Future Food* by Colin Judge. Harmony Books.
	Original Soft Cover Single Subject	*The Wild Palate* by Walter and Nancy Hall. Rodale Press.
1981	Best	*The New James Beard* by James Beard. Alfred Knopf.
	Basic	*The New James Beard* by James Beard. Alfred Knopf.
	American	*Honest American Fare* by Bert Greene. Contemporary Books.
	International	*French Regional Cooking* by Anne Willan. William Morrow.
	Single Subject	*The Complete Book of Pastry—Sweet & Savory* by Bernard Clayton, Jr. Simon & Schuster.
	Time-Conscious	*The New York Times More 60-Minute Gourmet* by Pierre Franey. Times Books.
	Natural Foods & Special Diets	*Madhur Jaffrey's World of the East Vegetarian Cooking* by Madhur Jaffrey. Alfred Knopf.

	Specialty	*Judith Olney's Entertainments* by Judith Olney. Barron's Educational Series, Inc.
	Original Soft Cover International	*American Food & California Wine* by Barbara Kafka. Irena Chalmers Cookbooks.
	Original Soft Cover Single Subject	*Appetizers* by Mable Hoffman. HP Books
	Original Soft Cover Specialty	*Christmas Feasts from History* by Lorna Sass. Irena Chalmers Cookbooks.

1982	Best	*The Book of Bread* by Evan and Judith Jones. Harper and Row.
	Basic General	*The La Varenne Cooking Course* by Anne Willan. William Morrow and Company, Inc.
	Single Subject	*The Book of Bread* by Evan and Judith Jones. Harper and Row.
	American	*Connecticut a la Carte* edited by Melinda M. Vance. Connecticut a la Carte of West Hartford, Conn.
	International	*Guiliano Bugialli's Classic Techniques of Italian Cooking* by Guiliano Bugialli. Simon & Schuster.
	Specialty	*John Clancy's Christmas Cookbook* by John Clancy. Hearst Books.
	Natural Foods/ Special Diet	*Better Homes & Gardens Cookbook* edited by Joyce Trollope. Meredith Corp.
	Original Soft Cover Basic/General	*Easy Basics for Good Cooking* by Janet Nix, Elaine Woodard, and other editors of Sunset Books and Sunset Magazine. Lane Publishing Company.
	Original Soft Cover Meat/Fish/Eggs	*The Great East Coast Seafood Book* by Yvonne Young Tarr. Random House.
	Original Soft Cover International/ American Regional	*Middle Eastern Cooking* by Rose Dosti. HP Books.
	Original Soft Cover Specialty	*Vegetable Cookery* by Lou Seibert Pappas. HP Books.

More Help: Suggestions for Further Reading

Appelbaum, Judith, and Nancy Evans.
HOW TO GET HAPPILY PUBLISHED.
Revised Edition. New York: Plume, 1982. You should enjoy this book for its upbeat, chatty approach and the candor with which Appelbaum and Evans examine trade publishing. Also, it is one of the most informative books available for the lay person on how the publishing industry works.

Balkin, Richard.
A WRITER'S GUIDE TO BOOK PUBLISHING.
New York: Hawthorn Books, Inc., 1977. Although you will find nothing really new here (perhaps because there is nothing new to find), this is a down-to-earth explanation of how to get published. The chapter on how to approach a publisher is valuable for its audience-oriented approach, and the chapter on how to negotiate a contract demystifies the legalities of signing with a publisher.

Bowker, R.R.
LITERARY MARKET PLACE.
New York: R.R. Bowker Company. Published yearly. This reference book should be available in your library. It lists publishers, printers, authors' agents, book reviewers, and book distributors, as well as a variety of other book-related information that will be useful to you in looking for publishers or helping to promote your book. Listings include names of people in key positions in publishing houses, and addresses and telephone numbers for all companies and individuals listed.

Coser, Lewis A., Charles Kadushin and Walter W. Powell.
BOOKS: THE CULTURE AND COMMERCE OF PUBLISHING.
New York: Basic Books, Inc., 1982. This book purports to show the inside operation of publishing houses, based on field research and interviews. Unfortunately, at least some of the editors interviewed gave smart-aleck answers, which, it appears, the writer took seriously. It does not deal directly with cookbook publishing, but it is worth reading to gain a general idea of all the steps involved in taking a book from idea to bound copies on bookstore shelves. Also, you get a glimpse into the personalities and social patterns of professional publishers.

Henderson, Bill, ed.
THE PUBLISH IT-YOURSELF HANDBOOK.
Wainscott, NY: Puschart Press, 1979. A more detailed look at the self-publishing process, written by one who has been there.

Kennedy, Evelyn Kirk.
COOKING FOR LOVE AND MONEY.
Whitehall, Va.: Betterway Publications, Inc., 1982. Kennedy's book deals mainly with finding and entering recipe and cooking contests, but it also contains a useful chapter on how to find other markets for your recipes and gives some examples of prize-winning recipes.

Lee, Marshall.
BOOKMAKING: THE ILLUSTRATED GUIDE TO DESIGN, PRODUCTION, EDITING.
New York: R.R. Bowker Co., 1978. A classic that tells you more than you can absorb about bookmaking. The discussions of decisions about type, paper, and illustrations are especially helpful to the self-publisher who is about to talk with printers.

Mathieu, Aron.
HOW TO WRITE, PUBLISH AND MARKET YOUR BOOK.
New York: Andover Press, 1981. About half this book is devoted to royalty (commercial) publishing; the rest discusses self-publishing and is valuable for its chapters on marketing.

Montgomery, Michael and John Stratton.
THE WRITER'S HOTLINE HANDBOOK.
New York: Mentor (New American Library), 1981. If you sometimes get confused about when to write "who" and "whom" or when to use "will" instead of "shall," this compact little grammar will get you out of trouble.

Phillips, G.M., Pedersen, D.J., and Wood, J.T.
GROUP DISCUSSION: A PRACTICAL GUIDE TO PARTICIPATION AND LEADERSHIP
Boston: Houghton-Mifflin, 1979. Phillips, Pedersen, and Wood offer plenty of helpful advice about working in groups and with committees. You have to take it seriously when you realize that the three of them managed to work together at least long enough to write the book.

Provost, Gary.
MAKE EVERY WORD COUNT.
Cincinnati, Ohio: Writer's Digest Books, 1980. This book tells how to use words in writing. It includes some exercises for mastering written language that are actually as much fun as parlor games, if you're in the mood. The book is really a fleshing-out and popularization of Strunk and White's little classic, *The Element of Style*. I think it's worth having whether or not you care about Strunk and White.

Rehmel, Judy.
SO, YOU WANT TO WRITE A COOKBOOK!
Box 1002, Richmond IN 47374: Judy Rehmel, 1982. This modest little book is

a self-published exploration of self-publishing, which goes into considerable detail on format, composition, and layout.

Richardson, Lou and Callahan, Genevieve.
HOW TO WRITE FOR HOMEMAKERS.
Ames, Iowa. Iowa State University Press, 1962. Although written primarily for practicing home economists, this book is full of information on managing advertising and getting publicity, as well as plenty of advice about testing and writing recipes.

White, Jan V.
GRAPHIC IDEA NOTEBOOK.
New York: Watson-Guptill Publications, 1980. Billed as "Inventive techniques for designing printed pages," this book offers ideas that are probably too far out for most cookbook designs, but it's worth looking at just to help you shake the old stereotypes about illustrations out of your head.

Writer's Digest (Paula Diemling, Ed.).
WRITER'S MARKET.
Cincinnati, Ohio: Writer's Digest Books. Published yearly. This is still the best listing available of who publishes what. Along with names, addresses, and telephone numbers, the listings give short descriptions of what each publisher is looking for.

INDEX

Other Books of Interest

Clutter's Last Stand, by Don Aslett—In this "ultimate self-improvement" book filled with anecdotes, cartoons, a "Junkee Entrance Exam," and "100 Feeble Excuses for Hanging Onto Junk," Aslett shows you how to judge, sort, and toss clutter to make life easier. 224 pages/$8.95, paper

Confessions of an Organized Housewife, by Deniece Schofield—Learn the secrets of successful household organization for every aspect of home-life: the kitchen, laundry, paperwork, sewing supplies, toys, and more to develop your own system of home management. 224 pages/$6.95, paper

Do I Dust or Vacuum First? by Don Aslett—In this lively book Aslett answers the 100 housecleaning questions he's asked most: how to keep no-wax floors looking like new, how to clean Venetian blinds, and more with a minimum of time, money, and energy. 156 pages/$6.95, paper

Extra Cash for Kids, by Belliston and Hanks—Here's more than 100 ways for kids from 8-16 to earn money during summer and spare-time hours doing everything from selling berry starts to making pet ID tags, with details on how to do the job, pricing, scheduling, advertising, and equipment. 185 pages/$6.95, paper.

How to Make Money Writing . . . Fillers, by Connie Emerson—Learn how short articles, greeting card verse, hints, recipes, puzzles, and contests can give you extra income with Emerson's advice on how to write and sell each type of filler. 266 pages/$12.95

How To Be A Successful Housewife/Writer, by Elaine Fantle Shimberg—A book for anyone trying to write at home, with tips on organizing your house and schedule, coping with distractions, setting up a home office, saving time to write, dealing successfully with editors. 254 pages/$10.95

Is There Life After Housework? by Don Aslett—Save up to 75% of the time you spend housecleaning as Aslett shows you how to use the techniques and tools of professional cleaners—including charts, diagrams, and illustrations to help you prevent housework and keep your house clean longer. 134 pages/$6.95, paper

Partnering: A Guide to Co-Owning Anything from Homes to Home Computers, by Lois Rosenthal—Here's practical advice on how to share the costs, the work, and the fun of co-ownership to buy that vacation home or appliance you're always wanted, with examples, interviews, sample agreements and a test for finding the right partner. 256 pages/ $12.95, paper

Use this coupon to order your copies!

— —

Please send me the following books: 1378

———— (1122) Clutter's Last Stand, $8.95, paper
———— (1143) Confessions of an Organized Housewife, $6.95, paper
———— (1214) Do I Dust or Vacuum First? $6.95, paper
———— (1246) Extra Cash for Kids, $6.95, paper
———— (1245) Extra Cash for Women, $6.95, paper
———— (1388) How to Make Money Writing . . . Fillers, $12.95
———— (1099) How to Be a Successful Housewife/Writer, $10.95
———— (1452) Is There Life After Housework? $6.95, paper
———— (1804) Partnering, $12.95, paper

Add $1.50 postage and handling for one book, 50¢ for each additional book. Ohio residents add sales tax. Allow 30 days for delivery.

☐ Check or money order enclosed   Please charge my: ☐ Visa   ☐ Master Card
Account # _____ Exp. Date _____
Signature _____ Interbank # _____
Name _____
Address _____
City _____ State _____ Zip _____
☐ Please send me your current catalog of Writer's Digest Books

— —

Send to: Writer's Digest Books   Credit card orders call TOLL-FREE
          9933 Alliance Road   1-800-543-4644
          Cincinnati, Ohio 45242   (in Ohio call direct 513-984-0717)
          (PRICES SUBJECT TO CHANGE WITHOUT NOTICE)